Library of
Davidson College

MULTINATIONAL INDUSTRIAL RELATIONS SERIES

NO. 5

PROFIT SHARING, EMPLOYEE STOCK OWNERSHIP, SAVINGS, AND ASSET FORMATION PLANS IN THE WESTERN WORLD

by

GEOFFREY W. LATTA

INDUSTRIAL RESEARCH UNIT
The Wharton School, Vance Hall/CS
University of Pennsylvania
Philadelphia, Pennsylvania 19104
U.S.A.

© 1979 by the Trustees of the University of Pennsylvania
MANUFACTURED IN THE UNITED STATES OF AMERICA
ISBN: 0-89546-015-7
ISSN: 0149-0818

Foreword

In 1972, the Industrial Research Unit began an ongoing research project dealing with the international activities of trade unions and the potential for multinational bargaining. This research has resulted in the publication of fifteen articles, the drafting of others in progress and a forthcoming book on multinational union-management activities. In addition, a Multinational Information Service has been established based upon the numerous contacts developed in Europe, Asia, Australia, and North and South America; the materials collected are, we believe, the most complete extant on international union and multinational corporation contacts and relationships. The project is under the joint direction of Professor Richard L. Rowan, Co-Director of the Industrial Research Unit, and the undersigned.

Another aspect of the Industrial Research Unit's multinational industrial relations project is the examination of the labor relations situation and climate in various countries. Thus, as listed on the back cover, studies have been published for Brazil, Mexico, Peru, and Venezuela. Others are in progress for Colombia, India, Spain, and the Philippines.

The Industrial Research Unit also makes special unpublished studies of labor conditions in various countries by request. The Unit's capability in this field has been greatly enhanced as a result of the Chase Manhattan Bank's gift of its international industrial relations library and extensive files. The Chase files, now carefully and continuously updated, were developed over a twelve-year period and are on a country-by-country basis from Abu Dhabi to Zambia. In addition to the industrialized countries, these files also include materials on all underdeveloped areas, with extensive coverage of current industrial relations developments, legislation, labor conditions, policies, and practices. These complement the Industrial Research Unit's already extensive materials on companies and unions.

This study, *Profit Sharing, Employee Stock Ownership, Savings, and Asset Formation Plans in the Western World*, begins a new phase of the multinational program. It is the first of several projected studies that will examine important industrial relations issues and compare their treatment among the major industrialized countries. Profit sharing, for example, is found principally in the United States, but also in other countries as well; in some, as in France, it is required by legislation. Plans for collective asset formation are a European creation, which in their most radical form would transfer profits in the form of company stock, not to employees, but to public corporations controlled by union officials. The latter plans are obviously envisioned not as a means of strengthening the capitalist system but rather as a method of turning over industrial control to union leaders.

The author of this study, Geoffrey W. Latta, examines the various types of plans for profit sharing, savings, employee stock ownership, and asset formation as found in the United States and the principal European countries, objectively assesses their purpose and performance, and compares and contrasts the different models and types. Programs in Latin America and Japan are briefly discussed in the Appendix. Thus, the scholar or company executive who is interested in the subject is provided with the basic facts and analysis for study or decision.

Mr. Latta was born and received his education in the United Kingdom. He received the Bachelor of Arts degree from Saint Catherine's College, Oxford University, in 1968 and the Master of Arts in Industrial Relations from the University of Warwick. Before emigrating to the United States, he worked for the Commission on Industrial Relations, on the faculty of the London School of Economics and Political Science, and as a national officer of the Engineers' and Managers' Association. In 1979, he received the Master of Business Administration degree from the Graduate Division of the Wharton School and is now a member of the industrial relations department of a major American-based corporation. He has previously authored seven articles dealing with various aspects of industrial relations and union policies.

Many persons were extremely helpful in providing information and making this study possible. In the course of the work, Mr. Latta visited with major corporate personnel in the United States and Europe, and all gave freely of their time and information. Since some prefer to remain anonymous, we are unable to list those in industry responsible for this assistance, but our appreciation is very great indeed. Mr. Latta also wishes to give particular thanks to Mr. G. F. Pecchioli of Shell International, who first suggested the study; to Mr. Bert L. Metzger, President, Profit Sharing Research Foundation, Evanston, Illinois; Dr. Hans-Günter Guski, Institut der Deutschen Wirtschaft in Köln, Director of its Department for Asset-Formation Policies; Dr. D. Snijders, Head of Economic Research,

Foreword

NV Philips Gloeilampenfabrieken, Eindhoven; Mme. Annie Benhamou, Director of International Affairs, Union des Industries Métallurgiques et Minières; and Mr. D. Wallace Bell, Director, Industrial Participation Association, London—all of whom provided substantial assistance in numerous ways.

Mr. Robert E. Bolick, Jr., Chief Editor of the Industrial Research Unit, edited the final manuscript and made up the index; Mrs. Margaret E. Doyle, Office Manager, handled the various administrative matters involved in the work; and the typescript was prepared by the Wharton Word Processing Center. The study was financed by special contributions from twelve corporate subscribers of the Industrial Research Unit's Multinational Research Advisory Group Information Services and from the Ford Motor Company Fund. The author is, of course, solely responsible for the study's content, including the accuracy of the research and the views expressed, which should not be attributed to the grantors or to the University of Pennsylvania.

Herbert R. Northrup, *Director*
Industrial Research Unit
The Wharton School
University of Pennsylvania

Philadelphia
May 1979

TABLE OF CONTENTS

	PAGE
FOREWORD	iii

CHAPTER

I. INTRODUCTION 1

    The Purpose of the Plans 1
    Profit Sharing 2
        Aims 3
    Employee Stock Ownership 6
        Aims 6
    Asset Formation 7
        Aims 8
    The Role of Government 8
        Collective Plans 8
    Nature of the Study 9

II. PROFIT SHARING IN THE UNITED STATES 11

    The History of Profit Sharing 14
        The Emergence of Deferred Profit Sharing 16
        Tax Support 17
        Current Growth and Problems 18
    The Nature of Deferred Profit Sharing 20
        Investment Policy 21
        Administration 22
        The Nature of Profit-Sharing Companies 23
        Union Attitudes toward Profit Sharing 24
    Conclusion 27

III. EMPLOYEE SAVINGS PLANS IN THE UNITED STATES 28

    The Number of Plans 29
    Tax Position 31
        Profit-Sharing Qualifications 32
        Employee and Employer Contributions 32

CHAPTER PAGE

    Taxes: Distribution during Employment 33
    Separation of Service: Tax Rules for Lump Sum Versus
        Installments 34
    Taxation at Death 35
    Special Tax Treatment: Employer Securities 35
    Summary of Tax Advantages 36
  Characteristics of Savings Plans and Recent Trends 36
    Groups Covered and Eligibility...................... 36
    Participation of Eligible Employees 37
    Contributions by the Employee...................... 38
    Contributions by the Employer...................... 38
    Voluntary Suspensions 39
    Contribution Investment........................... 40
    Investment Transfers 40
    Vesting Provisions................................ 41
    Forfeiture Allocation 42
    Periodic Distributions 43
    Voluntary Withdrawals............................ 43
    Voting Rights of Company Common Stock 44
    Forms of Distribution 44
  Benefits of Savings Plans 44

IV. STOCK-OWNERSHIP PLANS IN THE UNITED STATES 46

  ESOPs 47
  Development of ESOPs............................... 48
    The Number of ESOPs............................. 48
    Tax Considerations 49
  Legislation.. 49
    Regional Rail Reorganization Act, 1973.............. 50
    Employee Retirement Income Security Act, 1974 50
    Trade Act, 1974 51
    Tax Reduction Act, 1975 51
    Tax Reform Act, 1976 52
  Benefits and Advantages of ESOPs..................... 54
  Disadvantages of ESOPs 56
  Union Attitudes toward ESOPs....................... 58

CHAPTER	PAGE
Proposed Legislative Changes	59
Conclusion	60

V. **PROFIT SHARING IN EUROPE** 63

    Size and Character of Unions 63
    Economic Structure............................. 66
    Codetermination and Related Matters........... 70
    Investment in Europe 70
        United Kingdom Versus Germany 71
    Conclusion 72

VI. **GERMANY**...................................... 74

    Political Structure and Trade Unions........... 74
    Company Profit Sharing 75
        Participation Level........................ 77
        Contributions and Benefits 80
        The Largest Companies 82
        Company Profit Sharing: Final Comment..... 83
    Asset Formation 84
        DM 312 Act 84
        The 1965 Law............................. 85
        The 1970 Law............................. 86
    Collective Funds 87
        SPD Proposal............................. 87
        DGB Proposal 88
        SPD-FDP Proposal 89
    Conclusion 89

VII. **DENMARK AND SWEDEN**........................... 91

    Industrial Similarities........................ 91
        Unions and Politics 92
        Investment............................... 93
    Profit Sharing in Denmark 94
    Collective Asset Formation..................... 95

CHAPTER	PAGE

    The 1973 Bill. 96
    The Central Fund 97
    Control of the Central Fund. 98
    Employer Reaction. 99
    Other Attacks. 100
    Current Status 101

  Profit Sharing in Sweden. 101

  Collective Investment Proposals 102

    Underlying Philosophy 103
    Summary of the Meidner Plan. 104
    Employer Response 105
    The Mehr Commission and 1976 Elections. 107
    Revised LO Proposals 108
    Capital-Formation Levy 110
    Continued Aim 110

VIII. THE NETHERLANDS 112

  Trade Unions and Political Structure. 113

  Company Profit Sharing 115

  Savings Plans 117

    Vermogensaanwasdeling (VAD) 118
    1975 Proposals. 119
    1976 Proposals. 119
    Reaction to the Proposals 121
    Modified VAD 122
    1978 Proposals. 123

  VAD's Future and Impact 124

IX. UNITED KINGDOM. 126

  Trade Unions and Politics. 127

  Company Profit Sharing 128

    Cash Distributions. 130
    Imperial Chemical Industries (ICI). 132

  Share-Purchase and Share-Option Plans 136

  Government Initiative 137

    Reaction to the Proposals 140

Table of Contents xi

CHAPTER PAGE

    Government Action 141
    Collective Plans 142
    Conclusion 142

X. FRANCE 144

    Trade Unions and Politics 145
    Profit-Sharing Legislation 147
        Investment of the RSP 150
        Employee Accounts 151
        Tax Incentives 152
        Management of the Fund 152
    Effect of the Legislation 153
        Public Sector Coverage 154
        Investment Choice 155
        Overall Impact 156
    Savings Plans 156
    Proposals for Change 157
    Conclusion 159

XI. THE EUROPEAN COMMUNITY AND
    OTHER EUROPEAN COUNTRIES 160

    Switzerland 161
    Belgium 163
    Italy 163
    Ireland 164
    European Community 165

XII. CONCLUSION 167

APPENDIX 177

INDEX 183

LIST OF TABLES

TABLE　　　　　　　　　　　　　　　　　　　　　　　　　　PAGE

Chapter III

1. Date of Establishment of Savings Plans in Existence in 1977 30

Chapter V

1. Trade Union Membership 64
2. Economic Indicators, 1976–77 67
3. Labor Force Structure 69
4. Employment by Major Sector 69

Chapter VI

1. German Profit-Sharing Companies with Over 5,000 Participating Employees 78

LIST OF FIGURES

FIGURE　　　　　　　　　　　　　　　　　　　　　　　　　PAGE

Chapter II

1. Number of Profit-Sharing Plans Approved by Internal Revenue, Fiscal Years 1956–75 12
2. Average Number of Employees Participating in Profit-Sharing Plans, Fiscal Years 1956–75 13

CHAPTER I

Introduction

Diversification of the method of remunerating employees for their labor has become a significant feature of the employment relationship throughout Western Europe and North America in the latter half of the twentieth century. The nature and rate of growth of benefits have, of course, differed depending on the social and political structure of individual societies. For example, the considerable improvements that have occurred in the provision of vacations, protection of earnings during absence from work because of sickness or accident, pensions, and insurance benefits have varied from country to country because of the differences in, or lack of, legislation designed to meet similar needs.

In one sense, such benefits as those above, although vitally important, are negative ones, designed to protect employees from the undesirable consequences of certain situations. In contrast, other benefits have developed that are more positive in that they aim to motivate people to greater achievement. This range of benefits, consisting of profit-sharing, asset-formation, and employee stock-ownership plans, is the focus of this study.

THE PURPOSE OF THE PLANS

Plans for profit sharing, asset formation, and share ownership have developed rapidly in the United States and Western Europe over recent years. They are designed to distribute assets, usually in the form either of cash or of shares, to employees. Payments under the plans are separated from regular wages because the payments are intended for a different purpose. Share-ownership plans are based on the specific belief that it is socially and economically desirable for employees to hold stock. The advantages lie both in the provision of general support for the capitalist economic system and in the encouragement of employees' specific involvement in the economic fate of the company for which they work. Asset-formation plans, which include savings plans, are based on the desirability of providing special means and incentives to employees for saving money. The underlying assumption is that such plans increase the employees' propensity to save, and many plans provide mechanisms such as "blocking periods," during which the employee cannot withdraw his savings, to ensure the attainment of this objective.

The philosophical case for profit sharing is based on the belief that employees who contribute to a growth in profits should share directly in those profits. Profit sharing is intended to serve both as a reward for past effort and as a means of stimulating individual effort in the future. Although the relationship between employee effort or efficiency and profits may not always be direct, profit sharing relates employee remuneration to the short-term level of profits in a direct manner. In this sense, profit sharing differs from the normal wage system. It can be argued that the degree of profitability of a company determines in the medium and long term the level of wages that the company can afford to pay, and so profits and wage levels are related. The time required for profits to affect wage levels, however, makes it unlikely that employees will make this connection between profits and the level of wages. It is for this reason that many companies provide a separate payment related directly to profits, which makes the relationship between profits and remuneration more explicit.

PROFIT SHARING

Although it is rare for definitions to be entirely satisfactory, their omission is usually conducive only to confusion. The essence of profit sharing is captured by the current definition used by the Profit Sharing Council of America: "any procedure under which an employer pays or makes available to employees, subject to reasonable eligibility rules, in addition to prevailing rates of pay, special current or deferred sums based on the profits of the business."[1]

Some plans provide that payments should be related to profits by a direct formula, the simplest method being that a fixed percentage of profits should be distributed to employees each year. In some cases, the relationship is less direct, either being based on criteria that are not made explicit or being at the discretion of company directors.

Profit-sharing plans can be divided broadly into two categories. The first comprises plans that provide immediate cash benefits as soon as the relevant profits are known. A plan under which cash payments are made in March based on the profits for the year end-

---

[1] Bert L. Metzger, *Profit Sharing in 38 Large Companies,* Vol. I (Evanston, Ill.: Profit Sharing Research Foundation, 1975), p. 2.

Introduction

ing the previous December would be an example of this type. Plans in the second category offer deferred payments. Only after a specified period or in defined circumstances, such as retirement, can employees convert their holdings into cash.

Aims

Profit sharing is most widely applied in the United States, although throughout Western Europe, there are some companies that operate plans. In some countries, such as France, there is specific legislation supporting profit sharing. The aims and philosophical basis of profit sharing are generally the same in Europe as in the United States, with one important exception. In the United States, a number of profit-sharing plans are primarily designed to provide retirement benefits to employees. Such famous plans as that of Sears Roebuck fall into this category. The aim of relating retirement income to profits has been almost entirely unknown in Europe, where both public and private pensions have provided a defined level of retirement income. This income can come in the form either of flat-rate payments for all employees or varying payments related to length of membership in the pension plan and to salary level.

Although there is considerable variation in the reasons that lead employers to adopt profit sharing, there is a common ideological basis. The basic premise of such plans is the desirability of strengthening the capitalist economic system. It is perhaps not surprising in this context that the plans have been most favorably received in the United States, the country in which the capitalist ethic is the most strongly imbued in the widest section of the population. In Europe, Germany has seen the greatest development of profit sharing since World War II. Ideological support for profit sharing has, however, been matched by ideological opposition in Europe. The Communist-dominated union federations in France and Italy, the Confédération Générale du Travail and the Confederazione Generale Italiana del Lavoro, have both taken a hostile view of profit sharing, and even more moderate unions have viewed it with considerable mistrust.

Profit sharing seeks to emphasize the common interests of employees and employers and is based on the belief that it provides a mechanism that will enhance the identification of the former with the latter. If this sense of partnership is instilled in employees, it is believed that the results will include improved efficiency and work performance, as well as more harmonious labor relations within the company. Profit sharing is also seen as a means of strengthening the wider economic system by demonstrating the common interests of the two parties in industry. This philosophical basis helps to account for the almost evangelical fervor of some of the supporters of profit sharing. It also accounts for the degree to which the use of profit sharing relates to the wider social and political environment.

Illustrative of this relationship is the speech made in December 1960 by the chairman of S. C. Johnson and Son, a profit-sharing employer:

> We are today locked in a grim struggle—now ideological, but tomorrow it may be military—with a great foreign power whose ideals, philosophies, and treatment of the individual are contrary to our belief. Profit sharing helps give me confidence that we can win in this struggle. It seems to strike deeply and importantly at the basic roots of Communism. It is typically a practice of the American Free Enterprise System and is absolutely unknown to the Communist world. It is gratifying to note that the theory and practice of profit sharing is spreading rapidly in this country and is catching hold in a few other countries of the world. This could grow to be a major barrier to the Communistic inroads which even at this moment literally threaten our shores.[2]

It would, of course, be misleading to suggest that all employers view profit sharing in this light. Nevertheless, its incidence and popularity in the United States can be explained primarily by reference to the widespread belief in the existing economic system and the view that profit sharing reflects the ethos of that system.

Apart from profit sharing's wider social effect, many companies see it as a means of strengthening their own organizations' effectiveness. In his listing of the objectives of profit sharing, Knowlton placed at the head the development of a sense of partnership between employees and employers to increase employee interest in the company and to create a group incentive for greater productive efficiency.[3] In this sense, companies adopt profit-sharing plans for very practical business reasons.

Whether profit sharing does indeed meet these aims is an extremely difficult matter to assess and one to which this study will return at a later stage. It is true, as Bloom and Northrup have pointed out, that

---

[2] Quoted in A. C. Burrows, "Profit Sharing in the Joint Enterprise System," *Symposium on Profit Sharing and Productivity Motivation* (Madison, Wis.: Center for Productivity Motivation, School of Commerce, University of Wisconsin, 1961), p. 17.

[3] P. A. Knowlton, *Profit Sharing Patterns* (Evanston, Ill.: Profit Sharing Research Foundation, 1954), p. 55.

Introduction 5

profits have no necessary or close relation to physical production or employee effort—and this is one of the inherent weaknesses in profit-sharing plans. Employees may exert extra effort, yet profits may decline because competitive conditions compel a reduction in prices; on the other hand, despite a decline in physical production, profits may rise because the employer has made a favorable purchase of raw materials, or for many other reasons.[4]

In any case, supporters of profit sharing usually do not regard plans as a direct incentive to greater employee effort, a function that they consider performed best by piecework payment systems. Rather, they see the advantages of profit sharing to be those of motivating the employee as a member of the team and of creating a more positive working environment. They believe that profit sharing improves labor relations and shows that the company is a "good" employer. It must be remembered that many of the pioneer firms in profit sharing, such as Procter & Gamble, whose plan was introduced in 1887, were at that time far in advance of most other employers in their attitude toward employee relations.

A number of other advantages are claimed for profit sharing. It may be a factor in reducing labor turnover. It may be part of a wider employee benefits package and would have the advantage of being a fluctuating cost in relation to profit levels. Clearly, where profit-sharing plans have been the major vehicle for the provision of retirement benefits, this has been a matter of critical importance to the broader benefit system.

In the United States, profit sharing has sometimes been depicted as a means of maintaining a company's nonunion status, and traditionally, many profit-sharing companies have not been sympathetic to unions. As a major study in 1917 pointed out, "No profit-sharing firm is known to have in operation any system of collective bargaining or of definitely established friendly relations with trade unions."[5]

In later years, union opposition was often focused on profit sharing's alleged use as a device to prevent successful organization. Some evidence has been advanced that profit sharing may indeed help employers resist unionization.[6] A number of nonunion firms in the country are prominent profit sharers, including Sears Roebuck, Eastman Kodak, Winn-Dixie Stores, and Texas Instruments. It is

---

[4] Gordon F. Bloom and Herbert R. Northrup, *Economics of Labor Relations*, 8th ed. (Homewood, Ill.: Richard D. Irwin, Inc., 1977), pp. 146–47.

[5] Boris Emmet, "Will Profit Sharing Solve Labor Difficulties?" *Monthly Review of the U.S. Bureau of Labor Statistics*, Vol. V, No. 2 (August 1917), p. 249.

[6] Edgar R. Czarnecki, "Effect of Profit-Sharing Plans on Union Organizing Efforts," *Personnel Journal*, Vol. 49, No. 9 (September 1970), pp. 763–73.

important, however, to provide a balance to this and point out that profit-sharing plans exist in a number of unionized firms such as Zenith Radio and American Brands, and some plans, such as that for Xerox Corporation's blue-collar employees, are jointly administered by management and union.

In Europe, profit sharing, although not usually popular with unions, has rarely been directly linked to the maintenance of nonunion status. Employers have found its advantage to lie more in the fostering of a sense of partnership and identification with the company, and neither management nor labor perceives profit sharing to be incompatible with collective bargaining.

EMPLOYEE STOCK OWNERSHIP

As its name implies, an employee stock-ownership plan is any plan that provides for employees to become shareholders of the company by which they are employed. An employee can always choose to become a shareholder of his employer provided that the latter's stocks are publicly traded. The intention of specific plans, therefore, is to create an additional incentive to share ownership, usually by including some contribution from the employer, such as a discount price on shares.

The issue of eligibility to participate is not a major problem with profit-sharing or asset-formation plans. Some stock-option plans are, however, limited only to senior executives. In this study, any plan that is only designed for a small minority of an employer's labor force is excluded from consideration.

There is some degree of overlap between stock-ownership plans and deferred profit sharing. The latter may use company stock as a means of investment, and some stock may be ultimately disbursed to employees. In this study, if the amount of stock ultimately available to the employee is only a small part of his total entitlement and if the prime intention of the plan is other than making the employee a shareholder in the company, then it is considered a profit-sharing plan. Employee stock-ownership plans are defined here as plans that primarily provide a method, not necessarily related to profit levels, whereby employees can become shareholders of their employing company.

Aims

The motivation for introducing stock-ownership plans is frequently similar to the motivation for having profit sharing—that is, to create a sense of common identity between employer and employee.

Introduction 7

There is also the added factor of a sense of ownership arising from the holding of shares. Stock-ownership plans also have the advantage to the company of being a benefit that can, generally, be given without adverse effects on its liquidity position and that can provide a source of funds for investment.

Stock-ownership plans also have an ideological basis in the belief that the economic system will be strengthened if more people are given a direct stake in it as owners. This view is a political factor both in the United States and in Europe and is central to the attitude of pressure groups such as the Wider Share Ownership Council in the United Kingdom. It also accounts for the enthusiasm of some European centrist parties, such as the Free Democrats in Germany and the Liberals in the United Kingdom, for stock-ownership and profit-sharing plans.

There is an underlying assumption that the average employee may often be suspicious of share ownership and need encouragement to become a shareholder. Although stock-ownership plans have rarely run into great union hostility, there has been some criticism that they expose employees to a "double risk." Not only is an employee's future employment based on the well-being of his employer, but so is a part of his additional assets. The supporters of such plans see this, however, as a factor increasing the employee's motivation to work for the company's success.

ASSET FORMATION

Asset formation is defined here to cover plans that provide for employees to receive payments from their employer and to set aside part of their own remuneration in an account that is invested for a period of time before being made available to them, usually in the form of a lump sum or installment payments, or through an annuity contract. The most common examples in the United States of such provisions are savings and thrift plans. The essence of such plans is that the contributions should constitute a form of savings to which the employee does not have direct access for a specified period. Most plans define specific exceptions to this, of which the most common is a provision for withdrawal in the event of the employee's death. The employer's contributions are often based on the principle of "matching" the employee's savings, partially or fully, and are made without regard to current profit levels.

In Europe, there are in some countries legal provisions for employee savings, but without employer contributions. Instead, in the United Kingdom, Germany, and the Netherlands, the government grants a bonus related to the size of the employee's saving. This bonus is either paid in cash or given in the form of specific tax concessions. Where relevant, such plans are mentioned in the survey of individual countries.

Aims

The advantages of asset-formation and savings plans are not usually seen in the same light as those of profit sharing and stock ownership. They are based on the view that to have some additional incentive to save will be a useful fringe benefit welcomed by employees. Such plans involve very little risk to employees and serve as a low-cost fringe benefit that trade unions rarely consider inimical to their interests. As a result, these plans are not a controversial benefit in any major sense.

THE ROLE OF GOVERNMENT

In many countries, governments have considered to a greater or lesser extent that the aims of profit-sharing, stock-ownership, and asset-formation plans are desirable. They have, therefore, frequently made tax concessions available for plans to encourage their wider utilization. This has often made the support of such plans a political issue. Thus, the compulsory profit-sharing system in France owes much to Gaullist views of social order. In 1978, tax concessions for profit sharing were secured by the Liberal party in the United Kingdom as one of the prices for its continued support of the minority Labour government.

In Europe, a number of countries have seen plans as a useful source of funds for investment. The problem of the generation of investment in welfare-oriented societies is a major issue to which this study will return. In the United States, there has been a traditional incentive to save during working life to meet financial needs after retirement, but this motivation is much weaker in many European countries. Both in Europe and the United States, persistent shortages of private investment have been a major economic problem, and the creation of mechanisms whereby small investors can accumulate savings has been seen as one way of offsetting this difficulty.

Collective Plans

In recent years, there have been proposals in a number of European countries, particularly the Netherlands, Sweden, and

Denmark, for legislation to establish collective profit-sharing or asset-formation plans. The proponents of such measures have justified them partly by the need to generate additional funds for investment. Critics, however, have pointed out that such plans usually include trade union control over the investment funds. As such, they are seen as a means of enhancing the political and economic power of unions and not as a means of meeting individual economic aims.

Such arrangements have often been generally classified as profit sharing, but in addition to the direct union control, they differ from normal profit-sharing plans in two fundamental respects. First, they are multiemployer plans and draw on the profits of many companies to set up large composite funds. Second, they limit the holding of the individual worker, either partially or wholly, to a stake in the central fund rather than a holding directly with his own employer. The plans are also compulsory, with all companies above a certain size required to participate. Their aims are also quite different from individual company profit-sharing plans. They seek to alter the balance of economic power in favor of unions and to modify the existing economic system by redistributing wealth from stockholders to collective funds.

NATURE OF THE STUDY

This study seeks to compare and contrast the various wealth-creating benefits in different countries. A description of plans in the United States is followed by a survey of developments in Western Europe. Transnational comparisons always pose certain problems. It is extremely difficult both to convey all the elements that contribute to creating the values and structure of any society and to describe how social and cultural differences are reflected in the operation of apparently similar plans. The section on Europe is prefaced by a brief analysis of some of the salient differences between Europe and the United States, particularly in the systems of industrial relations and the structure of the economies. Such a description must necessarily take into account the varied cultural and political factors that affect this subject. The description of the types of profit sharing is made on a country-by-country basis, and developments at the European Community level are summarized separately.

The material for this study has been gathered from a number of sources, published and unpublished, in a number of languages. This has been supplemented by interviews and discussions with companies, union officials, academics, and other interested parties. The field has seen many rapid changes, which sometimes make definitive judgments difficult. One example may suffice: The VAD plan in the Netherlands has been the subject of considerable political debate over the period 1977-79, and a number of different versions of the plan have been put forward as the political situation has changed. The attempt to describe current phenomena inevitably poses such problems, especially when, as in this study, one seeks to indicate the possible pattern of future developments, as well as to describe the existing situation.

CHAPTER II

Profit Sharing in the United States

The United States has proved the most fertile soil for the growth of profit sharing. The concept has been extensively applied and widely supported. Its value has been seen as that of providing additional support to the capitalist economic system and of broadening the impact of that system. It has attracted a significant group of active supporters. The Profit Sharing Council of America (PSCA) is an active educational and lobbying group of companies that practice profit sharing. The Profit Sharing Research Foundation (PSRF), a publicly supported educational foundation, was formed in 1951, four years after the PSCA. Although it developed from the Planning and Research Committee of the PSCA, it is now a totally separate organization. The PSRF has published many articles and books on profit sharing that are an essential source of information on this field. Under its president, Bert Metzger, the PSRF has been actively involved in conferences and other educational work on the subject in the United States and abroad.

In total, it is estimated that about 339,000 American firms are profit sharers, of which about 100,000 have *immediate cash plans*.[1] Figures on cash plans, however, are not readily available. Figure II-1 indicates the steady growth of *deferred plans* in recent years, although there have been some setbacks associated with the decline in stock market levels and with the passage of the Employee Retirement Income Security Act (ERISA). Figure II-2 shows that, since 1966, there has also been a steady fall in the average number of employees covered by each plan, a decline indicating the spread of plans to smaller companies. There are also a number of plans that combine both deferred and cash-distribution elements. Eastman Kodak allows the employee each year to choose the proportions he wishes to allocate to cash and to deferred investment. Until 1960, its Wage Dividend Plan provided a cash distribution only, but the introduction of the Savings and Investment Plan allowed employees

---

[1] Bert L. Metzger, *Profit Sharing in 38 Large Companies,* Vol. I (Evanston, Ill.: Profit Sharing Research Foundation, 1975), p. 1.

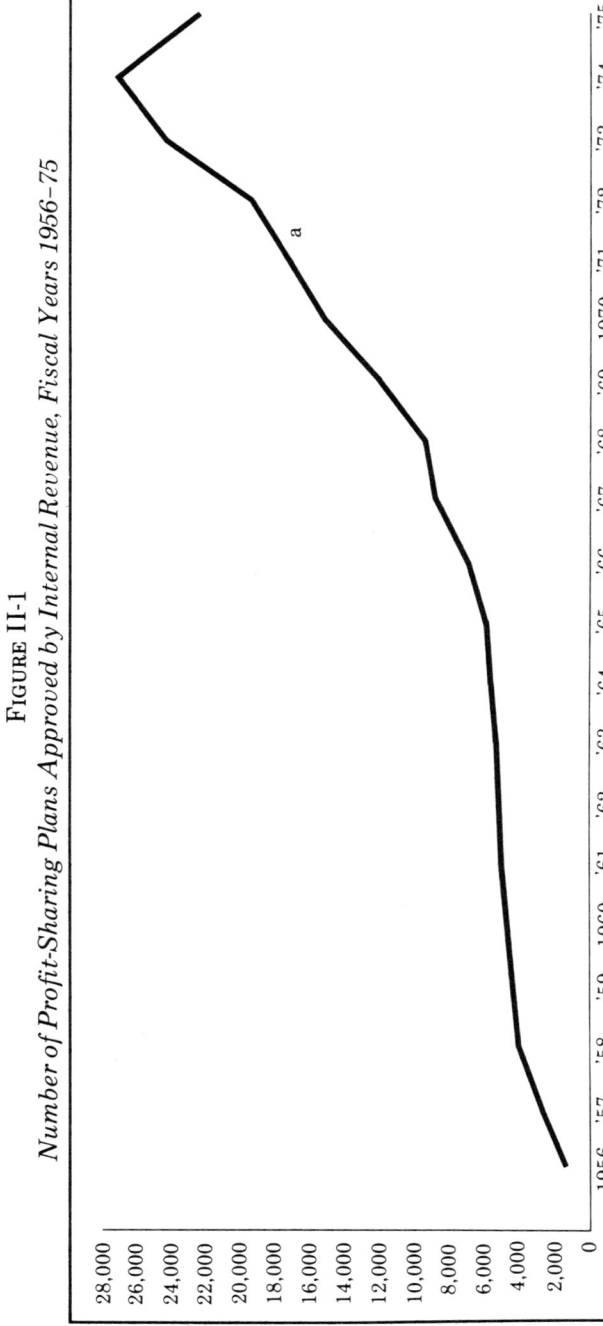

FIGURE II-1
Number of Profit-Sharing Plans Approved by Internal Revenue, Fiscal Years 1956–75

Source: Commissioner of Internal Revenue, *Annual Reports* (Washington, D.C.: U.S. Government Printing Office), for each year from 1956 through 1975.

[a]The data for 1971 to 1975 also include stock-bonus plans that were previously recorded separately. The average number of such plans over the five-year period 1966–70 was, however, only twenty-four per year, and the average number of employees covered was only 23,205.

Profit Sharing in the United States 13

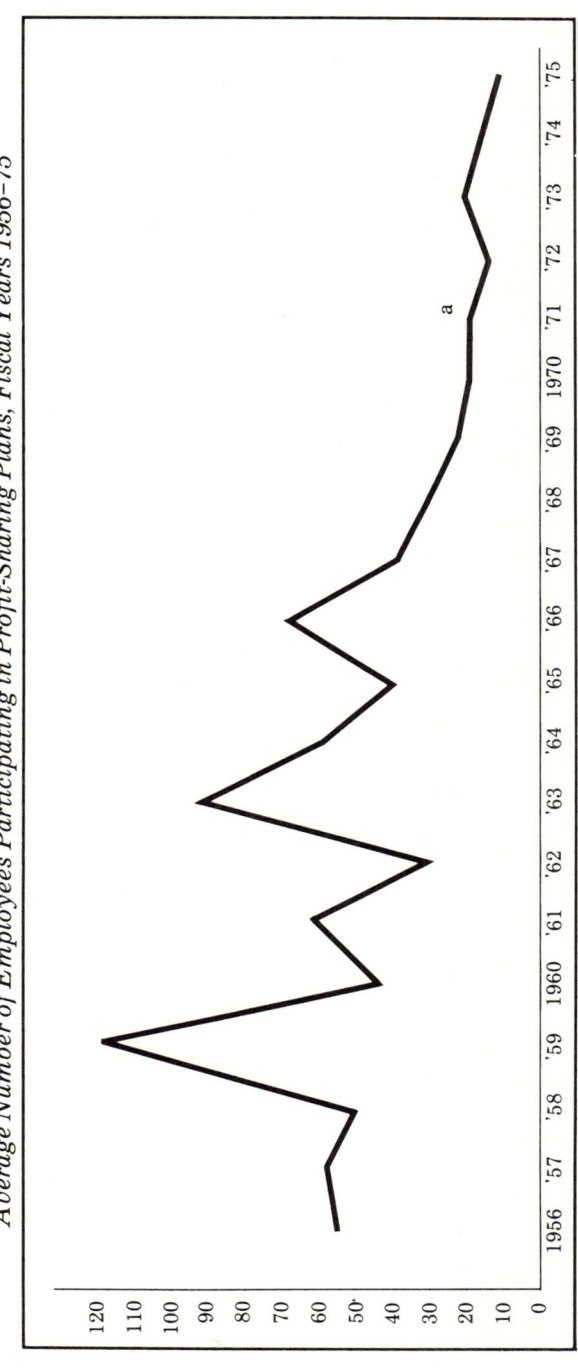

FIGURE II-2

Average Number of Employees Participating in Profit-Sharing Plans, Fiscal Years 1956-75

Source: Commissioner of Internal Revenue, *Annual Reports* (Washington, D.C.: U.S. Government Printing Office), for each year from 1956 through 1975.

[a]The data for 1971 to 1975 also include stock-bonus plans that were previously recorded separately. The average number of such plans over the five-year period 1966-70 was, however, only twenty-four per year, and the average number of employees covered was only 23,205.

to defer between 0 and 100 percent of the wage dividend. This chapter is not intended to provide an exhaustive account of the systems of profit sharing in the United States. There are many sources available to the reader who wishes to explore the subject more fully, a situation that distinguishes the United States from Western Europe. The chapter, therefore, mainly seeks to extract some of the salient points that relate to profit sharing and, in particular, seeks to highlight some of those features distinctive to American profit sharing.

THE HISTORY OF PROFIT SHARING

Historians of profit sharing have identified Albert Gallatin, secretary of the treasury under Jefferson and Madison, as the instigator of America's first profit-sharing plan, set up in 1797 at his glassworks in New Geneva, Pennsylvania.[2] It was only in the final decades of the nineteenth century, however, that profit sharing really began to develop. The origin of some of the early profit-sharing proposals was primarily religious. A group of Protestant clergy saw profit sharing as a possible antidote to some of the social problems that accompanied industrialization. A leading member of this group, Nicholas Paine Gilman, was the author of two books on profit sharing[3] and helped form the Association for the Promotion of Profit Sharing in 1892.[4] In 1889, Gilman identified thirty-four profit-sharing plans in the United States.[5] By 1896, however, a survey indicated that, of fifty plans, thirty-three had ceased entirely, and only twelve were fully operating.[6]

Much of this early movement was supported by people outside industry itself. One significant exception was Colonel William Cooper Procter, who was the main architect of Procter & Gamble's profit-sharing plan introduced in 1887. The plan divided net profits between the company and its employees in the same proportion as total wages bore to the total cost of production and marketing. Each employee received a semiannual cash dividend according to

---

[2] "Albert Gallatin," *Profit Sharing Trends*, Vol. XIV (March-April 1959), pp. 2-3.

[3] Nicholas Paine Gilman, *Profit Sharing Between Employer and Employee* (Boston and New York: Houghton, Mifflin and Company, 1889); Nicholas Paine Gilman, *A Dividend to Labor: A Study of Employees' Welfare Institutions* (New York and Boston: Houghton, Mifflin and Company, 1899).

[4] Kenneth M. Thompson, *Profit Sharing: Democratic Capitalism in American Industry* (New York: Harper and Brothers, 1949), p. 10.

[5] Gilman, *Profit Sharing Between Employer and Employee*, pp. 386-87, 389.

[6] Paul Monroe, "Profit Sharing in the United States," *American Journal of Sociology*, Vol. I (May 1896), p. 709.

the ratio of his wage to total wages.[7] Procter believed that profit sharing would increase employee involvement in the company and improve efficiency.

The growth of unions and the spread of worker unrest created a renewed interest in profit sharing during the early years of the twentieth century. Organizations such as the National Civic Federation saw profit sharing as a means of reducing labor problems.[8] As one supporter wrote, "By making the interests of employer and employee identical, profit sharing will tend to lessen antagonism and friction between owners and employed workers, and to substitute in their stead industrial harmony."[9]

The reaction of the trade union movement was not favorable. In 1916, Samuel Gompers, the president of the American Federation of Labor, said of profit sharing:

> This proposition has never been seriously considered by the organizations of labor. I desire to say further that it has come under my observation that some employers who have inaugurated systems of so-called profit sharing have pared down the wages of their employees so that the combined sharing of profits and their wages did not equal the wages of employees of other companies in the same line of industry. What we are especially interested in more than profit sharing is a fair living wage, reasonable hours and fair conditions of employment.[10]

Despite this opposition, the number of profit-sharing plans increased between 1910 and 1920. It was in this period that some of the most famous plans that still exist today were established, including those of Eastman Kodak (1912) and Sears Roebuck (1916). By 1916, however, a study by the Bureau of Labor Statistics could still locate only about sixty plans.[11] Two-thirds of these were less than ten years old, and only one plan was based on a signed agreement.

In the United States during the decade following World War I, emphasis shifted from profit sharing to employee stock ownership as a means of interesting employees in the success of companies for

---

[7] Alfred Lief, *It Floats* (New York: Rhinehart and Company, Inc., 1958), pp. 73-76.

[8] J. J. Jehring, "The Development of the Profit Sharing Idea in the U.S.," in *A New Approach to Collective Bargaining?* (Madison, Wis.: Center for Productivity Motivation, School of Commerce, University of Wisconsin, 1962), p. 12.

[9] Arthur W. Burritt et al., *Profit Sharing: Its Principles and Practice* (New York: Harper and Brothers Publishers, 1918), p. 78.

[10] The National Civic Federation, *Profit Sharing by American Employers* (New York: E. P. Dutton and Company, 1916), pp. 368-69.

[11] Boris Emmet, *Profit Sharing in the United States*, U.S. Bureau of Labor Statistics Bulletin, No. 208 (Washington, D.C.: U.S. Government Printing Office, 1917), p. 9.

which they worked. These plans provided that an employee's share of profits be distributed to him in the form of stock or credits on the purchase price of stock. Through such stock-ownership plans, corporations sought to promote industrial peace. It was hoped that the sense of proprietorship in the firm encouraged by stock ownership would evoke in the employee an increased loyalty to the interests of the business. Thus, an employee who was a stockholder would be less likely to go out on strike and more likely to take the viewpoint of owners or managers.[12]

The Emergence of Deferred Profit Sharing

Many of the plans established in this early period were not strictly profit sharing, and the latter term was often used loosely to describe any payments beyond the cash wage. In any case, the Depression years saw a period of relative inactivity on this front. Congressional interest in the topic in the late 1930s led, however, to a new growth of profit-sharing plans. In 1939, the Vandenberg-Herring Subcommittee of the Senate Committee on Finance reported on profit sharing and suggested that such plans were associated with labor peace, employee security, and business success.[13] Senator Vandenberg summarized the committee's investigation as follows:

> The committee finds that profit sharing, in one form or another, has been and can be eminently successful, when properly established, in creating employer-employee relations that make for peace, equity, efficiency, and contentment. We believe it to be essential to the ultimate maintenance of the capitalistic system. We have found veritable industrial islands of "peace, equity, efficiency, and contentment," and likewise prosperity, dotting an otherwise ... relatively turbulent industrial map, all the way across the continent. This fact is too significant of profit-sharing's possibilities to be ignored or depreciated in our national quest for greater stability and greater democracy in industry.[14]

This Senate report created additional public and management interest in profit sharing, particularly as a means of aiding industrial peace. Subsequent to, and partly influenced by, the favorable findings on profit sharing by the Vandenberg-Herring subcommittee, Congress passed legislation that provided tax advantages for qualified deferred profit-sharing plans. One survey found that, out of 209

---
[12] Burritt et al., *Profit Sharing*, pp. 85-88.
[13] U.S., Congress, Senate, Subcommittee of the Committee on Finance, *Survey of Experiences in Profit Sharing and Possibilities of Incentive Taxation* (Washington, D.C.: U.S. Government Printing Office, 1939), pp. 159-60.
[14] *Ibid.*, p. 5.

plans studied in 1945, 52 were established between 1940 and 1944, the period immediately after the report was published.[15]

World War II marked a departure from the old pattern of current-distribution, or cash, profit sharing. Federal regulations to control wage rates during the war encouraged the use of deferred profit-sharing plans. In an effort to stabilize wages and salaries, the government did not allow cash-distribution plans to be adopted after October 2, 1942. As long as the wage and salary controls were in force, only deferred profit-sharing plans that conformed to section 165(a) of the Internal Revenue Code (IRC) were allowed to be established.[16]

Tax Support

Still a significant incentive for initiating profit-sharing and pension plans was the tax advantage to both employers and employees. During the war years, the federal tax rates were sufficiently high that the tax advantages of qualified profit-sharing plans were a strong incentive to set up plans. If a plan met the Internal Revenue Service (IRS) requirements outlined in section 165(a) of the IRC, employers were permitted to deduct, as a wage cost, profit-sharing payments up to a maximum of 15 percent of total compensation.[17] Employees found the plans attractive because the deferred payments were not currently subject to income taxation and because lump-sum payments made at retirement could be treated as long-term capital gains.

Deferred distribution plans also provided a means of attracting and retaining workers during these years. Because wages and salaries were controlled and frozen to a large extent, employers were eager to find a permissible way to provide attractive benefits to hold skilled employees and attract desirable applicants. Consequently, many profit-sharing plans were adopted during the war for this purpose. Included among other fringe benefits instituted for employees during this time were pension plans to supplement the federal old-age benefits. Retirement-income plans financed by a portion of company profits were popular because they allowed the

---

[15] Bryce M. Stewart and Walter J. Cooper, *Profit Sharing for Wage Earners and Executives*, Industrial Relations Monograph, No. 15 (New York: Industrial Relations Counselors, Inc., 1951), p. 22.

[16] F. Beatrice Brower, *Sharing Profits with Employees*, Studies in Personnel Policy, No. 162 (New York: National Industrial Conference Board, 1957), pp. 8–9. The Internal Revenue Code can be found at 26 *United States Code* (U.S.C.) (1976).

[17] Brower, *Sharing Profits with Employees*, p. 9.

employer to provide benefits without assuming the obligations of fixed contributions as required by an actuarially determined pension plan.

The IRS approved 2,471 deferred profit-sharing plans between January 1, 1940, and August 31, 1946, of which over half (1,631) were established during the latter part of the war, September 1942 through December 1944.[18] Between 1946 and 1955, an additional 6,000 plans were approved.[19]

Current Growth and Problems

Figure II-1 illustrates the continued growth of plans and bears witness to the vitality of the profit-sharing concept. The recent history of profit sharing has not been an unqualified success. The decline in stock market values in the early 1970s created some problems. Profit-sharing plans actually held up better than pension plans during this period, but there were still some notable declines.[20] The assets of Sears Roebuck's plan declined from $3.8 billion in 1971 to $2.9 billion in 1973,[21] while the assets of the plan at Burlington Industries came down from $184 million to $153 million in the same period.[22] A number of companies met this situation by guaranteeing a certain minimum level of contributions irrespective of profit performance; Xerox Corporation and Zenith Radio are two examples.[23]

A major PSRF study has examined the question of whether participants benefit more from a profit-sharing plan or a pension plan in amounts of retirement income received. The study took a pension standard of 1.3 percent of final average pay per year of service, with final average defined as the best three consecutive years in the final five years of service, with no offset for social security benefits. It then compared the resulting retirement-income figure with a profit-sharing account balance converted to retirement income on the basis of a straight life annuity. Under this comparison, only six companies out of thirty-three studied generated lower benefits from profit sharing than from pensions. In practice,

---

[18] Stewart and Cooper, *Profit Sharing for Wage Earners and Executives*, p. 56.
[19] Gunnar Engen, "A New Direction and Growth in Profit Sharing," *Monthly Labor Review*, Vol. 90, No. 7 (July 1967), p. 4.
[20] James P. Roscow, "Profit Sharing Without Profit?" *Pension World*, Vol. 11, No. 3 (March 1975), pp. 9-10.
[21] Metzger, *Profit Sharing in 38 Large Companies*, Vol. I, p. 177.
[22] *Ibid.*, pp. 66-67.
[23] Bert L. Metzger, "PS Trends," *Profit Sharing*, Vol. 25, No. 2 (February 1977), pp. 26-31.

Profit Sharing in the United States

all of these six companies provided both profit-sharing and pension plans, with combined benefits exceeding the level of the pension standard. Among companies with pension plans, as well as profit-sharing plans, the thirteen out of nineteen that exceeded the standard did so by amounts ranging from 112 percent to 598 percent. Among those without pension plans, the figures ranged from 102 percent to 1,011 percent.[24]

Some profit-sharing plans have encountered more severe difficulties. Two companies, Marriott Corporation and Tappan Company, faced lawsuits arising out of the fall in value of employees' profit-sharing accounts.[25] In the former, a retiree had seen her account fall from a value of $17,764 in 1972 to $8,638 in 1975. Her suit charged that the corporation and the trustees of the plan had violated their fiduciary duties by investing too high a percentage of the plan's assets in the corporation's own stock. In this context, it is noteworthy that ERISA limits investment in own company stock to 10 percent of a pension plan's assets but imposes no similar restriction on profit-sharing plans.[26]

Some companies decided that, in the face of the adverse experience of these years, it would be better to close down their plans than to risk continuing problems. R. J. Reynolds terminated its plan in 1970.[27] Other companies modified their plans to take ERISA into account. Dart Industries fits into this category, and even Sears Roebuck has modified its profit-sharing plan. Some of profit sharing's advocates regarded the passage of ERISA as a setback to profit sharing.[28] This view was not universally endorsed, however.[29] Concern over the detailed issues arising out of ERISA may have slowed down the implementation of new profit-sharing plans, particularly as plan administrators awaited the issuance of clarifying regulations. In the absence of sufficient information, it was predictable that there would be a slowdown in the introduction of new plans. This situation may only be a short-term one, and once the effects of ERISA have been more clearly understood, the long-run trend of growth may resume. There is already evidence of a renewal

---

[24] Bert L. Metzger, *Profit Sharing in 38 Large Companies*, Vol. II (Evanston, Ill.: Profit Sharing Research Foundation, 1978), p. 48.

[25] "Employee Wrath Hits Profit Sharing Plans," *Business Week*, July 18, 1977, pp. 25-28.

[26] Employee Retirement Income Security Act, 29 U.S.C. §1107(a)(2) (1976).

[27] "Profit Sharing Plans Run into Trouble," *Business Week*, December 7, 1974, pp. 106-11.

[28] Robert D. Midkiff, "Helping Workers to Become Owners," in Bert L. Metzger, ed., *New Horizons for Capitalism* (Evanston, Ill.: Profit Sharing Research Foundation, 1977), p. 7.

[29] Bert L. Metzger, ed., *Pension, Profit Sharing, or Both?* (Evanston, Ill.: Profit

of this upward trend; during 1978, the number of approvals of profit-sharing plans reached a record 28,634.[30]

THE NATURE OF DEFERRED PROFIT SHARING

A 1973 PSCA survey of seven hundred plans indicated that a majority of those studied (54.1 percent) had the primary aim of providing a retirement benefit to employees, and in an additional 7.9 percent of the plans, this was a partial aim.[31] Many employers prefer to provide retirement income from a profit-sharing plan rather than a pension plan. This policy avoids the financial commitment and actuarial complexity of defined benefit pension plans and, in addition, provides an encouragement to employee performance, a provision absent in conventional pension plans.

The IRS rules for qualified profit-sharing plans influence eligibility provisions considerably. Plans must be established for the exclusive benefit of employees and their beneficiaries, and plans cannot discriminate in favor of highly paid employees. The test of discrimination is based on participation levels. A plan qualifies if it benefits at least 70 percent of all employees or over 80 percent of eligible employees, as long as at least 70 percent of all employees are eligible.[32] The 1973 PSCA survey found that 80.8 percent of the plans covered all employees, while 14.7 percent were limited to salaried or nonunion workers.[33] Service requirements are also used, the most common being one year, but 20.2 percent of the plans in 1973 had a shorter service requirement or none at all. Only 3.8 percent exceeded three years.[34]

Plans differ, of course, in the participation levels they attain. Where employee contributions are not required, participation is generally high, and the same applies if the profit-sharing fund is primarily intended to provide retirement benefits. Plans such as those at Sears Roebuck, Standard Oil of California, and Signode achieve a participation level of over 95 percent of eligible employees.

The majority of plans studied by the PSCA used a predetermined formula to assess the company's contributions, usually a percentage of profits before taxes. IRS rules require that the company con-

---

Sharing Research Foundation, 1975), pp. 3-4.
[30] Commissioner of Internal Revenue, *Annual Report, 1978* (Washington, D.C.: U.S. Government Printing Office, 1979), p. 100.
[31] Profit Sharing Council of America, *Guide to Modern Profit Sharing* (Chicago, 1973), p. 13.
[32] 26 U.S.C. §401 (1976).
[33] Profit Sharing Council of America, *Guide to Modern Profit Sharing*, p. 59.
[34] *Ibid.*, p. 61.

tributions should be "substantial and recurring,"[35] a requirement that is mainly designed to ensure that the plan is established on a permanent basis. The percentage of profits distributed tended to increase in the smaller companies.[36] The money was usually allocated to individuals in relation to pay level, although 34.1 percent of the plans included some service element in the calculation.[37]

In all profit-sharing plans, an employee's allocation becomes an entitlement that cannot be forfeited when it is vested. A few of the plans studied gave full and immediate vesting, but in most cases, vesting began only after two or three years' service and proceeded in accordance with a graduated schedule.[38] Full vesting typically was achieved over a ten-year period at a rate of 10 percent per year.

Employee contributions were mandatory in only 12.4 percent of the plans, but a further 39.2 percent of the plans provided for voluntary employee contributions, usually of amounts up to 10 percent of pay.[39] The use of employee contributions means that some profit-sharing plans have what could be termed a "savings plan" element and are therefore, in a sense, hybrid schemes. This is particularly true of plans in which the employee contributions are mandatory. The trend appears to run toward a more widespread use of employee contributions.[40]

The employee normally receives his share at retirement. Increasingly, there are provisions for loans and withdrawals from the plan. Partial withdrawal was allowed in 34.1 percent of the plans studied by the PSCA, and 30.5 percent of the plans allowed loans.[41]

Investment Policy

Profit-sharing plans vary in their investment policies. Many of the major plans have a diversified portfolio, including bonds and other companies' stock. Investment policies will differ according to whether a company believes in investing heavily in its own stock or seeks to avoid this. At one extreme, the Kellogg Company had only 2 percent of its plan's assets in Kellogg stock in 1973.[42] Other companies with under 10 percent include Xerox, Winn-Dixie Stores, and Chase Manhattan. Many companies, however, invest almost

---
[35] *Ibid.*, p. 37.
[36] *Ibid.*, p. 52.
[37] *Ibid.*, p. 69.
[38] *Ibid.*, pp. 87–92.
[39] *Ibid.*, p. 149.
[40] *Ibid.*, pp. 143–47.
[41] *Ibid.*, pp. 133–41.
[42] Metzger, *Profit Sharing in 38 Large Companies*, Vol. I, p. 37.

exclusively in own company stock—over 90 percent in the cases of Safeway Stores, Standard Oil of California, Eastman Kodak, and Carter Hawley Hale Stores. Companies of this kind believe that their policy encourages a feeling of ownership and community of interest. This high level of investment in own company stock in certain profit-sharing companies contrasts sharply with the previously mentioned ERISA requirements covering investment procedures in pension plans.

There has been a clear trend toward giving employees more choice in the way in which their allocation is invested. At Xerox each year, employees can choose how they want their entitlement invested, and they are free to spread this over all four options available to them. These are (1) a "General Fund," which is a diversified portfolio of stocks and bonds, (2) Xerox common stock, (3) a 9 percent "guaranteed fund," and (4) cash. The guaranteed fund was added in 1975 and now accounts for about 20 percent of investment of company contributions and over 90 percent of the employees' contributions.[43]

Administration

Plans are usually governed by an administrative committee or a board of trustees. In some cases, the plans are administered solely by managerial personnel. Some companies provide for employee involvement, and usually the employees are appointed by the board of directors. A few companies go further; for instance, Bell and Howell has group and divisional level profit-sharing boards with elected employee representatives.[44] In Motorola, two of the five members of the advisory committee that administers the plan are elected by participants, and a larger profit-sharing council, entirely elected, assists the advisory committee.[45] Xerox Corporation's unionized employees' plan is unusual in that it is managed by a committee of which one-half is appointed by the Amalgamated Clothing and Textile Workers' Union. The union representatives have made their impact felt on the plan, particularly on issues such as withdrawals. In some cases, the union has taken a less "liberal" attitude toward plan provisions than the company has. For instance, the company proposed a reduction in the time required for full vesting, but the union preferred a longer period because ad-

---

[43] Company official, interview in Stamford, Ct., April 27, 1978.
[44] Metzger, *Profit Sharing in 38 Large Companies*, Vol. I., p. 57.
[45] *Ibid.*, p. 135.

ditional forfeitures to the fund by leavers would be applied to benefit long-service employees.

The Nature of Profit-Sharing Companies

There has been considerable research on the type of industries in which profit sharing flourishes. One study indicated that, in 1967, retail trade and the banking industry had the highest percentage of employees covered by profit-sharing plans.[46] In retail trade, 44 percent of office workers and 27 percent of plant workers were involved. This finding is reinforced by the intuitive view of the industry as a profit sharer, which arises from the companies, such as Sears Roebuck, Carter Hawley Hale, Winn-Dixie, J. C. Penney, Safeway Stores, and Jewel, which have plans. Among banks, Chase Manhattan, Manufacturers Hanover Trust, and Bank America are noted profit sharers. In manufacturing, however, only 10 percent of plant employees and 15 percent of office employees were covered in 1967. In transportation, communications, and public utilities, the figures were even lower.[47]

Another analysis of profit sharing concluded that it was found most frequently "in industries where restrictive market structures generate substantial 'excess profits.' "[48] This study examined the number of employees who were covered by profit sharing in particular industries. Industries with over 25 percent coverage were photographic apparatus, oil, soap, and musical instruments. It seems possible to argue that some of these results were heavily biased by a single profit-sharing company, as with Eastman Kodak in photographic supply. At the other end of the spectrum, the results seem more valid, and industries such as steel, automobiles, shoes, and public utilities had a very low incidence of profit sharing.

There has been much effort expended to determine whether profit sharing improves a company's business performance. Metzger's study of large companies showed higher returns on sales and on stockholders' equity than for the relevant industrial grouping as a whole. He concluded that the findings "support other recent evidence that profit sharing companies, as a group, tend to outperform their non profit sharing competitors—and profit sharing contributes to this superior performance."[49]

This, of course, is the central issue. If those companies with profit

---

[46] Engen, "A New Direction and Growth in Profit Sharing," pp. 6–7.
[47] *Ibid.*, p. 6.
[48] Charles Schotta, Jr., "The Distribution of Profit-Sharing Plans: An Analysis," *Southern Economics Journal*, Vol. XXX, No. 1 (July 1963), p. 59.
[49] Metzger, *Profit Sharing in 38 Large Companies*, Vol. I, p. 4.

sharing do have higher returns, in which direction does cause and effect flow? Is there any relationship at all between the two phenomena? The oil industry is a significant profit sharer, but evidence that profitability is related to the existence of profit sharing seems slight. For the 1967-77 period, the aggregate average return of the three main profit-sharing oil companies was almost identical to the average return of the eight largest non-profit-sharing oil companies.

Evidence supporting the thesis that companies gain through profit sharing was gathered by a PSRF study published in 1971.[50] The study was restricted to the chain department store industry and updated previous work from the 1950s. The study concluded that profit sharing and employee stock ownership were "important contributing factors" to higher profits among profit-sharing companies when compared with non-profit sharers.[51] The study recognized that it is impossible to separate the effect of profit sharing from other factors and suggested that the existence of a profit-sharing plan reflects an able and enlightened management, which is likely to be commercially successful. In practice, profit sharing often forms part of a general managerial philosophy and a general policy on staff relations, which may well make this judgment correct. Profit sharing itself is, not the agent of change, but the reflection of it.

Union Attitudes toward Profit Sharing

Historically, American unions have not been enamored of profit sharing. The American Federation of Labor's first president, Samuel Gompers, went on record against such plans in 1916 and voiced his distrust of employers' motives and his preference for regular collective bargaining.[52] It was thought that plans were designed to make union organizing more difficult, and that typically, profit sharing was entirely outside the sphere of union control. William Green, Gompers's successor, summed this up in 1938 in his evidence to the Vandenberg-Herring Subcommittee of the Senate Committee on Finance:

> Labor is not opposed to principles involved in profit sharing, but it is opposed to the way in which it has developed and operated. So-called profit-sharing plans were mainly developed by corporations that at-

---

[50] Bert L. Metzger and Jerome A. Colletti, *Does Profit Sharing Pay?* (Evanston, Ill.: Profit Sharing Research Foundation, 1971).
[51] *Ibid.*, p. 84.
[52] The National Civic Federation, *Profit Sharing by American Employers*, p. 269.

tempted to substitute for real collective bargaining an arrangement termed "employee representation" which for the most part was the form without the substance.[53]

He went on to state that unions' priorities involved the establishment of effective negotiation over pay and conditions, and thereafter, profit sharing might enter into their consideration. In his evidence to the committee, John L. Lewis, president of the United Mine Workers, speaking on behalf of the Congress of Industrial Organizations, echoed this view:

> Labor cannot eat or live on hopes of participation in profit-sharing plans. Immediate higher standards of living achieved through collective bargaining with labor unions is the best guarantee policy for the continued expansion of industrial activity and profits from [sic] management.[54]

Attitudes, however, began to change after 1945. The International Union of Electrical, Radio and Machine Workers proposed a profit-sharing plan during negotiations with General Electric and Westinghouse in 1951 and subsequently made proposals to General Motors.[55] A Conference Board report in 1957 showed that 88 out of 204 companies studied that had profit-sharing plans were unionized, although only fifteen bargained on the subject.[56]

The agreement between the American Motors Corporation (AMC) and the United Automobile Workers (UAW) in 1961 was perhaps the first collectively bargained profit-sharing plan in a major industry. The plan provided for employees to share 15 percent of profits before taxes but after a deduction from profits of a sum equal to 10 percent of the company's net worth. Two-thirds of the company's contribution each year was used to improve and maintain employee benefits, and the remaining one-third was invested in AMC stock and credited to individual employee accounts to be held in trust. Individuals had the right to vote the stock in their accounts. Moreover, withdrawals of stock during employment could be made in designated circumstances and with committee approval.[57]

---

[53] U.S., Senate, Subcommittee of the Committee on Finance, *Survey of Experiences in Profit Sharing and Possibilities of Incentive Taxation*, Hearing, 75th Cong., 3d sess., 1938, p. 105.

[54] *Ibid.*, p. 190.

[55] I. B. Helburn, "Trade Union Response to Profit-Sharing Plans: 1886-1966," *Labor History*, Vol. 12, No. 1 (Winter 1971), pp. 75-76.

[56] Brower, *Sharing Profits with Employees*, p. 64.

[57] I. B. Helburn, *Progress Sharing at American Motors* (Madison, Wis.: Center for Productivity Motivation, School of Commerce, University of Wisconsin, 1964), pp. 12-25.

The plan was designed to meet the differing goals of the two parties. The UAW received improvements in fringe benefits and a portion of company profits for employees while agreeing to a reduction of time-paid-not-worked by five minutes, revision of inflexible seniority rules, and changes in production standards. These three concessions by the union were considered very important by the management to the competitive position of AMC.

AMC-UAW "progress sharing," however, did not meet with great success. The contract was ratified only after a second ballot, which still showed about one-third of the 10,000 voting members opposed. The plan paid a diminishing amount to employees in each year of the three-year agreement; consequently, the original progress-sharing plan was modified in 1964 to include a limited cash distribution. The company's sales and profit problems caused a seven-year lapse in profit-sharing payments to employees. In 1973, AMC distributed payments averaging $150 to 21,600 workers, which was the first such payment since the mid-1960s. As late as 1974, AMC tried unsuccessfully to drop the profit-sharing plan; that attempt became one of the disputed issues of the three-week strike.[58]

Although the attitude of unions toward profit sharing has mellowed, they remain skeptical. Schotta's study in 1963 showed that industries with strong unionization had little profit sharing.[59] His view was that industries such as steel and automobiles showed all the other necessary market conditions for a propensity to be profit sharers, and so the existence of unions was a major factor. A study in the 1960s, based on six years of comparative analysis of union election success, showed that the existence of profit sharing was associated with a lower level of union victories.[60] The author was quick, however, to point out that this did not establish a causal relationship.

Profit-sharing plans do exist in many unionized companies, and attitudes are not always hostile. Past rejection of profit sharing has often been based on practical considerations related to its antiunion uses rather than on ideology. Unions vary in their views, and there is no reason to believe that unions in the United States could not find profit sharing consistent with their general economic and social views.

---

[58] "AMC and UAW Reach an Accord On 2-Year Pact," *Wall Street Journal*, October 2, 1974, p. 4.

[59] Schotta, "The Distribution of Profit-Sharing Plans: An Analysis," p. 59.

[60] Edgar R. Czarnecki, "Profit Sharing and Union Organizing," *Monthly Labor Review*, Vol. 92, No. 12 (December 1969), pp. 61–62; Edgar R. Czarnecki, "Effect of Profit-Sharing Plans on Union Organizing Efforts," *Personnel Journal*, Vol. 49, No. 9 (September 1970), pp. 763–73.

CONCLUSION

In the United States, profit sharing has amply proved its resilience. Not only has it survived in the face of adverse economic conditions and union criticism, but it has prospered. Only in a country imbued with an economic philosophy that still stresses an individual's work achievement would this be possible. In Europe, where economic ideology is generally different, profit sharing has been unable to take such a firm hold.

Unlike profit-sharing plans, savings plans have flourished in both the United States and Europe. As we shall see, because savings plans encourage thrift and can offer various methods of investing employee savings, they have not aroused controversy on either side of the Atlantic.

CHAPTER III

Employee Savings Plans in the United States

Employee savings plans appear under a variety of names. They may be called savings plans, thrift plans, or investment plans, or they may include all or some of these in the title. The distinction between savings plans and stock-ownership plans may not always be readily apparent. Most savings plans include investment in company stock, either as one option or, in some cases, as the only method of investment. The names of many plans reflect this situation. General Motors's plan, for instance, is called a "Savings-Stock Purchase Program," and General Electric's is called a "Savings and Stock Bonus Plan."

There are two basic differences between savings and stock-ownership plans. The first is the manner in which the employee normally receives the assets that have been made available to him. Under a savings plan, he usually receives them either as a lump sum or as cash installments. In a stock-ownership plan, he generally receives the assets in the form of stock of his employer. Secondly, there is usually a difference in contributions. Savings plans require employee contributions, whereas such required contributions are rare in stock-ownership plans.

The neat analytical distinction between the two types of plans is not so easy to apply in practice. It is not clear that the employee is likely to perceive this distinction between the two types of plans. Savings plans that invest in employer stock usually allow the employee to direct the voting of his stock, and he is not usually under any compulsion to dispose of such stock until he wishes. Thus, if he wishes to keep the stock after retirement, and it is vested in him, he can do so. In this situation, he may feel just as much a shareholder as if a more direct stock-ownership plan had been used.

The basic requirement of a savings plan, as defined here, is that both employer and employee should make a contribution to the plan. It is also fundamental to such plans that the employee should be free to decide whether he wishes to join the plan or not. If he does decide to join, his contribution is usually deducted regularly from

Employee Savings Plans in the United States 29

his wages or salary. The company then matches all or part of the employee's contribution, and the combined sum will be invested by the fund in various ways. In some cases, the sole means of investment is company stock, but plans sometimes offer a range of alternatives, including investment in other securities, bonds, and guaranteed income funds.

Savings plans should also be distinguished from deferred profit-sharing plans. The typical deferred profit-sharing plan does not require employee contributions, and the company contributions are related to profit levels. In savings plans, the company contribution is basically a function of the level of the employee's contribution, and the main aim of such plans is to encourage employee thrift, not employee performance.

THE NUMBER OF PLANS

There has been a considerable increase in the number of savings plans for employees over recent years. In 1962, a Conference Board study reported that there were no more than 150 corporations with such plans.[1] The same study showed that, of the total number of surveyed companies with plans, 66 percent had adopted their plans after 1955.[2] The rate of growth seems to have continued, and a Bankers Trust survey in 1977 involved 236 plans, covering a total of 2.75 million employees, each plan with over 1,000 participants.[3] Using data drawn from this same study, Table III-1 gives the date of establishment of the largest savings plans. It shows that the largest plans generally were set up first, and the rate of growth among more medium-sized companies followed. It also illustrates a considerable slowdown in the creation of such plans since 1970. It is not clear whether this is due to market saturation or is a temporary phenomenon arising from adverse economic conditions and the passage of the Employee Retirement Income Security Act (ERISA).

Another estimate of the number of plans can be drawn from the survey of employee benefits made by the Chamber of Commerce. The 1975 survey showed that, of 761 employers, 18 percent had employee thrift plans. The incidence varied considerably among industries. Petroleum, with 56 percent, had the highest, a figure that is not surprising since Exxon, Shell, Standard of Ohio, and

---

[1] Harland Fox and Mitchell Meyer, *Employee Savings Plans in the United States*, Studies in Personnel Policy, No. 184 (New York: National Industrial Conference Board, 1962), p. 3.
[2] *Ibid.*, p. 12.
[3] Bankers Trust Company, *1977 Study of Employee Savings and Thrift Plans* (New York, 1977), p. 9.

TABLE III-1

Date of Establishment of Savings Plans in Existence in 1977

	Number of Plans				Cumulative Percentage of Plans			
Date	Over 20,000 Participants	10,000-20,000 Participants	5,000-10,000 Participants	1,000-5,000 Participants	Over 20,000 Participants	10,000-20,000 Participants	5,000-10,000 Participants	1,000-5,000 Participants
Prior to 1950	4	0	3	2	15	—	5	2
1950-55	7	5	6	5	41	17	16	6
1956-60	4	6	9	16	56	37	33	20
1961-65	5	5	15	23	74	53	60	39
1966-70	6	9	16	37	96	83	84	71
After 1970	1	5	6	34	100	100	100	100
Total	27	30	55	117	—	—	—	—

Source: Bankers Trust Company, *1977 Study of Employees Savings and Thrift Plans* (New York, 1977).

Standard Indiana, among others, have such plans. The chemical industry (37 percent), public utilities (33 percent), and insurance (29 percent) followed. No responding department stores or hospitals had plans, and the metal industries, metal products, textiles, and apparel all had under 5 percent.[4] The survey also gave information on the cost of thrift plans to employers. It showed that, on average for those employers with plans, the cost of company contributions to the thrift plan came to 1.5 percent of total payroll, ranging from 0.1 percent (primary metal industries) to 3.1 percent (metal products).[5]

TAX POSITION

The Internal Revenue Code (IRC) does not specifically provide for employee savings plans,[6] but the plan can be designed to qualify in one of three ways.[7] The savings plan can be qualified as a stock-bonus plan if the contributions of the company may, but need not, come from profits, and if the contributions are not used for any purpose other than providing the employee with common stock of the employer. The savings plan can also be a qualified money-purchase pension plan if company contributions are made according to a fixed formula that is not related to profits. A money-purchase plan is an arrangement whereby the employer's contributions, usually related to the employee's salary level, are allocated to the employee's account. This arrangement provides a simple method of accumulating funds for employees and avoids actuarial complexity. For the employer, it ensures that the pension cost of past service is fully funded, and that future cost is a fixed percentage of the payroll.[8] This plan then pays indeterminable benefits to employees as income after retirement. The third way that a plan may be qualified is as a profit-sharing plan, with company contributions from annual profits or retained earnings. Most savings plans are designed to qualify as profit-sharing plans, with contributions coming from current or accumulated profits.

A savings plan that is qualified as a profit-sharing plan is more flexible than a savings plan qualified as either a stock-bonus or

---

[4] U.S. Chamber of Commerce, *Employee Benefits 1975* (Washington, D.C., 1976), Tab. 15, p. 21.

[5] *Ibid.*, Tab. 16, p. 22.

[6] James A. Amdur, "Thrift Plans—Operation and Taxation," *Taxes*, Vol. 51, No. 10 (October 1973), p. 599.

[7] Bion H. Francis, *Employee Savings Plans—The Coming Trend in Retirement Planning* (Chicago: Advertising Publications, Inc., 1969), pp. 149–50.

[8] Dan M. McGill, *Fundamentals of Private Pensions*, 3d ed. (Homewood, Ill.: Richard D. Irwin, Inc., 1975), pp. 92–97.

money-purchase pension plan.⁹ A money-purchase pension plan does not allow the employee to withdraw employer contributions and increments during active employment; withdrawals of this nature are permitted under a profit-sharing plan. The qualified money-purchase pension plan does not allow the employer to vary the percentage of salary to be contributed from year to year; such an adjustment is permitted by a profit-sharing plan. The following discussion assumes that the savings plan is qualified as a profit-sharing plan under the IRC.¹⁰

Profit-Sharing Qualifications

To qualify as a profit-sharing plan under the IRC, the savings plan *must* meet certain nondiscriminatory criteria.¹¹ At least 70 percent of the employees must participate, or at least 70 percent of the employees must be eligible to participate in the plan, and 80 percent or more of those eligible must actually participate. These requirements are the same as those imposed on employee pension plans. If the plan does not meet the percentage requirements, then it must be demonstrated to the IRS that the plan does not discriminate in favor of the officers, shareholders, supervisors, or highly paid employees.

Employee and Employer Contributions

The employee contributions give rise to some important tax considerations. The Internal Revenue Service (IRS) has decided that a plan cannot have an excessively high employee contribution rate because it would be, in effect, a form of discrimination against the lower-compensated employee. Contributions of 6 percent or less of annual compensation have been deemed as *not* excessively high by the IRS, but any basic contribution over the 6 percent mark could be open to IRS scrutiny as a violation of section 401(a) of the IRC. Savings plans may provide for unmatched employee contributions in excess of the percentage necessary to participate. This benefits the employee because the trust acts as a tax shelter on fund earnings until the distribution of the account to the employee.

The nondiscrimination requirements are by no means purely theoretical. For example, until the early 1970s, under Exxon's Thrift Plan, originally established in 1936, employees could contribute

---
⁹ Amdur, "Thrift Plans—Operation and Taxation," p. 599.
¹⁰ *Ibid.*, pp. 599 ff.
¹¹ Internal Revenue Code, 26 *United States Code* (U.S.C.) §401(a) (1976).

Employee Savings Plans in the United States 33

2, 4, 6, 8, or 10 percent of salary, and the company matched this contribution to the extent of 60 percent. As a result of the IRS's view that this was discriminatory against the lower-paid employees, the company reduced the employee contributions to 6 percent but matched them dollar for dollar. Thus, the company ensured that, for the person who had been contributing at 10 percent and still wished to do so, the situation remained unchanged. Both before and after this change, additional unmatched contributions of a further 10 percent of salary by the employee were allowed. The strictness of IRS interpretation is illustrated by the fact that, prior to the change, 93 percent of the participants in the plan chose to contribute at the 10 percent level, and participation in the plan ran at 94 percent of eligible employees.[12]

Employer contributions are immediately deductible as a business expense, subject to certain limitations.[13] The employer is entitled to deduct up to 15 percent of the annual compensation paid to *participating* employees, with the allowable deductible amount increasing to 25 percent of this compensation *if* the employer also has a pension plan. The deduction for a contribution to benefit an employee is further limited to an amount that, together with other compensation paid, is "reasonable" in relation to the services actually rendered, the determination of what is reasonable being made by the IRS. The earnings from the investment of both the employer and employee contributions are exempted from income tax at this time.

Taxes: Distribution during Employment

There are two basic types of distribution that occur during employment: voluntary employee withdrawals and periodic partial distributions. With respect to voluntary withdrawals, the employee excludes from his gross income the portions of the withdrawals up to the point at which he recovers his own contributions, and any excess received is taxed as ordinary income. Most of the plans provide some restrictions on withdrawal to prevent the employee from being taxed under the doctrine of "constructive receipt." The IRC requires that the employee be taxed in the year that the amounts in the trust are made available or distributed to him.[14] This means that the employee may be taxed even if the funds are not distributed to him in the taxable year. The funds are not considered

---

[12] Company official, interview in New York, N.Y., March 30, 1978.
[13] 26 U.S.C. §404(a)(3) (1976).
[14] *Ibid.*, §402(a)(1).

"available" to the employee if substantial restrictions are placed on their withdrawal. When the employee withdraws only his own after-tax contributions, they are not then taxed, and the problem of constructive receipt does not occur.

The periodic partial distribution is taxed in a similar manner to the voluntary withdrawal. Distributions are excluded from the gross income of the employee up to the point at which he has recovered his contributions to the plan, and amounts received over this point are taxable as ordinary income. The problem of constructive receipt can enter here also. To prevent taxation under this doctrine, the employee should be given the right to defer receipt until a fixed later period or until termination of service. This decision must be irrevocable and should be made prior to the time that the funds are available to the employee. If the employee does not elect to defer, he can be deemed in constructive receipt because he had the right to receive the funds whether he actually exercised this right or not.

Separation of Service: Tax Rules for Lump Sum Versus Installments

Upon separation of service due to retirement, death, permanent disability, or other reasons, most plans give the employee the choice of receiving the distribution of his account in one of two ways: a lump sum or installment payments (including annuities). The tax rules for a lump-sum distribution state that the net employee contributions are not taxed because they were made with after-tax dollars.[15] In theory, the distribution resulting from employer contributions should be taxed as ordinary income, and the amount derived from increments on investment should be taxed at capital-gains rates. In practice, however, such distributions are treated more favorably because Congress has found it desirable to provide tax benefits to such plans. The distribution receives favorable tax treatment if (1) it occurs either at separation from service or after age 59½, and (2) it is a distribution of the total sum in the employee's account.[16]

Employees who joined a plan after 1974 and have five years of participation can have a lump-sum distribution taxed on a ten-year averaging rule, which decreases the tax liability that would have arisen if the total amount distributed had been added to the employee's regular income in the year of distribution. If the employee

---
[15] *Ibid.*, §402(e).
[16] *Ibid.*, §402(e)(4).

participated in the plan prior to 1974, that part of the distribution based on pre-1974 contributions is taxed at long-term capital-gains rates. The part attributable to post-1974 service is taxed under the new ten-year averaging rule.[17]

Installment payments are taxed in the same way as an annuity under section 72 of the IRC. The net employee contributions to the plan must be determined because the recovery period of these contributions is an important factor in assessing liability for taxation. If the employee will recover his contribution to the plan within three years of the beginning of the installment payments, then the amounts received are not taxed until after he has recovered his contributions. Subsequent payments are taxed as ordinary income. If the employee will not recover his contributions within the three-year period, a ratio to determine exemption from taxation is used. This ratio is composed of the employee's contributions in relation to his total account balance, and it is applied to the installment payments for each year. This computed amount, which represents the employee's contribution, is excluded, and the remaining portion is taxed as ordinary income.

Taxation at Death

Generally, upon the death of an employee, the amount in his account is distributed to a beneficiary in lump-sum form. For the purpose of federal estate tax, the value of a lump-sum distribution is includable in the deceased employee's estate, but an income tax deduction will be given for estate tax paid. The federal income tax treatment of lump-sum distributions is similar to that described in the previous section. Five thousand dollars is excluded from federal income tax as an employee death benefit if the account balance is paid in a lump sum in one taxable year to his beneficiary.[18]

Special Tax Treatment: Employer Securities

A special tax treatment occurs if the distribution to the employees is made in employer common stock or other employer securities. When the employee's account is distributed in total, the entire net unrealized appreciation is excluded, and any later transactions concerning the securities are taxed as long-term capital gains. For all other distributions, the net unrealized appreciation on the portion of securities acquired with employee contributions *only* is excluded.

---

[17] *Ibid.*, §402(a)(2).
[18] *Ibid.*, §101(b)(2).

This excluded portion is taxed as either long-term or short-term capital gains when sold, depending on the length of the holding period.[19]

Summary of Tax Advantages

The major tax advantages of an employee savings plan that is qualified as a profit-sharing plan are as follows:
1. Employer contributions are a tax-deductible business expense;
2. The trust that holds the contributions, investments, and earnings is tax-exempt;
3. Employer contributions and the earnings on both employer and employee contributions are not taxed to the employee until these funds are actually distributed to him;
4. When the employee is separated from the company and withdraws the funds accumulated to him, the lump-sum distribution receives favorable tax treatment; and
5. If the lump-sum distribution includes, or is in the form of, common stock of the employer, the amount subject to tax can be reduced by any unrealized appreciation on the stock.

CHARACTERISTICS OF SAVINGS PLANS AND RECENT TRENDS

One of the major sources of information on employee savings and thrift plans has been the series of studies conducted by the Bankers Trust Company, the fifth of which was published in 1977. The 1977 study was limited to plans with over one thousand participants but provided information on 236 plans and examined trends over the period 1972–77. The following account of plan characteristics draws heavily on this study.

Groups Covered and Eligibility

Most of the savings and thrift plans in 1977 offered membership to all employees (about 65 percent), although this constituted a slight decrease from 1972 (about 69 percent). The percentage of plans only covering salaried or nonbargaining unit employees tended to increase, but the majority of plans still included all employees. The use of a provision excluding members of a bargaining unit that does not accept the plan increased distinctly from 40 percent in 1972 to 48 percent in 1977.

Savings and thrift plans are required by law to comply with stated minimum standards for eligibility requirements set in 1974

---
[19] *Ibid.*, §402(a)(1).

under ERISA.[20] One requirement is that the plan must be open to any employee at twenty-five years of age with one year's service in the relevant group. An alternative requirement establishes eligibility after three years of service if the plan provides 100 percent immediate vesting. About 75 percent of the 1972 plans had standards more liberal than ERISA's, and only 20 percent of the plans contained more stringent requirements that had to be updated. Eighty-six percent of the 1977 plans studied had standards more liberal than ERISA's. Most companies have the definite aim of attracting as many company employees as possible to a plan.

There are two commonly used eligibility requirements: length of service and age. A length-of-service requirement was the most frequently used; 93 percent of the plans required one year or less. From 1972 to 1977, service requirements shortened. Forty-five percent of the plans in 1977 required exactly one year of service. The use of an age requirement was included only in just over 25 percent of the plans. The most commonly used age was twenty-one, but the trend was to shift the age either to eighteen or twenty-five. There was a small increase in plans that had neither service nor age requirements, although this still involved less than 10 percent of the total in 1977. The reason given for the use of some requirement is that it reduces administrative costs by excluding employees with the highest turnover rates.

Participation of Eligible Employees

Employee savings plans generally attract high participation, although there was a decrease from 70 percent to 50 percent between 1972 and 1977 in the number of plans with participation rates over 70 percent of eligible employees. Economic conditions, and particularly inflation, over this period seemed an important factor in discouraging involvement of any kind. Generally, newer plans lagged behind the older ones in levels of participation. About one-third of the plans had over 80 percent participation of eligible employees, and only one-sixth of the plans had less than 50 percent. Three of the most influential factors that affect the level of employee participation are the size of a company's matching contribution, the vesting provisions, and the number of different investment options. In general, there was high participation in plans that offered a high percentage of matching contributions by the employer, more immediate vesting provisions, and a greater

---

[20] Employee Retirement Income Security Act, 29 U.S.C. §1052 (1976).

number of investment options from which the employee could choose.

Contributions by the Employee

Contributions by employees to the savings plan are generally limited within some percentage range of the employee's compensation, e.g., 2 percent to 6 percent. The employer usually contributes a fixed percentage of this basic amount. Most plans permit the employee to make additional voluntary contributions above the basic percentage range, but these additional contributions are unmatched by the company. The percentage of plans with provisions for unmatched additional contributions increased from 29 percent in 1972 to 54 percent in 1977. These additional contributions benefit the employee in that the accumulated savings are in a tax-sheltered trust, and this trust receives favorable tax treatment if the savings are distributed at retirement. The 10 percent limit placed by the IRS on the additional voluntary contribution is added to the basic percentage to give a total maximum contribution percentage.[21]

The most common maximum figure for the employee's basic contribution is 6 percent. The trend has been to reduce contribution rates of above 6 percent because of IRS policy, which seeks to ensure that the plan does not discriminate in favor of higher-paid employees. There was not any great change in the percentage of 1977 plans with a rate lower than 6 percent. The use of a graduated employee-contribution scale based on service or membership, another provision subject to IRS scrutiny for discrimination in favor of higher-paid employees, has also declined.

About one-tenth of the plans in 1977 included a dollar limit in addition to a percentage maximum, but the use of such a provision has also decreased. The 1977 study recognized two types of dollar limitations: the use of a "flat dollar ceiling" or the use of a "specified level of recognized annual compensation up to which the elected rate of contribution is applied."[22]

Contributions by the Employer

In the overwhelming majority of plans, employer contributions are based on the amount of the employee contributions. In most cases, the matching contribution is a fixed percentage of the em-

---

[21] 26 U.S.C. §401(a)(13) (1976).
[22] Bankers Trust Company, *1977 Study of Employee Savings and Thrift Plans*, p. 17.

ployee contributions. Some plans use a range of percentages based on length of membership, length of service, or profits to match the employee's basic contributions. Seven percent of the studied plans used a definite profit-sharing formula to compute the company contribution. The companies allocated this amount either (1) in proportion to the employee's contribution, (2) in proportion to the employee's compensation, or (3) as a combination of contributions and compensation.

The matching percentage ranged from 25 percent to over 100 percent of employee contributions. The plans with the highest matching percentages also had the highest rates of participation, and a causal relationship can confidently be postulated. There is also a tendency for plans that cover all employees to have higher matching percentages than plans that are more selective in coverage. A graduated company-contribution scale, usually based on membership or length of service, was used in 10 percent of the 1977 plans. In the 1977 study, 23 percent of the plans included provisions for additional company contributions, depending on corporate profits. This was an increase from 20 percent in 1970, a rise caused by the fact that one-third of the new plans established in the 1972-77 period included such provisions. A majority (61 percent) of the plans in which employee contributions were matched at less than 50 percent provided for additional contributions.[23]

The cost of the plan to the employer is influenced by several factors. An important one is the number of eligible employees who choose to participate. The percentages that the employees decide to contribute also influence the cost. Another relevant factor is the number of forfeitures, if any, which are applied to reduce future company contributions. These three factors will influence cost decisions in the administration of the plan. The plans in the 1977 study had a median cost to the company of 3 percent of the covered payroll.

Voluntary Suspensions

Ninety-six percent of the 1977 plans studied allowed voluntary suspension of employee contributions, usually for any reason. In general, no company contributions are made to an employee's account during a suspended period. The trend was toward a liberalization of the restrictions placed on the voluntary suspensions; over one-half of the 1977 plans allowed the voluntary suspensions to

---

[23] *Ibid.*, p. 19.

occur more than once each year. If an employee voluntarily suspends his contributions, a time period is usually required to elapse, most often six months, before he may resume contributions. The percentage of plans with such a requirement, however, decreased from 90 percent in 1972 to 82 percent in 1977. There was also a decrease in the percentage of plans that terminated employee participation if the employee contributions were not made by the end of a maximum suspension period.

Contribution Investment

The investment of contributions in the past has mainly been in company stock. The developing trend in this area is to give more investment options and greater flexibility to the employees. Eighty-six percent of the 1977 plans, an increase in 11 percent from 1972, offered the employee some choice of investment options. These plans usually limited the employee's choice to the use of his own contributions. The company contributions were normally invested in employer stock. The percentage of plans that required at least partial investment in employer stock decreased from 68 percent in 1972 to 62 percent in 1977. In most other plans, investment in employer stock was one option, but 15 percent of all plans excluded company stock entirely as an investment option. Less than 10 percent of the plans used common stock as the only investment.

The number of investment alternatives has also increased, and most plans now offer three investment funds alternatives. The types of investment options that are offered have changed considerably. The trend is to change from fixed income funds, which were widely used in the past, to other types of funds. Guaranteed income funds are being increasingly used today, whereas in previous years, they were rare. Such funds may guarantee interest rates of up to 8 or 9 percent for periods as long as five years.[24] Diversified portfolios of equity and fixed income securities have become popular, although the use of United States government obligations has declined.

Investment Transfers

Most plans permit the employee to change the form of investment of future contributions from one option to another. Traditionally, however, the employee has not had the same degree of control over

---

[24] "Company Savings Plans Offer Big Tax Break; But for Some, the Bond Funds May be Better," *Wall Street Journal*, June 27, 1977, p. 28.

his accumulated account. The use of an investment-transfer provision in a plan allows an employee to change the investment of the accumulated contributions in his account from one fund to another, although the transfer may be limited to the employee's own contributions. The incidence of investment-transfer provisions increased sharply between 1972 and 1977, and in the latter year, such provisions were found in 57 percent of the plans. There is a growing tendency to limit transfers to one per year. Less than one-quarter of the 1977 plans limited transfers to a maximum of three in an employee's career. Almost all of the plans, which initially allowed the employee some choice in investment, also allowed him to change the investment at least once each year.

Three probable reasons for the increased use of investment-transfer provisions were offered by the Bankers Trust study. First, the provisions provide some defense against market volatility. Second, there is an increasing recognition by employers of the differing needs of their employees and how these needs change over the duration of a person's working lifetime. Finally, computerized systems have reduced the administrative problems created by investment transfers.

Vesting Provisions

All plans provide fully vested company contributions upon death, retirement, or permanent disability. An employee's own contributions are always 100 percent vested, and in some plans, the employer's contribution is also immediately fully vested in the employee, giving him an irrevocable right over his total account balance.

Vesting provisions in the absence of an immediate vesting system are therefore primarily designed to ascertain the employee's right on termination of service (other than by death, disability, or retirement) or the employee's right on withdrawal from the plan while still in the employer's service. There are two main types of vesting provisions: class and membership. Under a class system, the employer contributions for a specific period (e.g., one year) constitute a "class" and are vested after a designated period following the contribution date. Under this system, the employee is never fully vested because the most recent of his employer's contributions have not yet been vested. The contributions become vested at death, disability, or retirement, but withdrawal for any other reason involves the employee's forfeiture of part of the employer's contributions. Under ERISA, class vesting must be 100 percent vested five years after the close of the year in which the class was formed, but many plans use a shorter vesting period.[25]

The membership system provides the employee with vested rights to the company contributions after a specified period of service or plan membership, and unlike company contributions under class vesting, any company contributions after this period are immediately 100 percent vested. Membership vesting must meet one of three standards established by ERISA. Vesting must (1) occur after ten years, (2) be based on a five-to-fifteen-year graduated schedule, or (3) be based on a graduated "Rule of 45" schedule.[26] The ten-year provision has no vesting at all prior to the end of this period but then has full vesting in one operation. The five-to-fifteen-year graduated schedule requires 25 percent vesting by the first five years of service, 5 percent for each additional year up to and including the tenth year, and 10 percent vesting per year until it reaches 100 percent after fifteen years. Under the Rule of 45, an employee with at least five years' service receives 50 percent vested benefits when his age and years of service add up to forty-five, and 10 percent additional for each subsequent year.

Although membership vesting had declined since 1972, it was still the most frequently used method in the 1977 plans. Because of the amendment of older plans, there was a corresponding increase in the use of immediate vesting. The percentage of plans using immediate vesting doubled in five years, although the use was still small (12 percent). The percentage of plans using class vesting remained constant, but there was a trend toward the use of shorter time requirements, and in 1977, 40 percent of the plans had time requirements under three years. A two-year period was the median length for new plans using a class system. The overall trend was to use a graduated schedule as a part of membership vesting. Graduated schedules in class vesting were also used, but not as frequently as in plans with membership vesting.

Forfeiture Allocation

Some forfeiture of part of an employee's account will always arise upon termination of employment, other than by death, disability, or retirement, when vesting is based on a class system, and may arise under membership vesting, depending on the period of membership or service. Seventy-five percent of the 1977 plans used forfeitures to reduce future company contributions, and this provision also

---

[25] 29 U.S.C. §1053(c)(3) (1976).
[26] *Ibid.*, §1053(a).

reduced the effective cost to the company. Only about 10 percent of the plans allocated part or all of the forfeitures to the remaining employees, and this percentage had fallen since 1972.

Periodic Distributions

Some plans provide without penalty a regular periodic distribution of the employee's account to the employee as long as he is still in service. Usually, periodic distributions occur in plans using class vesting and are tied directly to the time required to vest completely. Before the class is fully vested, the employee is allowed the option to receive part or all of the class or to defer receipt of any portion until the termination of service. Only 28 percent of the 1977 plans had a distribution-in-service provision. The low utilization of this provision may be explained by the increasing tendency to use liberal voluntary withdrawal provisions.

Voluntary Withdrawals

Provisions for voluntary withdrawal were found in most of the studied plans in 1977. These provisions allow an employee to withdraw a portion of his account periodically, and the majority of the plans allowed withdrawals at any time during the year. The employee usually suffers a penalty upon withdrawal, both because of IRS rules and because of the plan's purpose of encouraging long-term thrift. Although some plans make the stipulation that withdrawals are only permitted in proven cases of hardship, no plan in the 1977 study totally prohibited a withdrawal of a portion of the employee's account. Within plans permitting voluntary withdrawals, the use of a provision allowing additional withdrawals in case of hardship was also increasing.

The maximum amount that an employee can withdraw has been fairly stable, but the penalties for maximum withdrawals have become less severe. From 1972 to 1977, there was an increase in the number of plans that allowed the employee to withdraw less than the maximum amount at a reduced penalty. About one-half of the 1977 plans allowed employees to withdraw all employee contributions and all vested company contributions, and only one-third of the plans limited the withdrawals to employee contributions.

Three different types of penalties are most frequently applied. The suspension-of-membership penalty prohibits the employee from contributing to the plan for a specified period, and the employee loses matching contributions during that time. If the termination-of-membership penalty is used, the employee is prohibited from participating in the plan for a specified time; and, for purposes of higher contribution matches or requirements for voluntary withdrawals, the employee also loses credit for participation in past years. Another frequently used penalty is a forfeiture of a portion of the employee's company account. The current trend is toward less severe penalties. The use of forfeiture and the use of a double penalty have both decreased, and there has been a corresponding increase in the use of the suspension penalty only.

Voting Rights of Company Common Stock

Approximately 70 percent of the 1977 plans gave the employee the right to vote his company common stock. This was usually accomplished by the employee's confidentially directing the trustee how to vote the stock. When the employee chose not to vote the stock, most plans permitted the trustee to vote undirected shares at his discretion. This practice, however, had decreased substantially since 1972. A few of the 1977 plans prohibited the voting of undirected stock, and the trend was to include a provision requiring the trustee to vote the undirected shares in the same proportion as the directed shares. The percentage of plans not giving the employee the right to vote at all had also decreased since 1972.

Forms of Distribution

There are several different forms that the distribution of an employee's account may take at the termination of service. The trend has been to permit alternatives to distribution in the form of one lump sum. The most common alternatives are installment payments, an annuity contract, or the purchase of an additional monthly retirement benefit through the employee pension plan. The annuity contract has been most frequently selected, the installment payment the second most frequently selected.

BENEFITS OF SAVINGS PLANS

Savings plans have proved a relatively simple and inexpensive benefit for employers to provide and have not aroused great controversy. They undoubtedly offer an encouragement for employees to save on a regular basis without significant risk. In plans offering a choice of investments, risk can be spread, but in any case, the employer's contribution acts as a buffer against any likelihood of loss by the employee.

Investment in the company's own stock is now often only one of the options, which overcomes the criticism leveled at some stock-ownership plans that they force workers to become shareholders against their will. Where a choice is provided, the employee can avoid investing in stock at times when the market is depressed. There is considerable evidence that employees are sensitive to economic changes. Thus, in Exxon's Thrift Plan, 75 percent of the participants held part of their portfolio in company stock in 1973, but this fell to 59 percent in 1977 with some slight increase thereafter.[27] There seems to be a general agreement that higher-paid employees are often more willing to accept the risks inherent in shareholding than are the lower-paid.

Savings plans also offer greater predictability of benefits than straight profit-sharing plans offer, although the benefits are usually smaller. The employee can plan major expenditures or face unexpected emergencies more satisfactorily. Participants regard this as a major advantage. Plans can frequently permit greater flexibility than profit-sharing plans; for example, one growing feature is the provision of loans to employees. In 1977, for instance, Exxon's plan, which had thirty-two thousand participants, made fifteen thousand loans, totalling $47.6 million.

There may also be less quantifiable advantages in having a savings plan. The plan may be seen as part of an overall benefits package, which may help enhance the company's image of being a "good" employer and may raise morale and reduce labor turnover. Insofar as the plan provides for stock ownership, it may help meet the goal of employee identification, which is felt to be the particular result of share ownership.

---

[27] Company official, interview in New York, N.Y., March 30, 1978.

CHAPTER IV

Stock-Ownership Plans in the United States

Like profit-sharing and savings plans, share-ownership plans come in a variety of forms.[1] Stock-purchase plans are one form, and there are a large number that are not funded and qualified under the Internal Revenue Code (IRC). One survey in 1966 suggested that 20 percent of the firms listed on the New York Stock Exchange had stock-purchase plans.[2] Some plans make no provision at all for employer contributions and merely give the employee administrative assistance in becoming a shareholder of his company. More generally, companies give a discount on the market value of the shares. For instance, under IBM's plan, employees can buy stock at 85 percent of the market value. Employees can put up to 10 percent of their salaries each year into such stock purchases.

Most stock-bonus plans are qualified by the Internal Revenue Service (IRS) under section 401(a) of the IRC. A stock-bonus plan is similar to a profit-sharing plan, except that employer contributions are not necessarily related to profit, and the benefits can be distributed only in the form of employer stock. A stock-bonus plan also must invest, at least in part, in employer stock. In 1975, the Treasury estimated that there were 7,250 stock-bonus plans, but these covered only four hundred thousand employees.[3]

Stock-option plans are virtually for senior executives only and so are not considered in this study. They give the employee an opportunity to purchase stock at current prices at some future date. If the market value of the stock rises, the option results in a capital gain for the employee; if the price falls, the option can be allowed to lapse.

---

[1] For a discussion of the types of stock-ownership plans, see U.S., Congress, Joint Economic Committee, *Employee Stock Ownership Plans (ESOP's)*, Hearing, 94th Cong., 1st sess., 1975, p. 11.

[2] Mitchell Meyer and Harland Fox, *Employee Stock Purchase Plans*, Studies in Personnel Policy, No. 206 (New York: National Industrial Conference Board, 1967).

[3] U.S., Congress, Joint Economic Committee, *Employee Stock Ownership Plans*, p. 90.

ESOPs

In recent years, the appellation of employee stock-ownership plan (ESOP) has been reserved for one particular type of share-ownership plan. In many respects, ESOPs are similar to traditional stock-bonus plans. An ESOP, however, must invest primarily in employer stock. A stock-bonus plan has to invest in employer stock to an extent sufficient to cover stock distributions but is free to invest part of its assets in other ways. It is also specifically recognized that an ESOP can be a technique of corporate financing, whereas a stock-bonus plan cannot be. As with regular stock-bonus plans, all distributions must be in the form of employer stock, and company contributions need not be based on profits.

The major element of an ESOP is that the employer contributes cash to a qualified tax-exempt trust (specially created under the plan) for the purchase of stock. The advantage here for the company is that it can deduct as a business expense a sum equal to the market value of the stock and so reduce its income tax burden. The stock is allocated to individual employees' accounts on the basis of such factors as salary level and length of service. Vesting and participation provisions must meet the standards laid down in the Employee Retirement Income Security Act (ERISA).[4] At retirement or at prior termination of service, the employee normally receives the stock that has been allocated to him. Some plans impose an obligation on the company to buy stock back at market value from the employee if the latter wishes to sell.

One major attraction of an ESOP to an employer is that it can be leveraged, that is, borrowed funds can be used to purchase new employer stock. Under such an arrangement, the trustees of the employee stock-ownership trust (ESOT) arrange for an appropriate lending institution to provide the ESOT with a loan, which is used to purchase company stock on the employees' behalf. The company guarantees the loan made to the ESOT by making contributions to the ESOT, and employer stock serves as collateral. The stock held by the ESOT is then allocated to participants as cash contributions are made on their behalf under the plan. These cash contributions made by the employer are tax-deductible and are used to retire both the principal and the interest of the loan. Although ESOPs do not have to be leveraged in this manner, the potential for this has helped their development.

---

[4] Employee Retirement Income Security Act, 29 *United States Code* (U.S.C.) §§1052–1053 (1976).

DEVELOPMENT OF ESOPs

The concept of ESOPs has become popular in recent years, and there has been a noticeable development of plans since 1970. This arises largely from tax incentives offered by Congress in various pieces of legislation. An active pro-ESOP lobby has developed, led in Congress by Senator Russell Long and outside by Louis O. Kelso, a San Francisco lawyer and consultant, whose name was given to the "Kelso plan," an important type of ESOP. Kelso has provided a theoretical justification for ESOPs[5] and has actively been involved in the practicalities of putting such plans into operation.

Kelso's views are tied to a belief that the source of wealth in society is derived primarily from the ownership of capital goods. The aim, therefore, is to turn employees into capitalists and expand the present narrow social base of share ownership. Kelso's views have generally been ignored or attacked by orthodox economists, who particularly assail both his assertion that there are two independent factors of production, labor and capital, and that new investment can be made out of "pure credit" without prior savings. Critical comments have been made by a number of economists, including Paul Samuelson,[6] but there has been no full study of the economic impact of ESOPs or of Kelso's economic theories. In any case, it is not clear that the validity of ESOPs necessarily depends on acceptance of Kelso's economic theories.

The Number of ESOPs

It is difficult to provide adequate figures for the total number of ESOPs in the United States at present because they are not recorded separately by the IRS. Estimates of the total number of ESOPs vary considerably. A leading consulting firm, which specializes in ESOPs, placed the figure at two hundred in 1977.[7] The Treasury estimated a rather higher figure of three hundred in 1975,[8] and

---

[5] See, *inter alia,* Louis O. Kelso and Patricia Hetter, *Two-Factor Theory: The Economics of Reality: How to Turn Eighty Million Workers into Capitalists on Borrowed Money and Other Proposals* (New York: Random House, 1967); Louis O. Kelso and M. J. Adler, *The New Capitalists, A Proposal to Free Economic Growth from the Slavery of Savings* (New York: Random House, 1961).

[6] U.S., Congress, Joint Economic Committee, *Employee Stock Ownership Plans,* pp. 257-61, 925; Dana L. Thomas, "Mighty Kelso—His Brainchild is Idea 'Whose Time Has Come,' " *Barron's,* July 21, 1975, p. 4.

[7] "ESOPs to Take Off, Consultant Predicts," *Business Insurance,* November 14, 1977, p. 30.

[8] U.S., Congress, Joint Economic Committee, *Employee Stock Ownership Plans,* pp. 90, 108.

another author has placed the figure at about eight hundred.[9] A survey in 1977 of 423 of the largest United States corporations revealed fifty-four ESOPs or TRAESOPs either in existence or in the course of being set up and 60 companies "actively considering" such plans.[10]

Tax Considerations

The increased interest in ESOPs has sprung primarily from the tax benefits that these plans have been granted under legislation since 1973. An ESOP must meet the qualifications laid down by section 401 of the IRC for all employee benefit plans that provide retirement income. Thus, the plan must be permanent in nature; it should not discriminate in favor of officers, shareholders, or highly compensated employees; and it must be for the exclusive benefit of eligible employees. Distributions from ESOPs can be in the form of employer stock, cash, or a combination of both. Prior to the Revenue Act of 1978, distribution could only be in the form of employer stock, although dividends could be paid in cash. As with all stock-bonus, profit-sharing, and thrift plans, annual employer contributions are set at a maximum of 15 percent of eligible employees' pay, or 25 percent if a money-purchase pension plan is included.

If the ESOP qualifies under section 401, two main benefits are derived. First, the employer may, for tax purposes, deduct his contributions up to the limit of 15 percent of the covered payroll. Second, the employee is not liable for tax on the company contributions or the earnings on those contributions until the stock is distributed.

LEGISLATION

A number of recent pieces of legislation have influenced the development of ESOPs.[11] In the period since 1973, this has resulted both in a clearer definition of ESOPs and in a heightened interest in their use.

---

[9] Ronald M. Bushman, "ESOPs: A Closer Look," *CLU Journal*, Vol. XXXI, No. 2 (April 1977), p. 33.
[10] James C. Hyatt, "Creating Capitalists—Employees of Many Big Companies to Get Stock Windfall From '75 Tax-Law Change," *Wall Street Journal*, June 15, 1977, p. 46.
[11] For a discussion, see Hewitt Associates, *ESOPs: An Analytical Report* (Chicago, Ill.: Profit Sharing Council of America, n.d.).

Regional Rail Reorganization Act, 1973

ESOPs were first legally defined by the Regional Rail Reorganization Act of 1973.[12] This act established the Consolidated Rail Corporation (ConRail), which assumed control of the Northeast and Midwest railway system. The new company was instructed to carry out a study of the potential value of using an ESOP and was given authority to buy its own common stock for its employees through an ESOP if it decided to implement one. The act, therefore, represented congressional interest in the use of an ESOP to help meet the capital requirements of the new corporation.

Section 716(e) of the act specifically recognizes ESOPs as an allowable corporate-financing technique. It also provides that the allocations of stock must be substantially proportional to the relative incomes of the participating employees. In addition, employee contributions cannot be required, although the act does not specifically prohibit them. These three features have also been included in subsequent definitions of ESOPs. In part because of union opposition, which branded ESOPs as "contrary to basic trade union principles," ConRail did not, in fact, use an ESOP as a method of financing.[13] Management commissioned consulting reports on the use of ESOPs and, as a result, rejected the concept further on the grounds that it would increase the requirement for government funding for ConRail and would not strengthen the company's financial position. It was also decided that an ESOP would not significantly improve employee motivation.[14]

Employee Retirement Income Security Act, 1974

The second piece of legislation affecting ESOPs is the Employee Retirement Income Security Act of 1974 (ERISA).[15] The definition of ESOPs found in ERISA has been officially added to the IRC. Section 1107(d)(6) of ERISA defines an ESOP either as a qualified stock-bonus plan or as a qualified stock-bonus and money-purchase plan, which is designed primarily to invest in qualifying employer securities. A qualifying employer security can be either stock or other equity securities, or a wide range of marketable obligations. The ESOT debt holdings cannot exceed 25 percent of the total assets of the plan or 25 percent of the total employer debt issue, and

---

[12] 45 *United States Code Annotated* §702(5) (1976).
[13] U.S., Congress, Joint Economic Committee, *Employee Stock Ownership Plans*, pp. 32, 293–95.
[14] *Ibid.*, pp. 641 ff.
[15] 29 U.S.C. §§1001–1381 (1976).

at least 50 percent of the debt issue must be owned by parties independent of the employer.

ESOPs are expressly exempted under section 4975(c)(2) from the prohibition against the lending of money or other extensions of credit between the plan and a party-in-interest. The ESOT can, therefore, borrow from the company to buy the stock. This exemption applies only under certain conditions. First, the loan must be primarily for the benefit of the participants or of their beneficiaries. This restriction can be a basis for controversy because there is no real definition of what is primarily beneficial to the employees. Secondly, the interest rate of the loan must not be deemed excessive by the IRS. Also, if any collateral for the loan is required, only qualifying employer securities may be used. This requirement gives added support to the ESOP because it enables the company to guarantee the loans.

Trade Act, 1974

The third act that defined ESOPs was the Trade Act of 1974.[16] Again, ESOPs were specifically recognized as a technique of corporate finance. The act defines a qualifying employer security as common stock, either of the employer or of a parent or subsidiary, that carries the same voting power and dividend rights as other common stock of that corporation. The Trade Act has two other requirements, including one that is already mentioned in the Regional Rail Reorganization Act. Employees *must* be allowed to vote stock allocated to their accounts, and there can be no reduction in pay or other employee benefits or the surrender of any other rights on the part of the employee as a result of the adoption of an ESOP.

The major provisions of this act deal with federal assistance to alleviate economic damage from foreign competition. As part of this, the act encourages ESOP formation by giving special preference for Department of Commerce loan guarantees to companies that agree to pay 25 percent of the principal of the loan into an ESOP which meets the act's criteria.

Tax Reduction Act, 1975

The Tax Reduction Act of 1975 probably stimulated more interest in employee stock ownership than any prior piece of legislation.[17]

---

[16] 19 U.S.C. §2372(f) (1976).
[17] W. Gordon Binns, Jr., "ESOPs: A Joint Piece of the Action," *Financial Executive*, Vol. XLIII, No. 9 (September 1975), pp. 48–54; P.L. 94–12, 89 *Statutes at Large* (Stat.) 26.

The then existing investment tax credit of 7 percent was increased to 10 percent for 1975 and 1976. For those years, a company could receive an additional investment tax credit of 1 percent if at least this amount were transferred to an ESOP, either in employer stock or in cash to purchase employer stock. This act, therefore, funded the ESOT through dollar-for-dollar tax savings, thus providing 100 percent government funding as opposed to the normal deductible funding for ESOTs. This new type of ESOP is commonly called a TRAESOP (Tax Reduction Act employee stock-ownership plan).[18]

The definition used by this act places more stringent requirements on a plan for qualification than those for the traditional ESOPs that qualify under section 401(a) of the IRC. This act's definition is similar to previous ESOP definitions in that it includes stock-bonus plans; stock-bonus and money-purchase pension plans; and, in addition, profit-sharing plans, provided primary investment is in employer securities. In addition, the act lays down that employee contributions cannot be required; existing employee benefits cannot be reduced; and employees must have the right to vote the stock allocated to them. The act defines qualifying employer securities as common stock or convertible stock of the employer or an affiliate, and employer contributions must be allocated to employees in proportion to pay on a nonintegrated basis up to a level of $100,000 per year. The allocated amounts must be fully vested immediately, and distribution of the allocations cannot occur until the end of the eighty-fourth month after the month in which the stock was allocated to the participating employees, except in the event of death, disability, or separation from service.

Even though the ESOP may not be qualified under section 401(a) of the IRC, it can still qualify as a TRAESOP if certain conditions are met. The plan first must meet all the additional requirements stated above. It must also comply with the restrictions on allocation found in section 401 of the IRC. Finally, the TRAESOP must meet the participation provisions of section 401 and comply with the limitations on benefits and contributions of section 415 of the IRC. But for all practical purposes, it is difficult for a TRAESOP to be qualified without also meeting the requirements of section 401.

Tax Reform Act, 1976

The Tax Reform Act, passed in 1976, extended through 1980 the additional 1 percent investment tax credit for contributions to a

---

[18] The acronym varies. They are also sometimes called TRASOPs or TRESOPs.

TRAESOP.[19] Companies with TRAESOPs also became eligible for up to 0.5 percent additional investment tax credit for the years 1977 through 1980 if their employees contributed a like amount.

Under the Tax Reform Act, TRAESOPs remain subject to the conditions laid down in the 1975 Tax Reduction Act, but certain additional features have been included.[20] Employees must have the option of matching the employer's contribution but cannot be required to do so. Employee contributions must be contributed before the end of the year in which the credit is being taken or must be pledged to be paid within two years after the end of that year, provided the pledge is made prior to the filing of the company tax return.[21]

TRAESOPs have also been made more attractive by a provision that a plan can be considered permanent even if contributions by the company are based on the availability of the investment tax credit. Previously, a plan that was held not to be permanent was disqualified under ERISA, but under the Tax Reform Act, the contributions can be contingent on the continuation of the additional investment tax credit. This major change ensures that the adoption of a TRAESOP does not automatically commit the company to long-run costs.

The act also benefits the company by providing reimbursement for the costs of establishing and operating the plan. The company is permitted to reduce the amount of its contributions to the plan by a percentage of the cost of setting up the TRAESOP, a percentage limited to 10 percent of the first $100,000 contributed plus 5 percent of the excess. Administrative expenses can be reduced by the lesser of (1) 10 percent of the first $100,000 plus 5 percent of the excess over $100,000 of dividends paid to the plan or (2) $100,000.

Several other provisions of the act have affected TRAESOPs. Stocks of "brother-sister" corporations, "second-tier" subsidiaries, and corporations that would have affiliated except for nonvoting preferred stock can be contributed to a TRAESOP in the future. The company is now permitted to withdraw from the plan amounts up to the recaptured tax credit if the amounts subject to recapture are separate from other plan assets, and if separate accounts are established for participants affected by the recapture.

A survey of TRAESOPs in 1977 by the consulting firm of Hewitt

---

[19] P.L. 94-455, 90 Stat. 1520-1933.
[20] "Investment Credit Rules Changed in Several Respects by New Law," *Journal of Taxation,* Vol. 46, No. 1 (January 1977), p. 29; Hewitt Associates, "Latest Tax Act Alters TRASOPS," *Business Insurance,* December 13, 1976, pp. 49-50.
[21] Hewitt Associates, "Latest Tax Act Alters TRASOPS," pp. 49-50.

Associates showed that the strongest interest in them came from large capital-intensive companies.[22] The firm surveyed both the largest one thousand companies, as listed by *Fortune*, and fifty major financial institutions. The most active interest was evinced by utilities and oil companies. By June 1978, there were 330 TRAESOPs in operation, and their growth rate was accelerating.[23] During 1978, 194 TRAESOPs were established, covering 185,929 employees.[24] The Revenue Act of 1978 extended the investment tax credit for TRAESOPs for a further three years until 1983.[25]

BENEFITS AND ADVANTAGES OF ESOPs

A number of benefits have been claimed for the introduction of an ESOP. The first is that employees will identify more closely with their company because now they will be part owners of it. Of course, this closer identification and its translation into improved working efficiency are difficult to detect. The plan's impact would perhaps depend on the amount of money involved and the size of the company, with identification increasing in smaller companies. An ESOP might, however, be a useful part of an overall package, which creates the attitude that an employer is a "good" one in regard to fringe benefits.

Tax advantages for companies also apply to ESOPs and TRAESOPs, and there can be a number of financing advantages for a company. For instance, a company could use an ESOP to refinance existing debts by means of the ESOT's borrowing the amount of that debt and purchasing stock. The new loan could be paid off with the pretax dollars from the deductible contributions to the ESOT. The loan could be retired more quickly, and the company could strengthen its balance sheet by lowering the debt-equity ratio.

In general terms, an ESOP enables a company to raise capital by creating an additional market for its stock and will ultimately increase a company's equity base. It can also improve a company's cash flow; if the ESOP receives direct stock contributions from the employer, the company receives a tax deduction equal to the fair market value of the contributed stock. Because there is no immediate cash outlay, the cash flow is increased by the amount of the tax savings.

---

[22] "AT&T to Establish an Employee Stock Plan," *Business Insurance*, May 30, 1977, p. 6; Hyatt, "Creating Capitalists," p. 46.

[23] Bert L. Metzger, *Participative Developments in the United States* (Evanston, Ill.: Profit Sharing Research Foundation, 1978), p. 18.

[24] Commissioner of Internal Revenue, *Annual Report, 1978* (Washington, D.C.: U.S. Government Printing Office, 1979), p. 100.

[25] P.L. 95-600, 92 Stat. 2763-2946.

There are a number of more exotic uses to which an ESOP can be put.[26] For example, a company could use an ESOP to acquire another company. The acquiring company would establish an ESOT, which would obtain a loan and purchase stock or assets in the company to be acquired. The ESOT would then exchange this acquired company's stock or assets for newly issued stock of the acquiring company. By using ESOT financing, the company has made an acquisition at reduced cost, since pretax dollars were used to retire the loan.[27]

A company could also use an ESOP to "spin-off" a subsidiary. First, the subsidiary would have to establish a separate ESOT, which would receive a loan, guaranteed by the parent company, which could be used to purchase the subsidiary's assets. The ESOT would then turn the assets over to the new company in return for stock in it. The new company's contributions to its own ESOT would then be used to repay the loan. The parent company would experience no dilution of earnings or equity because the stock would be issued by the new company. This procedure would, however, mean that the employees of the new company would eventually own part of the new company when the loan is retired.

This approach was used to accomplish a spin-off of South Bend Lathe from Amsted Industries.[28] By means of an ESOT, which was partly funded by the Economic Development Administration of the Department of Commerce, ownership in the company was transferred to employees. This transfer apparently had beneficial effects on the company's performance.[29]

An ESOP could also be used to transfer stock ownership from the major stockholders in a closely held company to the ESOT and thereby provide the major stockholders with liquidity. The company would set up an ESOT, which would acquire a company-guaranteed loan from a bank. The ESOT would use these funds to purchase stock from the major stockholders. The company would make its tax-deductible contributions to the ESOT, and the ESOT

---

[26] W. Robert Reum and Sherry Milliken Reum, "Employee Stock Ownership Plans: Pluses and Minuses," *Harvard Business Review*, Vol. 54, No. 4 (July-August 1976), pp. 139-41; Peter Hearst, "Employee Stock Ownership Trusts and Their Uses," *Personnel Journal*, Vol. 54, No. 2 (February 1975), pp. 104-6.

[27] Burton W. Teague, "In Review of the ESOP Fable," *The Conference Board Record*, Vol. XIII, No. 2 (February 1976), p. 11.

[28] John J. Ryan, "Saving Jobs—How and Why U.S. Helped 500 Workers Take Over a Machine-Tool Manufacturer," *Wall Street Journal*, August 16, 1976, p. 28; and Thomas, "Mighty Kelso—His Brainchild is Idea 'Whose Time Has Come,'" p. 3.

[29] Charles G. Burck, "There's More to ESOP Than Meets the Eye," *Fortune*, Vol. XCIII, No. 3 (March 1976), p. 172.

would retire the loan in the usual manner. By using an ESOT in this situation, the company can remain private without any direct cash outlay by the employees, who would eventually receive full ownership of the stock and the company. This approach was adopted in 1973 by the Mulach Steel Corporation, located in Bridgeville, Pennsylvania, when its owner, who was retiring, wanted to give ownership in the company to his employees rather than sell the business to an outside concern or liquidate it. An ESOP was established with full vesting after ten years, and ownership was thereby gradually transferred to the employees.[30]

DISADVANTAGES OF ESOPs

The major problem faced by ESOPs has been the variability in stock prices can create adverse employee reaction. An ESOP exposes the employee to a "double risk" because he relies on the company for his wages and for a part of his additional assets. This situation arises because the ESOP has to invest primarily in employer stock and securities.

A leveraged ESOP may experience dilution if the company contributes new shares to the ESOT and thereby increases the amount of outstanding shares and lowers earnings per share; this may create resentment among existing shareholders.[31] Dividends also pose certain difficulties. Under an ESOP, the tax-deductibility of the repayment of principal helps to offset dividend costs during the term of the loan.[32] Any dividends paid above the interest and principal are an extra cost, and even if they are substituted for interest and principal, they are not deductible for the corporation and so partially offset the benefit to the company of being able to deduct the principal payments. To the employee, the payment of dividends may be one of the attractions of an ESOP, although to the company, the ideal tax situation would be to pay no dividends at all. At the least, annual dividends should not exceed the annual tax savings from deducting repayments on the principal.[33]

ESOPs, therefore, are least beneficial in financial terms to large

---

[30] Keith W. Bennett, "ESOP's Fabled Benefits Catch Industry's Eye," *Iron Age*, Vol. 216, No. 4 (July 28, 1975), p. 22; Dana L. Thomas, "Explosive ESOTs—These Novel Financing Vehicles Begin to Create Controversy," *Barron's*, July 28, 1975, p. 5.

[31] Bart P. Hartman, David Laxton, and William Walvoord, "A Look at Employee Stock Ownership Plans as Financing Tools," *Management Accounting*, Vol. LVIII, No. 9 (March 1977), pp. 23–28.

[32] U.S., Congress, Joint Economic Committee, *Employee Stock Ownership Plans*, pp. 26–27.

[33] *Ibid.*, pp. 27–31.

publicly owned companies, which pay a relatively high level of dividends and also have alternative ways to finance expansion. For such companies, tax advantages can be outweighed by the costs of ESOP financing.[34] Proponents of ESOPs have, therefore, put forward suggestions for further tax changes, in particular to allow the payment of dividends on stock held by an ESOP to be tax-deductible in the same way as the interest and principal payments.

Closely held companies may encounter other problems. First, there is the issue of the valuation of stock. In a public company, this is not a problem because market price can be used. A closely held company needs an expert appraisal of the stock's value, and even then there is no guarantee that the IRS will agree with the valuation. The IRS can impose penalties for improper valuation, of which the most extreme would be that the plan could be disqualified, thus forfeiting tax benefits. IRS guidelines suggest that "good faith" is the key element in its acceptance of such valuations.[35]

Repurchasing stock from employees when they retire, for instance, may reverse some of the cash-flow advantages for the company, especially if it is closely held. If the employee receives a lump sum or installment payments when the stock is sold, the company may need a considerable amount of cash on hand to finance the repurchase, and it may not be possible to predict exactly when such financing will be required.[36] Moreover, in September 1977, the IRS issued regulations requiring an employer whose stock is not publicly traded to offer to repurchase shares from employees for up to fifteen months after their issue.[37]

Companies may face general problems with their fiduciary duty. The fiduciary of an ESOP, although free of ERISA's diversification requirements, must act in accordance with the so-called prudent man rule.[38] This could create problems in private companies facing economic difficulties, for there could be a conflict between the "prudent man" rule and the requirement that an ESOP should invest primarily in employer stock. Because of this potential conflict, some banks have been reluctant to act as trustees for an ESOP in a closely held company.[39]

---

[34] *Ibid.*, p. 43.
[35] Bushman, "ESOPs: A Closer Look," p. 35; U.S., Congress, Joint Economic Committee, *Employee Stock Ownership Plans*, p. 858.
[36] Bushman, "ESOPs: A Closer Look," pp. 34-35.
[37] Donald E. Sullivan, "ESOPs: Panacea or Placebo?" *California Management Review*, Vol. XX, No. 1 (Fall 1977), pp. 59-60.
[38] 29 U.S.C. §1104(a) (1976).
[39] Michael Lew, "ESOPs Under the New Acts," *Profit Sharing*, Vol. 24, No. 1 (January 1976), p. 29.

Although ERISA requires that an ESOP be for the exclusive benefit of employees, this has been interpreted by the IRS to mean primary benefit. The plan can provide indirect benefit to others and not violate the rule of exclusive benefit. Nevertheless, there can be possible conflicts of interest between the company's use of an ESOP as a financing technique and the employees' desire for a benefit.

UNION ATTITUDES TOWARD ESOPs

Traditional stock-purchase plans have usually been viewed by unions with relative disinterest, although not with any greater degree of hostility than traditional profit sharing. Such plans exist in a number of unionized companies without any apparent damage to collective bargaining.

ESOPs, however, seem to have created rather more controversy. In part, this appears to be the result of some of the consultants who "sell" ESOPs to companies. Thus in 1971, Alan E. Sapiro, then president of Kelso, Bangert and Company, said of such plans:

> They do a service to employees by building ownership in the company and do a service to companies themselves by building in significant ownership so that employees will begin to think and act a little more like owners and be a little less receptive to the inordinate blandishments of the unions.[40]

Kelso, Bangert and Company did not think of ESOPs as antiunion in themselves but agreed that there was greater interest in such plans in nonunion firms, an observation corroborated by another ESOP consultant.[41]

As has been pointed out, although the AFL-CIO had no official position on ESOPs, individual union leaders were skeptical of them.[42] Although unions have not actively campaigned against ESOPs, the element of risk for employees in such plans has been a particular target of criticism. For example, one AFL-CIO economist was quoted as saying of ESOPs: "This is profit-sharing with a vengeance. There's a great deal of potential for workers to get badly burned. I'd hate to think what would have happened to employees of the Penn Central or Pan Am if they'd had Kelso plans."[43]

It would, however, be incorrect to see ESOPs as incompatible

---

[40] "Getting Employees to Put up the Capital," *Business Week*, November 20, 1971, p. 91.
[41] Neil A. Wassner, "ESOPs: Can They Work for Your Corporation?" *Pension World*, Vol. 12, No. 6 (June 1976), p. 22.
[42] Teague, "In Review of the ESOP Fable," p. 13.
[43] "Worker's Capitalism—Free Distributions of Stock to Employees are Spurred by a New Tax Law Provision," *Wall Street Journal*, April 29, 1975, p. 23.

with unionization. A number of unionized companies have ESOPs, although in some of these cases, the ESOP has been used to transfer a significant degree of ownership to the employees, as at Mulach Steel Corporation and South Bend Lathe.[44] E-Systems, one of the pioneers of ESOPs, which set up its plan in 1973, is also unionized.

In addition, there are specific instances of union leaders' taking a more positive attitude toward ESOPs. A number of these instances have been cited by Louis Kelso to counteract the charge that ESOPs are antiunion.[45] Walter Reuther of the UAW spoke in favor of stock distributions, and in February 1972, Joseph Curran, then president of the National Maritime Union, specifically supported an ESOP for the passenger ship industry. Although most of the rail union officials opposed an ESOP for ConRail, the Brotherhood of Railway Clerks was a significant exception, and its then president, C. L. Dennis, supported the ESOP concept.

PROPOSED LEGISLATIVE CHANGES

There have been several recent efforts to aid ESOPs further by legislative changes. In 1975, Representative Frenzel introduced the Accelerated Capital Formation Bill (H.R. 462), which sought to abolish the 15 percent ceiling imposed on tax-deductible ESOTs and to grant a tax deduction for dividends paid on shares contributed to the ESOT. This bill broadly followed the lines of a measure (S. 1370) introduced in the previous session by former Senator Paul Fannin, although that had proposed to raise the limit from 15 to 30 percent rather than to abolish it entirely.[46] Neither of these bills progressed into law.

A further effort to introduce legislation came with the Javits-Humphrey Employee Stock Ownership Bill (S. 3300) of 1976.[47] The bill was designed by the sponsors "to facilitate employee stock ownership among organized labor through the time tested mechanism of voluntary labor management collective bargaining negotiations" and to give "the employees a 'piece of the action' in our American capitalist system."[48]

---

[44] Burck, "There's More to ESOP Than Meets the Eye," p. 172.
[45] U.S., Congress, Joint Economic Committee, *Employee Stock Ownership Plans*, pp. 289 ff.
[46] *Ibid.*, pp. 38-39.
[47] "Bill to Facilitate Stock Ownership by Employees Introduced in Senate," *Daily Labor Report*, No. 72 (April 13, 1976), pp. A4-A8; U.S., Congress, Joint Economic Committee, *Broadening the Ownership of New Capital: ESOPs and Other Alternatives* (Washington, D.C.: U.S. Government Printing Office, 1976), pp. 60-62.
[48] "Bill to Facilitate Stock Ownership by Employees Introduced in Senate," pp. A6-A7.

Specifically, there were four major provisions that concerned ESOPs. First, the bill proposed to include ESOPs within the scope of section 302 of the Taft-Hartley Act, which provides for jointly administered labor-management pensions and health and welfare funds established through voluntary collective bargaining. Second, a trustee would only be allowed to invest a maximum of 30 percent of the trust fund in employer corporate voting stock; the remainder would be invested in diversified corporate stock and fixed income securities. This portfolio would be selected and administered by the board of trustees. Third, the bill precluded the establishment of an ESOT for companies subject to the National Labor Relations (Taft-Hartley) Act unless the employer already had in effect an employee pension benefit qualified under ERISA. Finally, mandatory 100 percent vesting would occur after three years of employee participation. This bill also did not progress into law, but it is indicative of the continued legislative interest in the subject.

CONCLUSION

There is still a need for a thorough practical evaluation of the effect of ESOPs. Their popularity has grown considerably in the short space of time since Peninsula Newspapers introduced in 1957 what is often regarded as the first of the new ESOPs. Some analysts, however, have denounced ESOPs as a passing fad, bolstered by misleading claims. For instance, a critique by Triad Financial Reports attacked ESOPs on the grounds that, although they provided modest improvements in cash flow, they did so at the expense of reduced profits, dilution of prior ownership, reduced earnings on equity, and reduced stock values.[49]

Even though most analyses are skeptical of some of the more extreme claims made on behalf of ESOPs, few go as far as Triad. More typical is the conclusion of Don Sullivan of Towers, Perrin, Forster and Crosby, a benefits consulting firm, who concluded that ESOPs offered some advantages to small or medium-sized employers who were (1) unable or unwilling to raise capital by traditional means of borrowing or equity financing, (2) willing to adopt a qualified plan and meet its recurring contributions, or (3) desirous of transferring stock to their employees.[50]

Discussion about ESOPs often centers on the economic theories of Kelso himself. Paul Samuelson, for example, has written:

---

[49] U.S., Congress, Joint Economic Committee, *Employee Stock Ownership Plans*, pp. 55-56.
[50] *Ibid.*, p. 82.

Louis Kelso ... has made extensive claims for [ESOPs]. Often John-Law schemes, in which somehow, out of bank loans, equity is created from thin air, get involved in the profit-sharing Gospel. Those few economists who have audited the economic theories underlying the proposals and the claims made for them have generally not rendered favorable verdicts on them. I must concur in these negative appraisals.[51]

One report quotes an economist as saying, "Kelso really doesn't understand how the economy works."[52] It seems more worthwhile, however, to divorce Kelso's theories from the use of ESOPs. Whatever the merits of his views, companies have introduced ESOPs, and many of those companies have expressed favorable views of the plan's effects on the company's financial position and on employee morale. There is some evidence to support the view that companies with ESOPs are perhaps more profitable than conventionally owned firms.[53]

Therefore, it may be more useful to explore why certain companies feel that ESOPs are valuable and what kind of company will derive the most benefit from them. The clearest answer is a negative one. Virtually all parties agree that ESOPs are not feasible for companies in financial difficulties.[54] Most observers feel that closely held companies have the most to gain from ESOPs because they have fewer alternative sources of financing available to them, and because they are less concerned about the accounting impact of an ESOP in lowering earnings per share.[55] Large companies, on the other hand, can raise capital more easily and cheaply and may be uncertain of the reaction of existing shareholders to the creation of an ESOP.

It is also often stated that labor-intensive companies benefit more from ESOPs than do capital-intensive employers.[56] This arises because the contribution is related to payroll, and so labor-intensive companies can "shelter" a larger part of their taxable income than can capital-intensive ones. On the other hand, some observers believe that the opposite applies because labor-intensive companies

---

[51] Paul A. Samuelson, "Thoughts on Profit-Sharing," *Zeitschrift Für Die Gesamte Staatswissenschaft*, Special Issue on Profit-Sharing, 1977, p. 16.
[52] "Employee Stock Plans Begin to Catch Fire," *Business Week*, March 1, 1976, p. 60.
[53] Michael Conte and Arnold S. Tannenbaum, "Employee-Owned Companies: Is the Difference Measurable?" *Monthly Labor Review*, Vol. 101, No. 7 (July 1978), pp. 23-28.
[54] Hearst, "Employee Stock Ownership Trusts and Their Uses," p. 105.
[55] Wassner, "ESOPs: Can They Work for Your Corporation?" pp. 19-20.
[56] *Ibid.*, p. 22; Teague, "In Review of the ESOP Fable," p. 13; Bushman, "ESOPs: A Closer Look," p. 33.

could not give sufficiently large per capita benefits.[57] TRAESOPs, in particular, are seen as primarily beneficial for, and having chiefly been introduced in, capital-intensive companies, for they alone can make sufficient savings from the investment tax credit to make the adoption of a plan attractive.[58]

There has been considerable discussion about whether the use of an ESOP as a financing device conflicts with its claimed advantage of motivating employees. At best, the evidence from companies suggests that they take into account both aspects, although if the tax benefits were withdrawn, interest in ESOPs would probably wane considerably. It is significant that most analyses of ESOPs concentrate heavily on their financial advantages to companies and say little about advantages to employees.

Some consultants see ESOPs as most effective for companies with between fifty and five hundred employees.[59] Although it is true that many ESOPs have been set up in small companies, this is not universally the case. Perhaps the largest company to adopt a straight ESOP has been Gamble-Skogmo, the Minneapolis-based retailing company, which has eighteen thousand employees. In 1975, the company integrated an ESOP with an existing thrift and savings plan.[60] E-Systems of Dallas, one of the ESOP pioneers, has nine thousand employees.

The ESOP has undoubtedly struck a responsive corporate chord. Its twin appeal as a financing method and as an employee benefit has given it an advantage over other stock-ownership plans. It is not clear, however, that the momentum will be maintained. The largest employers have so far avoided ESOPs, except for those ESOPs created under the Tax Reduction Act; given the nature of TRAESOPs, there was probably some feeling that the company could not refuse a benefit that cost it nothing. As with savings plans, it is possible to argue that it is the large companies that set the pattern, and so it is unclear how extensively ESOPs will spread. Moreover, the ESOP experience covers only a short time span. The verdict on ESOPs, therefore, has to be left open at present.

---

[57] "Employee Stock Plans Begin to Catch Fire," p. 56.
[58] Linda Snyder, "New Wrinkles in Stock-Purchase Plans," *Fortune*, Vol. 97, No. 4 (February 27, 1978), p. 105; Hewitt Associates, *ESOPs: An Analytical Report*, p. 13; Bankers Trust Company, *1977 Study of Employee Savings and Thrift Plans* (New York, 1977), p. 38.
[59] "ESOPs to Take Off, Consultant Predicts," p. 30.
[60] Burck, "There's More to ESOP Than Meets the Eye," p. 133.

CHAPTER V

Profit Sharing in Europe

To assess the impact of profit sharing in Europe, it is initially necessary to consider the major differences that exist between Europe and the United States in their conduct of industrial relations and in their economic and political environments. Differences in the trade union movements, economic structures, investment practices, and the like explain much of the variations between European and American profit-sharing, employee stock-ownership, and asset-formation plans.

SIZE AND CHARACTER OF UNIONS

The first obvious difference between European and American industrial relations is the level of trade union membership (see Table V-1). Membership figures are notoriously unreliable, but there is probably no Western European country that has a lower percentage of union members in the labor force than that in the United States. One corollary of the figures shown in Table V-1 is that trade union membership in Europe has extended to many more white-collar, and even to managerial, employees than in the United States.

The figures in column 6 of Table V-1 seem the most realistic ones for assessing the real penetration of the trade union movement into the labor force. Figures for union membership are often quoted either against the total labor force or against total civilian employment. Unions generally organize only among employees and tend to exclude certain other categories, such as the self-employed, from their ranks. It is therefore significant in a country such as Ireland that, whereas the union movement would seem to organize only a minority of the total labor force, it is in fact one of the strongest in Europe when measured against its real potential membership. The actual union membership figures vary in reliability among countries. Those for France and Italy are probably the least accurate, but they do serve to reflect the relative strengths of the two labor movements.

The second major difference is that most unions in Europe are

TABLE V-1
Trade Union Membership

Country	Labor Force (Millions)	Total Employees in Labor Force[a] (Millions)	Trade Union Membership (Millions)	Trade Union Members as Percentage of Labor Force	Trade Union Members as Percentage of Total Employees in Labor Force
Belgium	4.03	3.15	2.11	52.4	67.0
Denmark	2.53	2.05	1.41	55.7	68.8
France	22.13	17.37	5.00	22.6	28.8
Germany	26.70	23.18	8.92	33.4	38.5
Ireland	1.14	0.74	0.45	39.5	60.8
Italy	19.62	14.24	8.37	42.7	58.8
Luxembourg	0.15	0.12	0.07	46.7	58.3
Netherlands	4.85	4.08	1.70	35.1	41.7
Sweden	4.15	3.75	3.02	72.8	80.5
Switzerland	2.94	2.55	0.90	30.6	35.3
United Kingdom	26.21	22.67	11.66	44.5	51.4
United States	96.92	87.79	20.20	20.8	23.0

Sources: Columns 2 and 3—International Labour Organisation, *1977 Year Book of Labour Statistics*, 37th ed. (Geneva, 1977). Column 4—Trade union membership figures estimated from trade union publications, government publications, and academic studies on trade unions within the individual countries.

[a]This column excludes from the total economically active population the self-employed, employers, family workers, and members of the armed forces.

explicitly identified with political parties, although the nature of the links varies. A number of countries have competing union federations defined by political ideology. In Italy, there are Communist, Catholic, and Socialist federations, although their links to the political parties contrast in their strength and nature, and the divisions are not clear-cut. The Communist Confederazione Generale Italiana del Lavoro (CGIL) maintains close links with the Italian Communist party but also draws some support from the Socialist party. The Catholic Confederazione Italiana Sindacati Lavoratori has tended to be associated with one particular wing of the Christian Democrat party. The smaller Unione Italiana del Lavoro has links both with the Social Democrats and the Republican party. Perhaps in response to the fragmented nature of the political system, too, unions have somewhat weakened their party ties over recent years and stressed common trade union action. This should not be interpreted, however, as a retreat from political commitment.

In France, there is a similar situation, although the Communist Confédération Générale du Travail has maintained even closer links with the Communist party than has the CGIL in Italy. The two other main federations are highly politicized, although they are not linked to any significant degree to political parties. In Belgium and the Netherlands, the union movement is also divided into competing federations. In Belgium, the two largest of these are Christian and Socialist, and in the Netherlands, the merger between the Catholic and Socialist federations, which will be completed by 1981, will leave the new body, the Federatie Nederlandse Vakbeweging, in competition only with the Protestant Christelijk Nationaal Vakverbond. Luxembourg also has competing Socialist and Christian federations. Switzerland has three separate federations, but of these, the Socialist federation is about twice as large as the Christian and white-collar ones combined.

In contrast, the United Kingdom, Germany, Sweden, Denmark, and Ireland all have one major union federation, which is broadly Social Democratic in orientation. Sweden is slightly different insofar as it also has two important white-collar union federations separate from the main Landsorganisationen i Sverige. In Germany, too, there is a separate white-collar federation and a separate civil service union group, although the numbers involved are not as significant a sector of the labor force as in Sweden.

In this second group of countries, the union federations maintain close links with the major Social Democratic parties, either formally or practically. Ireland is a slightly divergent case. Although the

Irish Congress of Trade Unions cooperates closely with the Irish Labour party, the party is the smallest of the three main Irish parties; in the 1977 general election, it secured only 17 out of the total of 148 seats in the Dáil Éireann (the lower house of the Irish Parliament).

The combination of the level of union membership and the unions' political role has given European unions political power greatly in excess of that enjoyed by American unions. The European unions' ideology has tended to increase their desire to participate in the wider political sphere, and in societies where a sizable section of the population supports Communist, Socialist, and Social Democratic parties, left-wing attitudes among unions are not regarded as a drawback by their members.

Within this context, it is perhaps easier to understand why and how unions are able to gain support for proposals, such as those on collective investment funds, which would seem extremely favorable to unions from an American viewpoint. American unions are very powerful politically, yet not nearly as strong in this regard as are unions in many European countries. For example, even in the overwhelmingly Democrat-controlled Congress of 1976-78, unions were unable to secure passage of amendments to the Taft-Hartley Act or to ease restrictions on picketing and boycotts by construction workers. In Europe, the balance of political power has often been in the opposite direction, and although employers are usually organized politically, they have not proved a particularly effective lobby.

ECONOMIC STRUCTURE

It is also highly significant that the economic structure in Europe has been considerably modified when compared with the American pattern. This modification is somewhat disguised by the information in Table V-2, which shows that the United States' level of government consumption as a percentage of Gross Domestic Product (GDP) is higher than those in many European countries. This is largely accounted for by the high level of defense expenditures in the United States, where there is only a limited amount of industry under public control. In most European countries, gas, electricity, rail, coal, postal, telephone, and air services are state-controlled. Automobile companies such as Renault in France, British Leyland in the United Kingdom, and Alfa Romeo in Italy are state-run. Other companies, such as Fiat and Volkswagen, have partial government stakes. Banks and financial institutions are sometimes

TABLE V-2
Economic Indicators, 1976-77

Country	Government Current Expenditure (Percentage of GDP)	Gross Fixed Capital Formation (Percentage of GDP)	Net Savings Ratio (Percentage of GDP)	Imports and Exports (Averaged as Percentage of GDP)	GDP per Capita ($ U.S.)
Belgium	17.9	20.6	22.1	50.8	6,710
Denmark	24.2	21.5	16.7	28.2	7,590
France	14.7	23.1	23.3	17.4	6,550
Germany	20.4	20.7	24.4	21.0	7,250
Ireland	19.5	24.5	17.8	47.2	2,510
Italy	14.0	20.3	20.2	24.6	3,040
Luxembourg	15.5	28.2	27.4	84.4	6,280
Netherlands	18.3	19.7	24.5	44.6	6,500
Sweden	25.6	20.6	20.6	25.5	9,030
Switzerland	13.4	20.7	26.3	26.2	8,870
United Kingdom	21.8	19.2	18.9	23.6	3,910
United States	18.7	16.2	17.4	7.0	7,910

Source: Organization for Economic Cooperation and Development, *OECD Economic Surveys* (Paris, 1978), for each country.

nationalized, and state industrial companies exist on the pattern of Statsföretag in Sweden, IRI in Italy, DSM NV in the Netherlands, and Elf Aquitaine and CFP in France. Industries that are not formally owned by the government may nevertheless rely heavily on government support, as American producers sometimes point out. The existence of the European Community (EC) and the extension of its influence have increased the pace of government economic intervention. These trends are least advanced in Germany and Switzerland, but in some other European countries, the "mixed economy" concept has profoundly modified the traditional capitalist economic system. This often makes comparisons with the United States economy rather difficult to draw.

The above factors have tended to decrease the interest in profit sharing in Europe and to provoke ideological opposition to it among unions, which is now less marked in the United States than formerly, although it has by no means entirely disappeared. There are also practical problems involved for European unions. Many have members in both the public and private sectors, and profit sharing may be seen as divisive between the two groups.

Table V-2 presents some of the salient points about the economies of Western Europe. Government consumption as a percentage of GDP is highest in Sweden and Denmark and lowest in Switzerland and Italy. There is apparently little correlation between this indicator and per capita GDP; Switzerland and Sweden occupy the two highest places despite their differing economic structures. Per capita wealth falls in a relatively narrow band for most European countries, with only the United Kingdom, Italy, and Ireland significantly below the average. The expression of income in United States currency, of course, makes exchange rates an important factor in the precise expression of these figures.

Information on savings and investment is not very conclusive. If one expected the savings ratio to reflect personal income, then Sweden and Denmark have lower savings ratios than would otherwise be the case. This would seem to bear out some of the criticisms of the adverse effect on savings of highly welfare-oriented societies. The United States, however, would also seem to show poorly in this regard, presumably for different reasons.

The importance of foreign trade to the economy is also illustrated in Table V-2. This serves mainly to show the degree of economic interdependence in Europe; for most countries, the major trading partners are other European countries.

Tables V-3 and V-4 give information on the structure of the labor force in different countries. Participation rates are lowest in the

TABLE V-3
Labor Force Structure

Country	Population (Millions)	Economically Active Population (Millions)	Participation Rate in Economic Activity	Employers and Self-Employed as Percentage of Labor Force
Belgium	9.82	4.03	41.0	12.1
Denmark	5.08	2.53	49.8	13.0
France	52.84	22.13	41.9	18.1
Germany	61.54	26.70	43.4	8.9
Ireland	3.09	1.14	36.9	23.1
Italy	55.27	19.62	35.5	20.3
Luxembourg	0.36	0.15	41.8	13.9
Netherlands	13.77	4.85	35.2	11.0
Sweden	8.24	4.15	50.4	6.9
Switzerland	6.41	2.94	45.9	10.4
United Kingdom	56.04	26.21	46.8	7.4
United States	214.65	96.92	45.2	7.7

Source: International Labour Organisation, *1977 Year Book of Labour Statistics*, 37th ed. (Geneva, 1977).

TABLE V-4
Employment by Major Sector
(Percentages)

Country	Agriculture	Manufacturing and Mining	Services[a]	Other[b]
Belgium	3.2	27.7	30.5	38.6
Denmark	9.3	23.2	36.1	31.4
France	10.8	27.3	27.8	34.1
Germany	6.4	36.2	27.0	30.4
Ireland	25.4	21.1	20.7	32.8
Italy	15.1	30.6	18.8	35.5
Luxembourg	7.5	33.6	24.0	34.9
Netherlands	6.1	24.5	26.8	42.6
Sweden	6.1	27.0	36.6	30.3
Switzerland	7.7	37.9	20.7	33.7
United Kingdom	2.5	34.2	28.3	35.0
United States	3.7	23.2	37.6	35.5

Source: International Labour Organisation, *1977 Year Book of Labour Statistics*, 37th ed. (Geneva, 1977).

[a] "Services" comprise finance, insurance, real estate, business services, and community, social, and personal services.

[b] "Other" comprises electricity, gas, construction, wholesale and retail trade, restaurants and hotels, transport, and communications. These may also be regarded as "services," and this figure combined with column 4 is often regarded as a measure of the total size of the "service sector."

poorer, more agrarian countries of Italy and Ireland and are highest in the richest countries—Sweden, Switzerland, and Denmark. The high percentage of self-employed in Ireland and Italy reflects the importance of their agricultural sectors. Self-employment is lowest in the United Kingdom and Sweden, two countries where tax structures are sometimes seen as inimical to individual entrepreneurship.

CODETERMINATION AND RELATED MATTERS

The movement in some countries toward union-controlled asset-formation plans needs to be seen in the light of the ongoing European debate on codetermination and related issues, which are often described by the term *industrial democracy*. The latter term covers a number of different systems and proposals. The German system of codetermination has attracted wide attention; in other countries, the unions have adopted aspects of the German system but combined them with a wider role for unions directly, as opposed to employees. The British unions' proposals for worker-directors, based solely on trade union machinery, are one example of this.[1]

The growth of union power in Europe has been accompanied by union involvement in increasingly wider spheres of economic activity. Proposals for collective union-controlled funds are therefore only a part of a wider trend. The weakness of French unions perhaps helps account for the lack of collective proposals in that country.

The increasing desire of governments to involve unions in wider aspects of economic planning is also a vital feature of recent years. This involvement has, in itself, forced unions to look more closely at issues with which they were not previously concerned. Many union movements are vitally concerned about altering the balance of economic power in their countries, and codetermination and collective asset-formation proposals are seen as two complementary ways of achieving this objective.

INVESTMENT IN EUROPE

One of the factors that acts both as a spur to profit sharing and as a constraint on its effectiveness is the relatively low interest in investing in shares among ordinary employees. Although the importance of such investment can be overstated in the United States, it remains the case that many more people with moderate incomes in

---

[1] United Kingdom, Department of Trade, *Report of the Committee of Inquiry on Industrial Democracy* (Chairman, Lord Bullock) (London: Her Majesty's Stationery Office, 1977).

the United States regard it as normal to buy company stock either directly or through some indirect means, such as mutual funds.

Collective investment funds have achieved some measure of governmental support precisely because they appear to provide a means for filling a vacuum in the investment area. The figures on share ownership in different countries are instructive. In the United States in 1977, there were approximately 25 million shareholders, or 1 person in 8.5 in the total population; West Germany, with 1 in 12, was the highest ranking major European country, and the United Kingdom, 1 in 26, and France, 1 in 44, trailed far behind.[2] These figures admittedly do not include investment via mutual funds, but holdings here are often small amounts, and it is arguable whether investors in mutual funds see themselves in the same light as regular shareholders. In the United Kingdom in 1976, only 1.1 percent of personal financial assets were held in unit trusts (mutual funds),[3] and investment in direct company shares involved over fourteen times more wealth. Naturally, with the usually smaller amounts involved in mutual funds, the number of investors would probably be relatively higher.

United Kingdom Versus Germany

Savings and investment policies generally in Europe exhibit marked contrasts. A recent comparative study of the United Kingdom and Germany has illustrated this point.[4] Since 1945, Germany has maintained a high level of investment in manufacturing industry. The government has held down domestic consumption, particularly in the 1950s, and has encouraged savings by legal enactment. Bank financing has been a key element in Germany's economic success and, in 1975, accounted for 25.9 percent of total funds available for industrial investment. Banks not only have lent money but also have attracted funds from small investors.

The situation in the United Kingdom contrasts markedly with this. Government policies have not focused on industrial investment, and tax measures have frequently discouraged it. Banks have not proved so ready to lend funds to industry and have not been the prime attractor of investors' funds. This role has fallen to the building (savings and loan) societies, which have invested

---

[2] "Proportionellement 2 à 5 Fois Moins D'Actionnaires en France Que Dans les Principaux Pays Occidentaux," *Intersocial* (Paris), No. 39 (June 1978), p. 36.

[3] "The Private Investor Grows in Wisdom," *Financial Times* (London), February 8, 1978, p. 17.

[4] J. M. Samuels and P. C. McMahon, *Savings and Investment in the United Kingdom and West Germany* (London: Wilton Publications, 1978).

basically in only one asset, housing. Life assurance and pension funds have also siphoned off customers from the banks and have proved conservative investors. The authors of the study also suggest that Britain is not a highly competitive country, and that companies often prefer to grow by acquisition rather than by an aggressive attempt to gain an increased market share or to break into new markets.

The level of private savings in the United Kingdom is much below that in Germany, while private borrowing is higher. Government encouragement of savings in the United Kingdom, such as the "Save As You Earn" plan, has been rather tentative and not too successful. Figures produced by the United Kingdom's Central Statistical Office on the use of personal savings show that, in 1976, investment in financial assets quoted on the Stock Exchange was £ 26.5 billion ($55.8 billion), only just ahead of the £ 26.1 billion ($54.9 billion) invested in building societies. Indirect investment through life assurance and pension funds was £ 37 billion ($77.9 billion). The proportion of wealth held by individuals in stocks and shares, moreover, fell from 24.6 percent in 1957 to 11.5 percent in 1976.[5]

In this regard, it is interesting that, in recent years, many German companies have instituted stock-ownership plans for employees as a way of raising additional capital, and this seems to have been well-received by the employees. The relatively high level of share ownership in the country as a whole must aid this favorable reception. In contrast, such plans have not flourished in the United Kingdom, although tax changes in 1978 may alter this. The lower level of share ownership, combined with a stronger anticapitalist ideology, has discouraged the use of such plans.

CONCLUSION

This chapter is an inevitably highly simplified sketch of an extremely complex area, but the information here provides some context for the following chapters on individual countries. The difficulty of determining the interrelationship of complex phenomena constitutes both a challenge and a danger to the observer. The challenge is to relate the data in a meaningful manner; the danger is to assume relationships where none can be proved, confident that they cannot be disproved. There remain many cultural, social, economic, and political differences among the European countries. For

---

[5] "The Private Investor Grows in Wisdom," p. 17. The exchange rate used is $1=£ 0.475 as of April 10, 1979.

those members of the EC, however, these may lessen over time. International regulatory action will also be spurred by the trade union movements of Europe. There exist a number of European trade union bodies, such as the European Trade Union Confederation and the European Metalworkers' Federation, that seem likely to increase the extent of economic standardization in Europe but may also serve to emphasize further the divergence of that continent's development from economic trends in the United States.

CHAPTER VI

Germany

In 1945, it would have been difficult to predict that in thirty years Germany would create the strongest economy among the major Western European powers. Germany's growth has been founded squarely on its strength in the manufacturing sector, which, with 34.8 percent of the total labor force, is second only to Switzerland's in providing employment. In some respects, together with Switzerland, Germany has been the most capitalistically oriented of Western European countries. Yet this tells only part of the story. Government consumption as a percentage of Gross Domestic Product (GDP) is relatively high (20.4 percent) and comparable to that of the United Kingdom. Social services are extensive, and payments are set at a high level. These welfare policies have not been accompanied either by a significant degree of public ownership of industry or by major controls on the operation of private companies.

Nine of the twenty-five largest European companies are German, including giants such as Siemens, Daimler-Benz, Hoechst, Bayer, BASF, and Thyssen. The industrial public sector is relatively small and extends to organizations in the transport and energy field. Saarbergwerke AG, which has some twenty-five thousand employees and is engaged in a wide range of activities, is state-owned, as is Salzgitter AG, which has over fifty thousand employees and is engaged in iron and steel and other industries. There is also a degree of public ownership in a number of other companies. Veba AG is 40 percent owned by the federal government, and the federal government has a 16 percent holding and the state of Lower Saxony a 20 percent holding in Volkswagen.

POLITICAL STRUCTURE AND TRADE UNIONS

Two groups of parties prevail in German politics. The Christian Democrats (CDU) and their allies, the Christian Social Union (CSU), are generally to the right; while the Social Democrats (SPD) at present govern with the support of the centrist Free Democrats

(FDP). The unions generally support the SPD and have close links with it.

The German trade union movement has a logical and unified structure generally lacking elsewhere in Europe. As reconstructed after 1945, the central union federation, the Deutsche Gewerkschaftsbund (DGB), has seventeen affiliated unions, the largest of which, Industriegewerkschaft Metall (IG Metall), has about 2.5 million members. Outside the DGB, there are over 1 million other trade unionists, the largest segments of whom are civil servants in the Deutsche Beamtenbund and white-collar workers who belong to the Deutsche Angestellten-Gewerkschaft.[1]

The unions enjoy considerable power both nationally and within companies, a power reinforced by the much-discussed German system of *Mitbestimmung* ("codetermination"). Employee representatives are elected at the board level and have a major influence over all aspects of company economic activity through the works councils (*Betriebsräte*). Although the representatives are formally elected by the entire work force, union-backed candidates are, in practice, usually chosen. The unions have generally adopted a politically moderate position and have consistently lent support to the country's economic development.

Investment in Germany has taken place through the period since the war despite a relatively weak risk-capital market. In place of stock-exchange financing, many companies rely heavily on bank financing and internal generation of funds. The relative unwillingness of Germans to use savings for investment in shares, often attributed to memories of the 1920s, may now be decreasing. Successive German governments have encouraged individual saving, and the unions have made proposals for collective investment funds, partly to fill a perceived gap in the German economy. Such proposals have been less prominent in the mid-1970s, but there has been a significant trend toward a growth of company profit-sharing and share-ownership plans, especially in many of the larger companies.

COMPANY PROFIT SHARING

In Germany, profit-sharing plans on an individual basis have been relatively scarce until recent years. There has, however, been a recent upsurge of interest in their use, partly because of legal changes

---

[1] E. C. M. Cullingford, *Trade Unions in West Germany* (London: Wilton House, 1976), pp. 11–15.

over the last few years that have given encouragement particularly to share-purchase plans.

The most important piece of legislation in this respect has been the 1959 Kapitalaufstockungsgesetz, which gives incentives to companies to issue shares to employees. A discount of up to 50 percent of the market price is permitted without the employee's becoming liable for tax on the benefits. Shares cannot be sold for five years, and the maximum gain from the discount cannot exceed DM 500 ($262) per year.[2]

There has been considerable research in Germany on these plans.[3] Guski and Schneider estimate that there are about seven hundred thousand employee stock owners and an additional one hundred thousand covered by other forms of equity participation. The total capital held by employees is now about DM 2,300 million ($1,207 million). A total of some 770 companies have been identified as having some form of equity participation, including 134 with employee stock-ownership plans. The latter are naturally concentrated among the larger firms.

The number of workers now covered totals about 6.2 percent of the eligible labor force, or around 800,000 employees. Because the public sector and some other areas are excluded from the legislation, only about 12 to 13 million employees are eligible. The ten largest employers in the country all have some form of capital participation. Of the plans, 50.3 percent began after 1971, and only 14.7 percent of them were established before 1960. In the face of economic recession, the pace of introduction of these plans has decreased since the period of major expansion (1968–74). Guski and Schneider found only two cases in which employers had abandoned profit-sharing plans.

In 82 percent of the *Aktiengesellschaften* ("limited companies") studied, plans had been introduced unilaterally by management, and only 16 percent had been discussed with the works councils. There was a much greater likelihood of prior discussions with works councils in small and medium-sized companies. It did not seem that the major reason for the introduction of plans was financial. In some smaller companies, the advantage of having an additional source of capital was a factor, but this did not apply in general to larger firms.

---

[2] Unless otherwise specified, the exchange rate used is $1 = DM 1.906 as of April 10, 1979.

[3] The most exhaustive recent account is contained in Hans-Günter Guski and Hans J. Schneider, *Betriebliche Vermögensbeteiligung in der Bundesrepublik Deutschland* (Cologne: Deutscher Instituts-Verlag GmbH, 1977). The subsequent figures on company profit-sharing plans are drawn from this source.

Their reasons were more connected with the desire to increase the identification of employees with the overall economic system by giving them a greater stake in economic development.

Some of the details of the plans are outlined in Table VI-1. The number of employees covered by plans varies considerably. Only 12.8 percent of the plans cover over ten thousand employees; 47.2 percent have between fifty and five hundred; and 8.2 percent, under fifty. The level of participation in plans also varies widely. Smaller companies have achieved higher participation; 61.8 percent have over 90 percent levels. In large companies, however, only 3.8 percent have over 90 percent participation, and 49.5 percent have under 30 percent. Even where there is a provision for free shares, only 85 percent of the employees take them. As Guski and Schneider comment, this is an instructive example that, even under the most favorable conditions, it is not possible to force people to become stockholders.[4]

Participation Level

There is a major difference in participation levels between blue-collar and white-collar employees. In only one case do a higher percentage of the former belong to a plan. This differential factor also influences the high levels of involvement in plans in the banking sector, with its large percentage of white-collar and managerial employees.

Participation depends on several factors. The state of the economy is an underlying influence and so is the employees' estimate of the economic position of the company. There is some tendency for initially optimistic expectations not to be realized, leading to a decline in participation. Guski and Schneider stress the importance of a well-organized educational and propaganda compaign by the company, preferably based on personal communications, which could help overcome initial distrust.

One of the major factors affecting participation is the attitude of unions and works councils toward plans. The opposition of certain unions, particularly IG Metall, has been a significant deterrent to participation and accounts, in part, for the lower level of blue-collar involvement. Unions' attitudes have been conditioned by a feeling that share-related plans could detract from collective bargaining and might, therefore, reduce pay increases and weaken union influence. Other criticisms include the belief that share plans expose employees to "double risk," hinder labor mobility, and create

---

[4] *Ibid.*, p. 45.

TABLE VI-1
German Profit-Sharing Companies with Over 5,000 Participating Employees

Company	Date of Introduction of Plan	Number of Employees	Number of Participating Employees	Value per Employee (DM)	Years Service Qualification	Years Blocking Period	Industry
Share-Purchase Plans							
Allianz-Versicherungs AG	1964	24,405	6,370	1,772	2.0	5.0	Insurance
BASF AG	1955	52,707	23,000	14,304	—	5.0	Chemicals
Bayerische Hypotheken-und Wechselbank	1965	10,700	7,500	3,882	—	5.0-6.0	Banking
Bayerische Vereinsbank	1967	9,086	7,000	5,895	1.0	5.0	Banking
Bewag AG	1971	6,000	5,400	1,489	—	5.0	Utility
Commerzbank AG	1965	19,668	11,000	1,400	—	5.0	Banking
Continental Gummiwerke AG	1971	18,878	11,537	671	1.0	5.0	Rubber
Daimler-Benz AG	1973	122,775	12,192	628	1.0	5.0-6.0	Vehicles
Deutsche Bank AG	1974	40,898	33,200	1,246	1.0	5.0	Banking
Dresdner Bank AG	1970	24,692	15,000	1,116	1.0	5.0-6.0	Banking
Hamburgische Electrizitätswerke AG	1971	5,600	5,000	3,648	1.0	5.0-6.0	Utility
Hoechst AG	1960	90,000	40,000	2,378	9 mos.	5.0	Chemicals
IBM Deutschland	1958	24,890	11,328	8,160	1.0	—	Data Processing
Mannesmann AG	1957	85,600	40,000	1,086	1.0	5.0	Steel
RWE	1958	20,627	17,920	2,497	—	5.0	Utility

Rosenthal AG	1963	7,958	5,500	1,337	—	5.0-6.0	Ceramics
Rutgerswerke AG	1974	6,380	6,129	863	10 mos.	5.0	Chemicals
Siemens AG	1969	201,300	100,000	7,090	3 mos.	5.0	Engineering
Thyssen Gruppe	1976	137,000	70,000	600	1.0	5.0	Steel
Veba AG	1965	69,825	25,858	1,013	—	2.0-6.0	Chemicals
Volkswagenwerk AG	1961	176,824	63,500	1,325	—	2.0	Vehicles
Employee Funds and Debentures							
Deutsche Philips GmbH	1970	32,700	30,100	1,993	—	5.5	Electrical
BMW AG	1974	28,989	6,600	1,695	1.0	6.0	Vehicles
Nixdorf Computer AG	1972	7,238	6,794	1,014	6 mos.	20.0	Computer
Bayer AG	1953	64,370	72,000[a]	2,592	—	1.5	Chemicals
Chemische Werke Hüls AG	1970	15,020	16,000[a]	327	1.0	3.0	Chemicals

Source: Hans-Günter Guski and Hans J. Schneider, *Betriebliche Vermögensbeteiligung in der Bundesrepublik Deutschland* (Cologne: Deutscher Instituts-Verlag GmbH, 1977).

[a]Includes pensioners.

divisions between employees of profitable companies and those in other sectors, such as public service.[5]

Many plans impose a service qualification that employees must fulfill in order to be eligible to join. About 40 percent of the plans have opted for a one-year service requirement, although a significant number impose no qualification period at all. Only 30 percent have a period of over two years, and only 1.3 percent exceed five. The provision of a longer qualification period would tend to diminish participation, but not necessarily by as much as might be expected, especially in smaller companies with low labor turnover. Among the latter, two-thirds of the companies with three-year qualifying periods have still achieved over 50 percent participation, although only three-eighths of the larger companies have. There has been a tendency over recent years for large companies to reduce or to abolish service qualifications. For example, Rosenthal AG, the ceramic manufacturer, imposed a five-year limit until 1971 but now has no qualification period at all. Some companies also impose age qualifications; the most common age is eighteen or twenty-one. Hettlage KGaA, which has a minimum age of twenty-eight, is a rarity.

Contributions and Benefits

The nature and method of contributions are not standardized. Among limited companies that have plans based on share purchase, the normal practice is to make the shares available to employees at a discount, which is legally limited to a maximum of 50 percent of current market price if the employee is to take advantage of the tax concessions offered. The 50 percent discount level has become the most common practice. There are other policies, however, which range from very small discounts to some exceeding 50 percent. There is also provision for the free distribution of shares on a one-time basis, and this is used by some companies to give shares to employees on such occasions as birthdays. The company will often meet any additional purchase costs that the employee has to bear from buying stock, although sometimes this has to be repaid to the company.

Where there are share-purchase plans, there are a number of methods that companies use to decide how much money to make available to the plan each year. In many companies, the relationship is to profits, which are often divided equally between workers and shareholders. In this context, profits are not usually calculated on a

---

[5] Hermann Adam, "Probleme der Vermögensbildung aus der Sicht der Gewerkschaften," *Aus Politik und Zeitgeschichte*, September 10, 1977, p. 11.

net after-tax basis but are composed of "distributable profits," which consists of after-tax profits minus interest on capital, a risk premium on capital, and remuneration for general management. The individual's allocation usually depends primarily on his wage level, but length of service is also taken into account in 28.6 percent of the plans. In smaller companies, the plans often provide for payment to employees in cash, employee loans, or, in some cases, debenture bonds. The allocation is based directly on profit level in 22.8 percent of such companies, but 44.9 percent opt to pay at a fixed rate, which is usually oriented to the National Bank Rate (e.g., 3 percent above it). A mixed formula is used in 32.3 percent of smaller companies.

In order to enjoy tax exemption under the Kapitalaufstockungsgesetz, the employee must hold his shares for a five-year blocking period before disposing of them. Some plans have even longer blocking periods; 10 percent of share plans have periods that exceed six years. In smaller companies that rely on loan systems (i.e., the employee's holding is lent to the company for it to invest), blocking periods are often longer and exceed ten years in 20.3 percent of the cases. Exceptions are often allowed in the event of death or illness-induced retirement.

The total size of the employees' holdings naturally depends on the size of payments and the participation level. The possibility of workers' obtaining a majority through share acquisition is not borne out by the evidence. It has been argued in the context of parity codetermination that even a small employee shareholding could tip the balance in situations in which employee representatives hold 50 percent of the seats on the supervisory board. This possibility is negated, however, by the fact that section 133 of the Aktiengesetz provides that decisions of shareholders' meetings should be by majority vote.[6] In 53.6 percent of the large companies, the total worker ownership of shares is under 1 percent, and only in 4.3 percent of the companies does it exceed 10 percent. In small and medium-sized companies, 68.1 percent have under 15 percent ownership, although in 3.1 percent of the cases, the employees have an absolute majority holding.

Some of the latter, however, may be unusual companies. For example, Photo-Porst AG, which was owned by Hannsheinz Porst, has 75 percent of its capital owned by the employees, but this has largely been a policy decision by Porst, who has been described as a "millionaire Marxist."[7] Since 1972, all profits have been allocated to

---

[6] Rudolf Mueller and Evan G. Galbraith, eds. and trans., *The German Stock Corporation Law*, 2d ed. (Frankfurt am Main: Fritz Knapp Verlag, 1976), p. 167.

[7] "La Participation Salariale," *Intersocial* (Paris), No. 34 (January 1978), pp. 19-22.

the employees above an interest on capital set at 3 percent above the bank rate. Seventy-five percent of the allocable profits is distributed in equal amounts to all employees, and the remainder is distributed in relation to salary. The management of the company is formally elected by the employees, who are involved in making most key decisions.

Another example of a company with a majority holding by employees is Joh. Friedrich Behrens, whose employees own 84 percent of the company's capital.[8] The company manufactures paper clips and office equipment and has a total labor force of 450. The company assumed its present form in 1945 when purchased by Karl Backaus, who believed that this form of industrial democracy would prevent any recurrence of fascism in Germany. The company, however, has run into economic difficulties recently, and after a number of employees cashed in their holdings, a decision was made to transform it into a limited company. Its democratic managerial structure has been retained, but the participating workers receive shares in the company as individuals, and their holdings are no longer under the control of a collective fund.

In general, the level of holding per employee is not very high. In only three large companies does the holding per employee exceed DM 10,000 ($5,247). The highest of these is at the Württembergische Bank, where the 100 participants (under 20 percent of employees) have holdings of an average of DM 25,800 ($13,537). Nineteen large companies have holdings of less than DM 1,000 ($525). Some eighteen smaller companies, including Porst and Behrens, have average holdings per employee of over DM 10,000 ($5,247). The highest figure here is DM 76,000 ($39,877), which is an average held by each of the 25 participating employees of Küba Kühlerfabrik, which has a total labor force of 420 and limits participation by salary level. Its nearest rival, Raspe and Paschen, a Hamburg export company, also hardly qualifies as a real profit sharer because its plan is open only to executives with ten years of service. As a result, only 4 of its employees (out of 40) participate. Each, however, has an average holding of DM 50,000 ($26,235).

The Largest Companies

In order of sales, the ten largest German companies are Siemens AG, Volkswagenwerk AG, Hoechst AG, Bayer AG, BASF AG, Daimler-Benz AG, Thyssen AG, Veba AG, AEG-Telefunken, and

---
[8] *Ibid.*

Mannesmann AG. All have some form of profit-sharing plan and are analyzed here as a distinct group. In addition, several of the large foreign corporations operating in Germany have profit-sharing plans for their German subsidiaries.

Among the ten companies, four instituted plans in the 1950s, four in the 1960s, and two in the 1970s. Participation rates vary widely. Only two companies (Bayer and Thyssen) exceed 50 percent; four have rates of between 40 and 50 percent; and two, between 30 and 40 percent. Participation at Daimler-Benz is only 10 percent, although it has been reported that 25 percent of white-collar staff and only 6 percent of blue-collar participate.[9] AEG-Telefunken's plan is only a partial one for its cablemaking division, and it achieves a participation rate of only 0.6 percent.

The holding per employee ranges from DM 388 ($204) (AEG-Telefunken) to DM 14,304 ($7,505) (BASF) per employee. Five of the companies fall between DM 1,000 and DM 3,000 ($525–$1,574). This does not only relate to the length of operation of the plan. Three of the four plans dating from the 1950s have under DM 3,000 per employee.

Four plans have no service qualification at all, and the only company with a qualification period exceeding one year is AEG-Telefunken. Nine of the companies distribute the employee's holding in the form of shares, and for the other (Bayer), this is one of three options. This choice may help account for the fact that Bayer has the highest participation rate of any company. Seven of the companies distribute the shares at a price calculated as a percentage of the current market price. For the tax reasons outlined above, a discount of 50 percent is common. Three companies fix a set price each year, but again, this usually works out to be about a 50 percent discount on market price. In addition, most of the companies will meet any incidental purchase costs incurred upon the acquisition of the shares.

Company Profit Sharing: Final Comment

Capital-sharing plans have, in recent years, gained an active body of support. Small companies may have been attracted to plans by the advantages that they offer in providing finance and in overcoming the difficulty of raising capital externally; this motive, however, is not significant in large companies. The tax benefits are

---

[9] "German Social Partners Look at Private Share-Purchase Plans," *Business Europe*, February 11, 1977, pp. 44–46.

also an important advantage, and in the long term, proponents also see potential improvements in productivity and motivation of employees.[10] The movement in favor of capital sharing has been particularly aided by one organization, the Arbeitsgemeinschaft zur Förderung der Partnerschaft in der Wirtschaft, which publicizes and encourages developments in the fields of codetermination, asset formation, and capital sharing.

ASSET FORMATION

In addition to the plans outlined above, there are legislative provisions in Germany on employee asset formation. These are sometimes integrated with profit-sharing arrangements but usually exist in their own right. From the early 1950s, there were proposals for the establishment of a mutual fund for employees based on employer contributions. For example, in 1957, Bruno Gleitzke, the head of the Trade Union Institute of Economic Science, proposed a "social capital" plan, whereby part of the capital growth of companies would be transferred to collective funds.[11] The unions, however, could not agree on a common policy, and there was little political momentum behind the proposals.

The Christian Democrat government meanwhile adopted a policy of encouraging personal savings. The 1952 House Savings Law offered premiums on savings connected with house purchase, and the 1959 Savings Premium Law provided premiums for savings contracts.[12] Both of the laws are still in force and operate as amended in 1975. The House Savings Law gives a premium of 18 percent of savings plus 2 percent for each child below eighteen years of age. The Savings Premium Law gives 14 percent plus 2 percent for each child under eighteen. In both cases, the maximum allowable savings is DM 800 ($420) per year if unmarried and DM 1,600 ($840) if married.

DM 312 Act

The acts of the 1950s were the precursors of the 1961 "DM 312" Act, the First Asset Formation Act. This specifies that workers can voluntarily set aside up to DM 312 per year ($78; 1961) for savings,

---

[10] Hans-Günter Guski, "Vermögensbeteiligung in der Möbelwirtschaft," *AGP-Mitteilungen*, No. 207 (May 1, 1977), p. 4.
[11] Solomon Barkin and Derek Robinson, *Workers' Negotiated Savings Plans for Capital Formation* (Paris: Organization for Economic Cooperation and Development, 1970), p. 13.
[12] *Ibid.*, p. 15.

if their employer so agrees, and will receive income tax relief on such payments. In addition, both employer and employee are freed from the obligation to pay social insurance contributions on the DM 312.[13] The savings must be placed in various specified forms of asset. The main benefit arises from the stipulation that, in addition to the individual's savings, the state will pay a special premium, usually 20 percent of the amount saved, if the employee holds his savings for five and one-half years. Thus, the government's main aim was to stimulate individual personal savings. There is no provision in the legislation for collective bargaining on asset-formation plans, and an employee can withdraw his holding at any time.

The legislation was subjected to criticism, particularly by the Construction Workers' Union, whose president, Georg Leber, was an advocate of collectively bargained asset-formation plans. In 1964, his union published the "Program for the Promotion of Construction Workers' Savings," which put forward a policy whereby the employer would pay an amount equal to 1.5 percent of the employee's pay into a fund jointly managed by unions and employers. The fund would invest the contributions and would issue certificates to employees showing their entitlement, which normally could not be cashed in until retirement. The employees would participate irrespective of their personal wishes.[14]

Criticism of the legislation also received support from a survey, published in 1965, that showed the limited impact of the 1961 legislation.[15] Only in 2.1 percent of undertakings had management offered to apply the DM 312 law, and only in 1.2 percent had the offer been accepted. In participating firms, only 10 percent of employees had decided to save, and there was a preponderance of white-collar employees in this total. It should be pointed out, however, that the 2.1 percent of firms that offered to participate employed 20.3 percent of the 12 million workers covered by the inquiry.

The 1965 Law

The so-called Leber plan received a mixed reception. Employers disliked the union influence over the fund's management and felt profits might be affected adversely. Union support for the plan was also muted, although in 1964, the DGB did issue a general policy

---

[13] Derek Robinson, *Incomes Policy and Capital Sharing in Europe* (New York: Barnes and Noble, 1973), p. 111.
[14] Barkin and Robinson, *Workers' Negotiated Savings Plans for Capital Formation*, pp. 16-17.
[15] Cullingford, *Trade Unions in West Germany*, pp. 85-92.

statement in support of capital accumulation.[16] Nevertheless, the proposals were instrumental in securing an amendment to the law in 1965, when the Second Capital Formation Act was passed. This extends tax concessions to plans set up as a result of collective bargaining and which involve employer contributions. The law also extends the plan to the public sector. If the full tax benefits are to be enjoyed, savings must be blocked for a period, usually of six to seven years. The special premium paid by the government remains payable to the employee.

By 1967, thirty-three agreements covering 1.7 million workers had been signed, but over 90 percent of these were in construction; the only other significant agreements were for the clothing industry and the Saar coal-mining industry. In construction, even though the agreement provided for both employer and employee contributions, only a minority of those formally covered actually chose to participate in the plan.

The 1970 Law

In June 1970, the Third Capital Formation Act was passed. The main effect of this was to raise the limit from DM 312 to DM 624 ($171; 1970) on annual payments that would receive tax concessions. These payments can be applied to employees earning up to DM 24,000 ($6,581; 1970) per year in taxable income if unmarried and DM 48,000 ($13,162; 1970) if married, with an additional allowance of DM 1,800 ($494;1970) for each child. The savings are, however, liable to income tax and social insurance contributions, although as a partial compensation, the bonus payable by the state was raised to 30 percent, or 40 percent with three or more children.

It is evidence of the changing political situation that the Third Act was introduced by a Social Democrat government, acting in conjunction with its coalition party, the Free Democrats. In addition, union interest in the plan grew, and this resulted in more collectively bargained plans. The most significant development in this regard was in the metal industry. IG Metall had been one of the unions that had been least enthusiastic about asset formation. Possibly under pressure from its membership, however, it signed an agreement that took effect in July 1970 for a six-year period.[17] The agreement covered 4.2 million employees and was estimated to cost DM 8 billion ($2.19 billion; 1970) over the six-year period, equivalent to an average pay increase of 2 to 4 percent. The union insisted on

---

[16] Barkin and Robinson, *Workers' Negotiated Savings Plans for Capital Formation*, p. 18.

[17] Robinson, *Incomes Policy and Capital Sharing in Europe*, p. 119.

securing from the employers a promise that the payments were to be regarded as totally separate from the rest of the wage agreement. IG Metall insisted that, unlike the agreements signed in the construction industry, the plan should require no payment by the employee. In common with other agreements, the deal specified a range of investment alternatives, and the blocking period consequently varied. The union was keen that employees should invest via the Trade Union Bank, but the preference of workers lay, in fact, in investment methods that were more readily transferable into cash. As a result, savings were generally paid into ordinary bank accounts or into loan societies to aid in acquiring property mortgages, or were used as premiums for life insurance policies.

Further collective agreements in 1970 in the chemical industry in Hesse, Rhineland-Palatinate, and Lower Saxony also included asset-formation provisions, and in succeeding years, many other plans were introduced, with the number of workers covered rising from 5.7 million in 1969 to 19 million in 1974.[18] This latter figure represented about 85 percent of the total German labor force.

COLLECTIVE FUNDS

At the same time as the scope of the DM 624 law was being extended by collective bargaining, an active debate within the unions and the Social Democratic party was developing on the potential for collective investment funds. Much of this debate was generated by arguments concerning the distribution of wealth in Germany. The unions alleged that the wage earners had little real wealth and quoted figures purporting to show that 1.7 percent of the population owned 70 percent of the country's private productive wealth. As Guski has pointed out, however, private productive wealth accounted for only 19 percent of the country's total wealth, and so the ownership of the 1.7 percent was really about 13 percent (70 percent multiplied by 19 percent).[19] Guski and other observers have recognized the need to provide means for accumulating capital, particularly among wage earners, who in the context of a welfare system have a much lower propensity to save than the self-employed.

SPD Proposal

In 1973, the SPD party conference in Hannover overwhelmingly approved a policy on collective asset formation. All employers with

---

[18] Hans-Günter Guski, *Vermögensbildung—Bilanz und Perspektiven* (Cologne: Deutscher Instituts-Verlag GmbH, 1975), p. 69.

[19] *Ibid.*, pp. 39–42.

taxable profits in excess of DM 400,000 ($149,645; 1973) per year would have to set aside a fixed percentage of profits that would be transferred to collective funds. The level of company contributions would be set to yield DM 5,000 million ($1,871 million; 1973) in the first year and would be paid in the form of shares. The plan was limited to employees earning less than DM 36,000 ($13,468; 1973) per year or DM 48,000 ($17,957; 1973) if married. Employees would receive certificates in the central fund but would be unable to cash in their holdings for a period of seven years.

The plan's supporters claimed that it would not affect the liquidity of companies, but critics attacked the plan as a major disincentive to traditional share investors. In addition, a growth in the shareholding of the central fund was envisioned that would increase its holding to 25 percent after about fifteen years, and the fund would attain a majority after forty years. Although the funds were to be run by people elected by the employees, it was clear that, as with the works councils, the vast majority of those actually chosen would be union-backed candidates. As such, the plan was attacked both for the accretion to union power that it represented and for constituting a step toward the socialization of the means of production.

DGB Proposal

In April 1973, the DGB Executive Committee narrowly approved a policy document on asset formation that was similar to the SPD plan, except that the funds were to be run by union officials only. Moreover, dividends would not be credited to individual employees as in the SPD plan but would be used to provide further funds for investment. The DGB plan incurred even greater hostility than that of the SPD. Guski called it a "fig leaf" behind which lurked the old socialist aims of controlling the means of production.[20]

The policy had some major union opponents. Both IG Metall and the major public sector union, Gewerkschaft Öffentliche Dienste, Transport und Verkehr, saw it as politically unrealistic and as a diversion from the goal of parity codetermination. IG Metall also attacked the concept of compulsorily including all employees in the plan and took the view that the priority should be to maximize immediate income.

---

[20] *Ibid.*, p. 116.

SPD-FDP Proposal

Politically, the SPD needed to take cognizance of the views of its coalition partner, the Free Democrats. The FDP had always favored a wider distribution of wealth and had also espoused the central fund concept, based on a levy of company profits provided that the company made a profit of at least DM 3 million ($1.16 million; 1974). In addition, the FDP sought to enable small firms to pay their contributions in cash and so avoid diluting ownership.

The coalition, as a result, arrived at a compromise proposal that was put forward in 1974. This plan included all limited companies with annual pretax profits in excess of DM 400,000 ($154,321; 1974) and all other companies with profits in excess of DM 500,000 ($192,901; 1974). The contribution rate would rise up to 10 percent if profits exceeded DM 1 million ($385,802; 1974). The planned yield of this levy was at least DM 5 billion ($1.93 billion; 1974) per year. Limited companies would be required to distribute the payment in the form of shares but could, for payment of a 15 percent surcharge, distribute in cash. All employees with an income of below DM 36,000 ($13,889; 1974) per year (single) or DM 54,000 ($20,833; 1974) (married) could participate. In addition, the salary cutoff point could be raised by DM 9,000 ($3,472; 1974) for each dependent child. As a result, the vast majority of the labor force would be covered. The maximum contribution per employee was set at DM 212 ($82; 1974), and the employee would receive certificates in a central fund, and his holding would be blocked for seven years.

It is no surprise that the plan met with considerable opposition and was not pursued. Opposition came from employers and the CDU/CSU block in the Bundestag. The divisions within the trade union movement itself also contributed to the demise of the plan.[21]

CONCLUSION

Over the last few years, attention has swung back to further developments in the DM 624 legislation and to advances in the field of company profit sharing. The latter has been aided by tax decisions over recent years. In 1974, the Finance Court ruled that specified "worker-loans" should not be subject to income tax, and in February 1978, the Federal Social Security Court ruled that such

---

[21] "Compulsory Asset Formation No Longer Threatens German Employers," *Business Europe*, August 5, 1977, pp. 243–45.

"worker-loans" would be free of social security taxes while invested.[22] Whether collective programs again will be pursued will probably depend much on the extent of union interest, which, in 1978-79, was largely concentrated on codetermination and on issues relating to employment.

---

[22] "Neue Wege für die Vermögensbildung," *Blick Durch die Wirtschaft* (Frankfurt am Main), February 17, 1978, p. 1.

CHAPTER VII

Denmark and Sweden

Because both Denmark and Sweden are Scandinavian countries, there is a temptation not to draw distinctions between them. One important corrective to this attitude is to point out that Denmark is a member both of the European Community (EC) and NATO, while Sweden belongs to neither. Furthermore, the history and cultural heritage of the two countries are quite different.

INDUSTRIAL SIMILARITIES

Although it is important to distinguish between the two countries, there are many reasons that justify analyzing them together. The economic, social, and political structures of the two countries exhibit many similarities. Table V-2 shows that, of all major Western countries, Denmark and Sweden have the highest levels of government consumption as a percentage of Gross Domestic Product (GDP). They also have the highest overall participation rate in the labor force, which results entirely from the high level of female participation, over 40 percent, in both countries. Sweden has the longest life expectancy figures in the world, and Denmark is not far behind. As a result, both have male labor force participation rates close to the European average and behind those of such countries as the United Kingdom and Switzerland.[1]

The industrial deployment of the labor force is also comparable. In Denmark, agriculture accounts for 9.3 percent of the labor force; manufacturing, 23.1 percent; services, 36.1 percent; construction, 8.1 percent; and distribution, 14.4 percent.[2] In Sweden, agriculture, with 6.1 percent, is slightly less important; manufacturing, with 26.5 percent, is slightly more important; but services (36.6 percent), construction (7.1 percent), and distribution (14.2 percent) are very similar.[3]

---
[1] International Labour Organisation, *1977 Year Book of Labour Statistics* (Geneva, 1977), pp. 38, 45.
[2] *Ibid.*, pp. 128-29.
[3] *Ibid.*, pp. 154-55.

Unions and Politics

In both countries, the labor force is highly unionized, with a rate of membership of over 65 percent, which places the two in Belgium's company as the Western leaders in this regard. The unions play an important role both politically and economically and have strong influence over the Social Democratic parties of the two countries. In Sweden, between 1932 and 1976, the Social Democrats enjoyed governmental control that was only briefly interrupted for three months in 1936. In 1924 in Denmark, the Social Democrats became the country's largest party in votes and have been in government on their own or as part of coalitions for forty of the fifty years between 1929 and 1979. Their position has been somewhat eroded since 1968, but they have currently been back in government since 1975. In August 1978, the Social Democrats entered into a coalition with the Liberal party, which seems to have produced some friction between the unions and the Social Democrats. The coalition was greeted by a wave of strikes, and unions have expressed fears that the necessity of reaching agreement with the Liberals will reduce the Social Democrats' willingness to espouse the unions' political objectives.

During the course of their political dominance, the Social Democrats in both countries have erected elaborate welfare states, which offer a wide range of benefits to their citizens. These benefits have been financed by a high level of government expenditures made possible by high and sharply progressive personal taxation. In Sweden's case, personal taxation reached a level of 45 percent of Gross National Product (GNP) in 1974 and is a major factor in the ratio of household savings (between 8 and 10 percent from 1974 to 1976), which is low compared to the ratios of other European countries.[4] In this regard, Denmark's tax system is less sharp and influences the considerably higher rate of household savings out of disposable income (between 16.8 percent and 19.1 percent from 1973 to 1976).[5]

Although there is a tendency to see both countries as strongly "socialist" because of their welfare provisions, neither country traditionally has had a high degree of state control of manufacturing industry or of the financial and banking sector. Statsföretag AB, the Swedish state holding company, with interests in a number

---

[4] Organization for Economic Cooperation and Development, *OECD Economic Surveys: Sweden* (Paris, 1977), p. 8.
[5] Organization for Economic Cooperation and Development, *OECD Economic Surveys: Denmark* (Paris, 1977), p. 44.

Denmark and Sweden

of industries including mining, chemical, and textiles, was the only significant exception to this generalization. Ironically, this situation changed during the period when the Social Democrats were not in power in Sweden, 1976-78. The coalition of three center and right-wing parties placed the shipbuilding industry under government ownership and took a major stake in the steel industry. A number of commentators have pointed out that this represented a larger increase in state ownership in two years than the Social Democrats had attempted in forty-four.

Investment

Denmark has faced considerable problems in recent years in attracting sufficient investment. The annual growth rate of investment between 1963 and 1975 was only 2.7 percent,[6] and both private savings and private investment declined between 1960 and 1977. Despite its much lower level of personal savings, Sweden achieved a higher growth rate of investment (4.2 percent per year) between 1963 and 1975.[7] Sweden's relative success in this regard sprang largely from its ability to devise alternative sources of investment. In particular, a major source of investment has been the Swedish pension fund system. Not only has this helped maintain the level of investment in Sweden, but it has also contributed to what a survey by the Organization for Economic Cooperation and Development described as the "striking" factor of Sweden's investment record: its stability over time.[8] Some 34 percent of the National Pensions Insurance Fund, a total of Kr 9,500 million ($1,860 million; 1971), went into investment in industry between 1959, when the fund was created, and 1971.[9] Because the fund has been growing steadily since its inception, it can be assumed that its financing role will increase. The use of the pension fund and other investment mechanisms, such as AB Sveriges Investeringsbank, the investment bank set up in 1967, is the precursor to some of the collective investment proposals that have emerged in Sweden in recent years.

Denmark has not had such an active governmental policy in the promotion of investment, and this has been one of the bases for

---

[6] Organization for Economic Cooperation and Development, *OECD Economic Surveys: Sweden*, p. 9.
[7] *Ibid.*
[8] *Ibid.*
[9] Marie Norgren and Christian Norgren, *Industrial Sweden* (Stockholm: The Swedish Institute, 1971), pp. 87-88. The exchange rate used is $1=Kr 4.859 (Sweden).

proposals for collective investment funds in that country. As a result, much of the financing for investment has been supplied directly by banking institutions, and these institutions have labored under governmental restrictions. In general, however, Denmark has not witnessed as high a level of governmental economic intervention in industry as has Sweden. While the latter has adopted selective subsidy policies for certain industries, Denmark has avoided giving significant aid to even the struggling textile and shipbuilding industries.

PROFIT SHARING IN DENMARK

Voluntary profit sharing within companies in Denmark and the formation of "social funds" designed to provide a range of welfare benefits to employees have been promoted and encouraged by a law passed in 1957. A profit-sharing board established at the national level has the responsibility of advising companies contemplating the introduction of such plans. The board consists of an independent chairman appointed by the government and of representatives of both employee and employer organizations.[10]

Since 1957, approximately fifty companies have instituted profit-sharing plans. The majority of these require that shareholders be allocated an initial percentage of profits, but the amount in excess of this basic level must be divided evenly between shareholders and employees. The plans differ in the use to which the money is put. In some companies, the total amount is contributed to individual employees; in others, the money is paid into a collective social fund.[11]

One example of a company plan is that of A/S Atlas, a household appliance manufacturer with eight hundred employees.[12] The company inaugurated its profit-sharing plan in 1950 but brought it within the framework of the new law in 1957. The company sets aside an initial percentage of profits for shareholders that equals half the Danish Bank Rate plus 0.25 percent, subject to a minimum level of 2.75 percent. Thereafter, the company makes available for employees a sum equal to the amount paid out in dividends. One-half of the sum is paid in cash to employees; those with over twenty-five years' service receive larger proportions of this half than the other employees receive. The other half is paid to a social welfare

---

[10] "Profit-Sharing in Denmark: A Review of Some Company Schemes," *European Industrial Relations Review*, No. 13 (January 1975), p. 14.
[11] *Ibid.*
[12] "Profit Sharing in Denmark: The Atlas Scheme," *European Industrial Relations Review*, No. 27 (March 1976), pp. 8-10.

fund, which can pay benefits at its discretion. Both the plan as a whole and the fund are managed by an elected committee of three blue-collar employees, three salaried employees, one manager, and one director. The amount paid to the plan naturally varies and has been zero in some years (e.g., 1968 and 1969). In 1974, however, payments amounted to Kr 2.1 million ($344,545; 1974).[13]

Royal Porcelain Manufacturing introduced a plan in 1973 for its eighteen hundred employees.[14] After an initial allocation to shareholders based on the Danish Bank Rate, further profit is divided equally between shareholders and employees. This calculation leads to smaller payments than those at A/S Atlas. The employee's share is paid entirely in the form of a five-year debenture with an interest rate set at 2 percent above the bank rate. There is a minimum service requirement of three years for membership eligibility.

The number of companies adopting profit sharing under the 1957 provisions has been small. Union disinterest has been cited as a factor in limiting the effect of the law, particularly in larger companies. The main union federation, Landsorganisationen i Danmark (LO), has been increasingly critical of the limited impact of the legislation, but the major Danish employers' confederation, Dansk Arbejdsgiverforening (DA), has continued to support it.

COLLECTIVE ASSET FORMATION

The attitude of both parties in recent years has been reflected in the emergence of union and government proposals for collective investment funds. These proposals had their origin within the Danish Union of Engineering Workers, which, with one hundred thousand members, is the third largest in the country. In 1969, the union adopted a policy document drafted by a former prime minister, Viggo Kampmann. The proposal provided for funds both at company and national level but gave no individual withdrawal rights to employees. Company contributions to the funds would be made in relation to profits.[15]

The national trade union movement debated this proposal in conjunction with its interest in gaining board-level representation. The LO established its own committee to examine the issue under the chairmanship of a former minister of finance, Henry Grünbaum. This committee reported to the 1971 LO congress, where its report

---

[13] Unless otherwise specified, the exchange rate used is $1=Kr 5.285 (Denmark) as of April 10, 1979.
[14] "Profit-Sharing in Denmark: A Review of Some Company Schemes," p. 14.
[15] Dansk Arbejdsgiverforening and Industrirådet, "Co-Worker, Co-Owner," Discussion Paper on Economic Democracy (Copenhagen, 1972), pp. 40-41.

was accepted by the overwhelming vote of 1,096 to 4.[16]

The proposals adopted in 1971 differed in several respects from those put forward by the Danish Union of Engineering Workers. In particular, all employees in the country would be given individual certificates, which would represent their holdings in the plan, but these would be subject to a blocking period of five years. The LO also decided to support contributions related to a company wage bill, partly because of difficulties in integrating the public sector in the plan. The plan would start with a levy of 1 percent of the wage bill, which would rise to 5 percent after eight years.[17] The LO stated clearly its ideological aims in putting forward its proposals in the 1971 resolution:

> The wage-earners must demand a share in the capital growth to which they contribute through their work. The LO should make efforts to ensure that the wage-earners get influence and co-determination in the management of enterprises and co-ownership rights to the means of production.[18]

The 1973 Bill

As a result of the LO's proposals, the Social Democratic government placed before the Danish Parliament (Folketing) its "Joint Ownership (Employees) Bill" in January 1973, clarifying and expanding the LO's proposals.[19] With this bill, the government sought to establish an "Employees' Investment and Dividend Fund," collectively owned by all wage earners. The plan was to include all employees aged between eighteen and sixty-six, for whom the employer would be liable to pay contributions to the "Labour Market Supplementary Pension Scheme." This would include public and private sector workers and exclude only those who worked less than fifteen hours per week. The fund would be financed by employer contributions based on total wage bill. In 1974, the employer's contribution would have been 0.5 percent of that year's total wage bill, and the contribution would rise to 5 percent after ten years. The employer would receive tax benefits on his payments. Although the government followed the LO's lead in not relating the plan to profits, it promised to investigate the future possibility of supplement-

---

[16] Landsorganisationen i Danmark, *Co-Ownership Co-Determination: The Danish Government Bills on Economic and Industrial Democracy* (Copenhagen, n.d.), p. 5.

[17] Derek Robinson, *Incomes Policy and Capital Sharing in Europe* (New York: Barnes and Noble, 1973), p. 91.

[18] Landsorganisationen i Danmark, *Co-Ownership Co-Determination*, p. 6.

[19] Denmark, Ministry of Labor, *Economic Democracy: Introduction and Bill* (Copenhagen, 1973).

ing or replacing part of the wage-related contributions with profit-related payments. The wage-related formula was, however, seen as a means of simplifying the participation of public sector employers in the plan.

The application of the money raised would differ among types of company. Limited companies with a payroll of over fifty would be required to pay two-thirds of their contribution in the form of shares, which would be allocated equally to the employees of that company, while the remaining one-third would be paid into the central fund. It was estimated that this arrangement would cover about twenty-eight hundred organizations. Approximately twenty-six hundred companies, with between twenty and fifty employees, would be given the option of leaving two-thirds of their contributions in the enterprise as share capital provided that they agreed to accept the same rules for employee participation as applied to companies with over fifty employees. This was an effort to encourage smaller companies, legally exempt from the proposed bill, to follow the legal provisions of the Danish Companies Act, which came into force in January 1974 and established a system of worker-directors. Companies with less than twenty employees would pay their two-thirds internal allocation in cash.

Employees would receive certificates each year specifying their entitlement under the plan. These certificates could not be negotiated or borrowed against, but after seven years, the employee would have the right to withdraw his holding plus dividends and interest. Withdrawal would also be allowed at age sixty-seven or in the event of death. At the time the holding is cashed in, the employee would be liable for tax on his income at a flat rate of 35 percent.

The intention of the plan was to provide a steady increase in employee shareholding in companies. There was, however, a restriction preventing employee shareholdings from exceeding 50 percent of the total shares of any company. Once this limit is reached, future payments would have to be in the form of cash or loans. The loan system would also apply to the public sector enterprises, with a provision that up to two-thirds of contributions could remain in the undertaking in that form.

The Central Fund

Although the bill prescribed that a sizable part of the contributions would be held inside the individual companies, the right of control over these investments would be held by the central fund in the employees' names during the seven-year blocking period. As a result, the assets of the fund would be expected to grow very rapidly. It was expected that, by 1988, the fund would hold 35 percent of all Danish share capital, with the fund's total assets coming to Kr 88.70 billion ($16.78 billion). This growth was posited on the assumption of annual increases of 9 percent in wages, annual interest rates of 9 percent, and dividend rates of 4.5 percent per year.[20] It was recognized that much would depend on the rate of employee withdrawal at the end of the seven-year period. The calculations were based on the assumption of a 100 percent withdrawal rate and so could understate the fund's growth.

Control of the Central Fund

If effected, this plan would give tremendous economic power to the central fund. The fund would be governed by a council of sixty members appointed for three-year terms, thirty-six of whom would be appointed by employee organizations and twenty-four by the government. Of the former, the LO would appoint eighteen members, while the other seats would be spread among other bodies. The employers would be entirely excluded from representation. The council would elect a managing board of ten members (six union, four government), which would have the main responsibility for the daily handling of the fund's affairs.

The government also recognized the need for parliamentary surveillance over the fund. It provided, therefore, for the election of a seventeen-man board of supervision from among the members of the Folketing. This board could demand any information from the fund and would transmit to the Folketing the accounts and annual report of the fund together with its own comments.

The unions and government suggested that the bill would not only help democratize the ownership of the means of production but would also provide much-needed funds for capital investment.[21] The collective fund was commended on the grounds that it would give employees a stake in industry without hindering labor mobility and without exposing an employee to risk in the event of economic difficulties experienced by his employer. Although the fund would hold shares in individual companies, voting rights attached to these shares could be exercised by the employees in the particular com-

---

[20] *Ibid.*, pp. 33-43.
[21] Bernt Schiller, "Industrial Democracy in Scandinavia," *Annals of the American Academy of Political and Social Science*, No. 431 (May 1977), p. 69.

pany. The government and unions felt that this would reduce criticism that the plan was distant from individual workers.

Employer Reaction

These proposals encountered considerable criticism. The employers saw the proposals as marking a further socialization of the economy while giving unions undue economic power. The employers had already produced their own ideas for action in 1972 in response to the LO's initiative.[22] They agreed with the unions that it was desirable to increase employee savings to help relieve the prevailing shortage of capital in Denmark, and they had become worried over the previous twenty years about the low propensity to save that resulted from Denmark's highly developed welfare system. The employers, too, felt that it would be beneficial to give workers a broader identification with industry and even felt that there was scope for a more equitable distribution of wealth, which they believed could no longer be furthered by taxation because the level of tax payments had become so high that it stifled individual initiative.

There was agreement, therefore, on some of the objectives of reform, but disagreement on the means of implementation. In particular, the employers felt that, if employees were to have equal rights with existing shareholders, they should also have equal risks. They particularly opposed the collective fund concept. They felt that this forced employees into participation against their will and would not, therefore, increase employee involvement in industry. They believed that the existence of a central fund would prevent an employee's identification with the profit performance of his own company.

The employers were also strongly critical of the assumption that the plan would increase industrial investment. According to them, the fund might not invest in industry, and any gains would be negated by the flight of capital abroad. They felt that what was required was a fundamental change in the government's attitude that would alter the existing tax disincentives to share investment. That the unions supported a compulsory plan seemed to the employers to prove that there was a lack of incentive to save voluntarily. As they said:

> Economic democracy, however, is meaningless if the attitude of government and employee organizations to investment in private industrial establishments and the yield from such investment is negative

---

[22] Dansk Arbejdsgiverforening and Industrirådet, "Co-Worker, Co-Owner."

and results in discriminatory provisions. Economic democracy cannot, therefore, be realized unless there is a fundamental change in this attitude.[23]

The employers' own proposals were designed to give workers the opportunity to acquire shares voluntarily in their own companies. The employers opposed strongly any form of profit sharing based on cash payments but otherwise adopted a flexible approach. They also recognized the added risk element in share purchase from one's own employer and advocated the creation of mutual funds to circumvent this problem.

After the government introduced its bill, the employers repeated many of their criticisms. They described the bill as a "rash experiment"[24] and to their previous criticisms added opposition to relating payments to the wage bill. They felt that such a policy discriminated against labor-intensive companies in contributions, although it favored them in capital accumulation. They warned that, because contributions were wage-related, employers would have an additional incentive to hold down wage rates. The employers were also alarmed at the explicit statement by the unions that investment by the central fund "might involve motives other than profit."[25] Environmental improvements and regional development were mentioned in this context.

Other Attacks

The proposals were also attacked from other quarters, as one academic commentator has pointed out: "The Danish proposal has met criticism from the left which has described economic democracy as a kind of first aid for crisis-ridden monopoly capitalism."[26] This accusation emanated particularly from the extreme left Socialist People's party (which currently has seven members in the Folketing). The LO, hotly contesting this interpretation of its policy, claimed that the plan would "result in the creation of a society based on the ideas of democratic socialism of a more equal distribution of prosperity and of economic influence."[27]

---

[23] *Ibid.*, p. 33.
[24] Dansk Arbejdsgiverforening, *The Consequences of Economic Democracy* (Copenhagen, n.d.), p. 1.
[25] Landsorganisationen i Danmark, *Co-Ownership Co-Determination*, pp. 24-25.
[26] Schiller, "Industrial Democracy in Scandinavia," p. 70.
[27] Landsorganisationen i Danmark, *Co-Ownership Co-Determination*, pp. 25-26.

Current Status

In any case, the 1973 election intervened to hinder any progress on the bill, although in 1975, the Social Democrats tried unsuccessfully to resurrect it during the course of negotiations over the formation of a coalition government. The unions have remained committed to the plan, and as a result, the minority Social Democrat government announced late in 1977 that it was appointing a tripartite commission to report on the issue of economic democracy. This report was published in 1978, but it restricted itself to a survey of the different options without making any firm recommendations.[28] The creation of the Social Democrat-Liberal coalition has made political action unlikely, since the Liberals oppose the unions' economic democracy proposals. Perhaps for this reason, the LO changed its tactics, and in November 1978, it put forward proposals on this subject to the employers directly during the opening rounds of national pay talks. The employers refused to negotiate on the issue, and the unions dropped their claim on this subject. In doing so, however, the unions made it clear that they had not abandoned economic democracy as an ultimate goal, and the issue seems destined to recur in Danish politics.

PROFIT SHARING IN SWEDEN

Although there are a few profit-sharing plans at the company level in Sweden, they have not proved particularly popular. In his work on Swedish industrial relations, Johnston drew attention to the attitude of the major employers' federation, Svenska Arbetsgivareföreningen (SAF): "SAF considers that profit-sharing is a typical bargaining issue, and that profit-sharing schemes, of which few exist in Sweden, are contrary to the whole rationale of the collective bargaining system."[29] Nor have the unions seemed eager to put forward proposals in this area for somewhat similar reasons.

Among the few profit-sharing plans in Sweden is that at Skandinaviska Enskilda Banken (SEB), which has 6,750 employees, and which, in 1977, established a plan on a trial basis for three years.[30] Each employee receives an individual share, which is placed in a

---

[28] "Economic Democracy: The Options Assessed," *European Industrial Relations Review*, No. 60 (January 1979), pp. 8-9.

[29] T. L. Johnston, *Collective Bargaining in Sweden* (Cambridge, Mass.: Harvard University Press, 1962), p. 258.

[30] Curt G. Olsson and Torsten Carlsson, "Profit Sharing and Participation in Capital Formation," *Skandinaviska Enskilda Banken Quarterly Review*, No. 3-4 (1977), pp. 67-77.

fund run by the Swedish Union of Bank Employees. The profit to be distributed is

> 20 percent of what remains after the bank's operating profit has been reduced by the approved shareholders' dividend, the tax calculated on this dividend and such appropriations to the untaxed reserves so that these grow on a percentage basis as much as the balance sheet total. The profit share must never exceed 20 percent of the dividend.[31]

The fund purchases shares of the bank in the market and, during a five-year blocking period, reinvests the dividends. At the end of five years, an employee can decide whether to sell the shares or leave them invested in the fund until retirement. Any employee with two years' service is eligible to participate and, if he does participate, receives an annual statement of the shares accruing to him. The allocation is not salary-related.

The plan was introduced after discussion with the union, but the SEB made it clear that the plan was under its discretion and could be revoked. It specifically reserved the right to do this if any profit-sharing plan were introduced by legislation or by a collective agreement. In this, the bank was safeguarding its position if the Meidner plan, discussed below, should become law, a position buttressed by the provision of a three-year trial period for the company plan.

Svenska Handelsbanken, which has five thousand employees, also has a profit-sharing plan on somewhat similar lines. In its plan, however, the individual profit shares are not made available until retirement age is reached, and at that time, the payment is made in the form of cash rather than of shares.[32]

COLLECTIVE INVESTMENT PROPOSALS

In recent years, Sweden has witnessed active proposals for collective investment plans. The 1971 conference of the major union federation, Landsorganisationen i Sverige (LO), asked economist Rudolf Meidner to conduct a study and put forward suggestions designed to answer a number of questions. Between 1945 and 1966, Meidner had been director of the research department of the LO; currently, he is senior adviser to that organization. The committee headed by Meidner issued its proposals in 1975, and after some modification, these were presented to the LO congress in 1976, where they were unanimously endorsed.[33]

---

[31] *Ibid.*, p. 68.
[32] *Ibid.*, p. 74.
[33] Rudolf Meidner, *Employee Investment Funds* (London: George Allen and Unwin, 1978). This is the English translation of the 1976 report.

The main issues that his committee examined were (1) how to complement the unions' wage solidarity policy, (2) how to counteract the concentration of wealth resulting from the existing methods of financing industrial organizations, and (3) how to increase employees' influence over the economy by coownership of productive capital.[34]

Underlying Philosophy

The importance of the wage solidarity policy must be stressed. Swedish unions have long pursued a policy of coordinating their bargaining strategy to ensure a more egalitarian wage structure. This policy was instituted in the early 1950s and concentrated union attention on reducing differentials and on aiding the lower-paid. The aim of the policy was described by a report to the 1971 LO congress:

> The aim of the wage policy of solidarity is to create fair relations between wages. A corollary to this is that the trade union movement does not demand equal wages for everyone. Its wage policy is based on the principle of differentiation of wages according to the nature and demands of the job.... On the other hand, the wage solidarity policy rejects wage-setting based on the varying profitability and wage-paying ability of different economic sectors. Wage-setting based on the profitability of companies means that employees with low wages are being forced to subsidize stagnant or poorly managed companies.[35]

The proposals for collective investment funds were founded on the situation that the unions felt had resulted from this policy. They believed that efficient companies were earning "excess profits" because unions were not basing pay claims on the companies' ability to pay. Investment funds were seen as a way of using these excess profits for the unions' benefit. The specific proposals also constituted an effort to reduce further the effect of economic differences between disparate groups of employees.

The proposals were also designed as a means of giving unions and employees a greater say in the allocation of profits for investment purposes. It was also Meidner's view that the plan would offset the effects of the concentration of ownership of capital in a few hands. The committee pointed out that, although seven hundred thousand Swedes owned shares, 3 percent of shareholders owned 66 percent of the outstanding shares.[36] Because employee influence would not be

---

[34] *Ibid.*, p. 15.
[35] Lennart Forsebäck, *Industrial Relations and Employment in Sweden* (Stockholm: The Swedish Institute, 1976), p. 77.
[36] Meidner, *Employee Investment Funds*, pp. 35-37.

increased, the committee rejected proposals for a higher corporation tax as a means of tapping excess profits. The report also did not favor plans to transfer money to inefficient companies; this was contrary to the unions' desire to see a strong and viable economy in Sweden.

The proposals entirely rejected the concept of individual profit sharing, which was felt to tie workers to their particular company and to undermine the solidarity of wage earners as a whole, and which was also felt not to offer any significant increase in employee influence over decision making within companies. Therefore, unlike plans in other countries, the plan contained no provision for individual employees to withdraw capital from the investment fund.

Summary of the Meidner Plan

Under the plan, all firms with fifty or more employees would be required to set aside 20 percent of their profits in the form of new shares, which, while remaining as equity capital within each firm, would be owned by a "central equalization fund." The calculation of profit would be after depreciation but before appropriations.[37] Special proposals would prevent multinational companies from transferring profits overseas to avoid paying their contributions.

The central equalization fund would be run by a board composed solely of union representatives. The fund would own the shares and would receive the dividends from them, which would be used in roughly equal proportion either to buy additional stock in companies or to make payments for such purposes as union members' education and research.

As the shares are turned over to the fund, its stake in the individual company would of course steadily increase. The Meidner report estimated that it would take between twenty and seventy-five years for the fund to acquire a 50 percent stake in a company, depending on the company's level of profitability.[38] The shares owned by the fund could not be sold, so collective ownership would be retained.

In addition, as the fund's holding increased, the local union would be permitted to appoint a delegate to the company board. Once the fund's holding exceeded 20 percent of the shares, additional board members would be appointed by a "branch fund," composed of an equal number of representatives of the unions in the particular

---

[37] Svenska Arbetsgivareföreningen, *The Development of Workers' Participation in Sweden*, SAF Document 139 (Stockholm, 1977), p. 7.
[38] Meidner, *Employee Investment Funds*, p. 59.

Denmark and Sweden

company and representatives of other unions, as well as a number of representatives of the community as a whole. The local union would have the right to veto such appointments.

The unions supported the proposals as an extension of "industrial democracy" and as a means of providing a countervailing force to the power of private capital. They claimed that their proposals would aid investment and encourage economic growth.

The unions ran into certain internal problems in framing the plan, however. Some unions expressed criticism that ownership would only develop rapidly in the profitable sectors and claimed that this was unfair to workers in low-profit or nonprofit organizations. In response, the LO stressed that the dividend income of the fund could be used to buy stock in less profitable companies and linked its fund proposals to its wage solidarity policy. Problems were recognized in relation to the accounting policies of multinational companies, and it was suggested that legislation might be needed to prevent them from declaring low profits. For private firms, Meidner proposed ways of forcing them to go public, but the subject remained ambiguous.

Employer Response

The employers' response was highly critical. In 1974, even before the Meidner plan was published, the SAF, in conjunction with the Sveriges Industriförbund, a body that represents employers in the economic sphere, had appointed a task force to study the long-term implications of collective asset formation. The group was chaired by Erland Waldenström, who is both chairman of Gränges, Sweden's largest steel company, and first deputy chairman of the SEB. The committee, which also included other businessmen and academics, published its report in May 1976.[39]

The report looked at a number of means of achieving profit sharing and recommended that a voluntary system be chosen, preferably based on the payment of a percentage of employee salary, rather than a percentage of company profit, to purchase shares. The government should encourage such plans by granting tax concessions. The money would be paid into a company fund, and after the end of a blocking period, the employee would have the right to withdraw his savings. The best plan would aim to increase the employee's work motivation and his feeling of solidarity with his employer.

---

[39] Svenska Arbetsgivareföreningen and Sveriges Industriförbund, *Company Profits, Sources of Investment Capital, and Wage-Earner Funds* (Stockholm, 1976).

Perhaps recognizing that proposals for a savings plan with only employee contributions fell rather short of the union demands, the report did accept that there might be scope for profit-sharing plans. Ideally, these should allocate one-third of profits above a certain threshold to the employee fund. The suggested threshold was a rate of return on capital equal to the annual rate of inflation plus 2 percent. At the annual inflation level in May 1976, which was 11.1 percent, many companies would have been exempted from making any payments at all. This would be reinforced by basing the calculation on an average of the previous five years' profit.

The report recommended that profit sharing should be implemented only in companies with a high level of earnings; otherwise, it would discourage regular investment. In any case, profit sharing had the inherent disadvantage that it could not be applied to the public sector or to parts of the private sector such as cooperatives.

The report was somewhat lukewarm to profit-sharing plans and pointed out that a strikingly small proportion of Swedish employees were covered by such systems. The most that the report would say was that companies with profit-sharing plans believed that they had a positive effect on relations between the company and the employee.

The Meidner plan was attacked in detail. The Waldenström report held that it would lead to the collapse of the existing market for risk capital and would confiscate the assets of existing shareholders. The attack was extended to suggest that the implementation of the Meidner plan would lead to the collapse of the existing Swedish economic system. Foreign investment would disappear, and the unions would gradually take over control of the economy.

The SAF pointed out that Sweden was already suffering many economic problems, not the least of which was a decline in investment since the mid-1960s. Increased balance-of-payments deficits and higher public sector borrowing had added to these difficulties. Companies had experienced a steady decline in levels of profitability, and these problems could only be accentuated by the Meidner plan. By providing an adequate return for investment, higher profits would be the most effective means of encouraging a broader share ownership.

The Waldenström proposals were also felt to have positive economic advantages, insofar as increased savings might stabilize the rate of inflation, an effect totally absent from the Meidner proposals. The report suggested measures to avoid a situation in which any employee-run fund could build up a majority shareholding in any company. It was also felt that individual funds should operate quite separately to avoid any risk of concentration of power. The SAF's conference in September 1977 clearly reaffirmed the employers' opposition to the Meidner proposals as a grave threat to the Swedish economy and society.

The Mehr Commission and 1976 Elections

On adopting the proposals, the LO sought to persuade the Social Democrat party (Socialdemokratiska Arbeterpartiet, SAP) to endorse them. The government referred them instead to a Royal Commission on "Employees and the Growth of Capital," chaired by Hjalmar Mehr and including both union and management representatives. The commission was asked to report by 1979, although it does not seem certain at present that it will meet this deadline.

The Meidner proposals were a factor in the 1976 election, and it has been widely suggested that their unpopularity led to the SAP's losing power for the first time in forty years and being replaced by a coalition under the Center party's leader, Thorbjörn Fälldin. Meidner himself has admitted that there was a lack of coordination between the unions and the SAP, and that the debate of the plan was "confused and vulgar, dominated by slogans more than by rational arguments."[40] Of the argument that blamed the SAP's defeat on the plan, he concluded, "Although this hypothesis can hardly be proved, it sounds far from absurd."[41]

The new coalition faced a number of problems in maintaining its own internal cohesion. The coalition clearly did not support the Meidner plan, but its constituent parties did not agree on a common solution to the investment problem, nor did they agree on a common definition of what the problem was. The result was that the government outlined some very tentative proposals in 1977 for employee savings, which bore some similarity to the Waldenström report. In March 1978, these proposals were put into the more definite form of a bill offering tax concessions to stimulate individual savings plans.[42] The bill included provisions for individual savings accounts, which could be used to purchase shares and would be subject to a five-year blocking period.

---

[40] Rudolf Meidner, "Employee Investment Funds and Capital Formation—A Topical Issue in Swedish Politics," *Working Life in Sweden*, No. 6 (June 1978), p. 5.
[41] *Ibid.*
[42] *Ibid.*, p. 6.

Revised LO Proposals

During their unaccustomed period of opposition, the SAP and the LO have been reconsidering their policy with the aim of avoiding the problems that they faced in the 1976 election campaign. A joint committee, whose members included Meidner, published their report in February 1978.[43]

The report stressed, even more than Meidner's original proposals, the preeminent role of wage policy in the thinking of the labor movement. It pointed out that profitable companies make larger profits than they would otherwise because of the unions' wage solidarity policy, which restrains wage claims in the more profitable sectors. The unions wished to use these "surplus profits" for the benefit of employees. The need for investment and the need for a wider spreading of economic power were still major factors as well.

The report stressed that Swedish investment and savings had declined and that industry needed to be rejuvenated. The report was critical of the Center government's proposals:

> Everyone agrees on the need to increase capital formation in the Swedish economy. The disagreement arises on the way in which saving should be increased. The traditional non-socialist approach is that of private saving. One alternative suggested is to increase individual saving by introducing favourable terms, savings premiums and tax relief. The labour movement sees this as a costly alternative for the taxpayer and one whereby the benefits will be reaped by those who can afford to save, i.e. those with high incomes.[44]

The report also took the view that increasing profits is not a desirable means of generating investment and so produced some new proposals of its own. The report suggested that all companies that are either quoted on the stock exchange or that have over five hundred employees should set aside 20 percent of their pretax profits to be paid into an employee investment fund administered by union and employee representatives. Companies would issue shares to the fund to the value of the amounts that were allocated. The level of five hundred employees was much higher than in the original Meidner proposals, although it would still include two hundred companies, which employ one-third of the Swedish labor force. The level reflected a reconsideration of the difficulties of including smaller firms, where the calculation of what constituted profits might pose problems. The 20 percent contribution level

---

[43] Landsorganisationen i Sverige and Socialdemokratiska Arbeterpartiet, *Employee Investment Funds and Capital Formation: Draft by Joint LO and Social Democrat Party Task Force* (Stockholm: Landsorganisationen i Sverige, 1978).
[44] *Ibid.*, p. 4.

would be fixed for five years and would then be subject to review by the Parliament.

For smaller firms, the report proposed that they could voluntarily join the plan if their unions agree. Unions and management would settle on the implementation of the plan, including issues such as the way in which the company books should be kept, how the managing director's salary should be fixed, and how unions should be guaranteed a sufficient say in the running of the company. Firms would be encouraged to join by being given a tax exemption on their contribution to the fund.

Small firms not joining the main plan would be subject to a payroll tax, which would be set at 1 percent of their covered payroll. The proceeds of this tax would be paid into a special fund to promote codetermination in the small firms involved in making these payments. This fund would finance a range of training, research, and advisory services designed to assist unions in furthering codetermination.

The report's authors believed that they had weighted these two alternatives in such a way that participation in the employee investment fund would be attractive to companies:

> Affiliation to a profit-sharing system has hardly any disadvantages. . . . It is conceivable that in the future, smaller companies will be queuing up to join—or at least after the employee investment funds system has been in force for a while.[45]

Companies owned by the state or local government and cooperatively owned companies would not be required to participate but could do so if they wished.

The investment fund concept followed the original Meidner proposals in not providing for individual share ownership. The structure of the funds, however, was altered considerably. The funds would be managed by twenty-four regional councils to which local unions would appoint about three hundred delegates. Unions would be allowed to elect representatives regardless of whether or not their own members were actually employed in a company that participated in the investment fund. Voting at a participating company's annual meeting would be divided equally between the regional council and the employees of the company until the fund owned 40 percent of the shares. Thereafter, additional voting rights would be exercised solely by the regional council. Dividends on shares owned by the fund would be used to pay for the running of these councils.

---

[45] *Ibid.*, p. 8.

The report recognized the criticism leveled at the concept that it would reduce dividends for existing shareholders and lead to a flight of capital overseas, and suggested, therefore, one means of eliminating the risk of this happening. Dividends paid out on shares owned by employees should be deducted from the 3 percent levy payable by all companies for capital formation, which the report proposed, and in addition, dividends would be deductible from taxes.

Capital-Formation Levy

The capital-formation levy was a new proposal introduced by the report. This levy would be used to finance "development funds," which would provide capital for investment on a less cautious basis than the pension funds. The levy would be set at 0.75 percent of payroll in the first year and rise to 3 percent after four years.

The money would be paid into two national funds during the first five-year period; a decision would be made thereafter on whether further funds were needed. One of the national funds would have a majority of representatives of public authorities, the other a majority of employee representatives. A small part of this levy would be made available to the twenty-four regional funds. The regional funds would manage the capital-formation-levy assets through a board consisting of a majority of representatives of public authorities and a minority of employee representatives. By adopting the payroll basis rather than the profit basis, the task force imitated the Danish solution to the problem of incorporating the public sector into the plan.

Continued Aim

The unions felt that the new proposals offered a more moderate approach than the original Meidner plan but were still well-removed from the individual approach of the Center party and the Waldenström report. The aim of the new proposals was still a major political change. The president of the LO, Gunnar Nilsson, was reported to have described the intention of the proposals in the following terms: "We want to abolish the existing power structure in the companies, and replace it by a greater say for all employees."[46] The proposals did have one distinct political advantage. The major

---

[46] "New Swedish Push for Workers' Funds," *International Trade Union News* (International Confederation of Free Trade Unions), March 15, 1978, p. 4; "Modell 'Meidner II' zur Gewinnbeteiligung in Schweden," *Gewerkschafts Report*, No. 4 (June 1978), p. 38.

white-collar union federation, the Tjänstemännens Centralorganisation (TCO), had not been happy about the original Meidner proposals and had put forward its own views.[47] The TCO wanted the plan to be based on payroll-related contributions as well as profits, probably because of its important public sector membership. The TCO also stressed that it saw the aim of such proposals as aiding investment rather than redistributing wealth, although they fully supported funds' being collectively owned and under union control. The development funds proposed by the LO/SAP report would seem to meet this objective, and the report also explicitly recognized the need for greater capital formation. The TCO also opposed the concept of industrywide funds. It supported a regional basis for their establishment because it apparently believed that this would lead to less inequality between funds. In the light of these views, it seems probable that the LO and TCO can reach agreement to support the new policy. The TCO's own policy, however, is subject to review by its 1979 congress, so the matter is by no means finally settled.

The proposals were actively debated within the LO, which generally welcomed them. The SAP, however, adopted a more cautious approach with its eye on the 1979 election campaign. In June 1978, the party executive voted to postpone a decision on the proposals until the 1981 party conference. The LO is reported to have accepted this postponement,[48] which pushes the possible implementation of the proposals further into the future. The issue was further confused by the collapse of the coalition government in October 1978 and its replacement by a minority Liberal administration under the leadership of Ola Ullsten. This might improve the Social Democrats' chances of winning the 1979 election, and if it weakens the other political parties, it may pave the way for a revival of the Meidner proposals.

---

[47] "Developments on Capital-Sharing Front," *European Industrial Relations Review*, No. 50 (February 1978), p. 8.
[48] "Swedish Left Retreats on Worker Shares," *Financial Times* (London), July 4, 1978, p. 2.

CHAPTER VIII

The Netherlands

In many respects, the Netherlands might seem a very typical European country. It has suffered from most of the economic problems that have become prominent in the 1970s. Private investment and profits have been depressed, and unemployment and inflation have risen steadily. In the 1960s, the country seemed a model of steady economic growth, rising living standards, and labor peace, which was reflected in the country's ability to match pay increases with improvements in productivity. The exploitation of natural gas reserves also supplied the economy with an additional stimulus.

Government expenditure has risen as the Netherlands has established a welfare state with extensive benefits. The level of employer contributions to the social security system has been a factor in the Netherlands' becoming one of the highest wage-cost countries in Europe. As a recent survey by the Organization for Economic Cooperation and Development stated:

> While in the mid-1960s, hourly wage costs in industry were on a par with those in Italy, by 1975 they were one of the highest in the world. Up until the early 1970s, this rapid growth was associated with superior productivity performance.... After 1971, this favourable trend was reversed, and unit labour costs began to climb relative to other countries, without, however, wiping out all the earlier gains. The deterioration in the relative competitive position can mainly be attributed to the steep rise in employers' social security contributions.[1]

The structure of the labor force follows the general European pattern, but as Table V-3 shows, the country has a low participation rate in the labor force. This results partly from the longevity of the Dutch population and partly from the fact that the Netherlands has a lower female participation rate than any other country included in this study. The agricultural sector is relatively small.

A traditionally good record in relation to investment and savings

---

[1] Organization for Economic Cooperation and Development, *OECD Economic Surveys: Netherlands* (Paris, 1977), p. 23.

has been somewhat undermined since 1970, in part because Dutch companies have invested heavily overseas, and because foreigners have been reluctant to invest in the Netherlands. This reluctance has been based largely on high production costs and the expense of social security payments, as well as on apprehension about the power of Dutch unions and the impact of collective asset-formation measures.

Overseas investment by Dutch companies is aided by the fact that the Netherlands' leading companies are in many ways the most international in the world. Three of the five largest companies outside the United States are partially or completely Dutch-owned. Unilever and Shell are both joint British-Dutch ventures, and Philips is wholly Dutch. The internationalism of Dutch companies is also illustrated by the next largest Dutch companies. Akzo, the chemical company, has operations in forty-five countries, and Estel NV is a joint Dutch-German steel company. The Dutch part of the latter company is formed by Hoogovens BV, and the German part consists of Hoesch Werke AG.

The sixth largest Dutch company, DSM NV, which manufactures chemicals and allied products, is owned by the government and has about thirty thousand employees. The public sector in the Netherlands is not, however, very large. The government does have a majority shareholding in the national airline, KLM, but has generally not taken over a significant part of the manufacturing sector.

The Netherlands, as Table V-2 shows, is heavily dependent on foreign trade. By far its most important trading partner is Germany, which accounts for approximately 40 percent of Dutch exports and imports. In general, the Netherlands has had balance-of-payments surpluses in the 1970s both on current account and on invisibles.

TRADE UNIONS AND POLITICAL STRUCTURE

The overall level of trade union membership is not high by European standards. Two features of the role of unions have been notable in the Netherlands. The first is the extent of integration of Dutch unions into the national political structure. The most visible effect of this process has been the series of centralized wage agreements, for which the country has been often praised. The degree of centralized decision making has been remarkable in its own right, although in the 1970s, the system has had to be modified to meet current conditions. This decline of central regulation dates back to 1964-65 and was partly caused by membership pressure on union leaders. Efforts to revive a central wage accord in 1974-75 were not successful, although as in many European countries, the government has intervened increasingly in wage issues. The unions' centralized policies resulted in a low level of strike activity in the 1950s and early 1960s but made the unions vulnerable to pressure by the rank and file. An increase in strikes in the period of 1964-65 was followed by three years of relative calm, but after 1969, strikes again increased. The Netherlands, however, still ranks with Germany, Denmark, and Sweden at the low end of the European spectrum in number of strikes.

The union movement has been traditionally divided into three federations. The largest of the three is the Socialist federation, the Nederlands Verbond van Vakverenigingen (NVV); the second largest is the Catholic federation, the Nederlands Katholiek Vakverbond (NKV); and the smallest is the Protestant Christelijk Nationaal Vakverbond (CNV). Over the period 1947 to 1967, the relative sizes of these three organizations remained fairly stable. Of those workers who belonged to unions affiliated to one of the three federations, 46 percent were in the NVV, 35 percent in the NKV, and 19 percent in the CNV.[2]

A continuing feature of the industrial relations situation has been the attempt of the three federations to overcome their traditional rivalries. In 1971, the federations issued a common program for action and entered into various joint working arrangements. In 1974, however, a preliminary federal arrangement for the three federations was rejected by the CNV. This agreement led to the formation in January 1976 of the Federatie Nederlandse Vakbeweging (FNV), which embraced the NKV and the NVV. This body has gradually brought its two constituent parts into closer liaison, and the merger is intended to be complete by 1981.[3] A number of white-collar and other organizations are outside both the FNV and the CNV. The largest of these is the Raad van Overleg Middelbaar en Hoger Personeel, formed in 1974. The FNV, however, now holds a dominant position in Dutch union affairs.

The unions have not had links with political parties as close as in many other countries. One of the main reasons for this lack of close identification lies in the fragmented structure of Dutch politics. In the 1959 election, eight parties won seats in the Second Chamber of

---

[2] John P. Windmuller, *Labor Relations in the Netherlands* (Ithaca, N.Y.: Cornell University Press, 1969), p. 183.

[3] "Study About Unification NVV-NKV," *FNV News*, No. 9 (November 1978), pp. 2-5.

the Dutch Parliament, but of these, two parties dominated, the Labor party and the Catholic People's party. During the 1960s, the political situation became more volatile, and by 1972, fourteen parties were represented. Whereas in 1959, the two major parties secured 65 percent of the seats, they secured only 47 percent in 1972, and the Catholic People's party suffered the major drop in support.[4] The voting system in the Netherlands, which consists of a very pure form of proportional representation, was a major factor in this fragmentation.

In the 1977 election, the number of party groups fell to eleven, but this was largely because three of the religious parties, including the Catholic People's party, combined to form a Christian Democrat grouping. In 1977, the Labor party won 53 out of 150 seats in the Second Chamber; the Christian Democrats won 49; the Liberals, 28; and eight other parties shared the remaining 20 seats.[5] This fragmentation has made it less easy, and less beneficial, for unions to ally closely with particular parties. The NVV has traditional links with the Labor party, and the CNV now generally favors the Christian Democrats. Dutch politics tends to be based on a high degree of shared values. Thus, although the Labor party was the major supporter of collective asset-formation plans, the Christian Democrat coalition government introduced similar legislation in 1978, although in a rather modified form.

COMPANY PROFIT SHARING

The available evidence indicates that a number of Dutch firms have voluntary profit-sharing plans. Philips's 65,000 employees receive an annual bonus payment, which is usually related to dividends paid and has in recent years averaged 6 percent of salary. In addition, an annual bonus of f 400 ($195) is paid to all employees over the age of twenty-two, with younger workers receiving f 350 ($170).[6] Unilever's 10,900 employees receive semiannual bonuses totalling 8.33 percent of annual profits. At Enka Glanzstoff and Akzo, 12,000 workers receive semiannual bonuses—the first based on 0.5 percent of the dividends paid, the second based on 2 percent of annual profits. KLM's 9,500 employees receive an annual bonus

---

[4] "Netherlands," *The Statesman's Year-Book 1973-74* (New York: St. Martin's Press, 1973), pp. 1173-74.
[5] "Netherlands," *Europe Brief Notes*, No. 553 (1977).
[6] Philips's company official, interview in Eindhoven, Netherlands, December 27, 1977. The exchange rate used is $1=f 2.05 as of April 10, 1979.

of 2 percent of profits up to an individual maximum of f 1,250 ($610).[7] In the cigar industry, the annual bonus is 3.3 percent; and at Firestone, 5.5 percent.[8]

Many Dutch plans are based on a salary-related bonus, and over a period of time, this has often come to be seen as an entitlement rather than as a payment that fluctuates with differing profit levels. Some plans are an exception to this. OCE-Van der Grinten NV, a manufacturer of office materials and reprographic equipment, which is based at Venlo, distributes to its Dutch employees 25 percent of the company's worldwide profits multiplied by the fraction that Dutch workers constitute of the overall company's employees. At present, this fraction is 2,250 out of 6,450, or about 7/20, and this yields a distribution to the company's Dutch employees of about 8.75 percent of total company profits.[9]

A recent survey on profit sharing was conducted by the leading Dutch employers' organization, the Verbond van Nederlandse Ondernemingen (VNO), in conjunction with the Nederlands Christelijk Werkgeversverbond (NCW).[10] The survey, published in 1976, showed that, out of the 4,504 companies that responded, 2,771 (62 percent) had some form of profit-sharing payment, and this covered in total about five hundred thousand employees. In 48 percent of these plans, however, a fixed payment was made, while in only 34 percent of the cases did the payment fluctuate with the company's profits. In the other cases, the payment was not directly related to profits.

The survey focused on the "pure" profit-sharing plans, in which payments were profit-related. These involved 314,000 employees out of 700,000 covered by the inquiry. It is fair to point out that only about one-half of the companies affiliated to the VNO and NCW responded to the inquiry, but most of the nonrespondents were assumed not to have profit-sharing plans. The nonrespondents also tended to be small companies, and the results were not therefore representative of companies with under fifty employees. Taking account of the nonrespondents, it was estimated that a total of 350,000 Dutch workers were covered by pure profit-sharing plans. The average payment equaled 3.3 weeks' pay, or just over 6

---

[7] "Savings and Profit-Sharing Schemes in the Netherlands," *European Industrial Relations Review*, No. 45 (September 1977), pp. 13-15.

[8] Philips's company official, interview in Eindhoven, Netherlands, December 27, 1977.

[9] *Ibid.*

[10] "Half Miljoen Werknemers Kreeg in '75 6% Extra," *Onderneming* (Verbond van Nederlandse Ondernemingen), November 5, 1976.

percent of annual pay. In terms of the duration of the plans, some 21 percent had operated for six years or less.

SAVINGS PLANS

The Netherlands also has a legal framework for savings plans, most of which include contributions by both employer and employee. The 1965 decree on company savings lays down rules related to three kinds of plans.[11] The first are bonus-savings plans, which involve employees' paying a sum of up to f 750 ($366) per year into a savings account, which can be invested either in the shares of the company or elsewhere. If the worker keeps the whole sum invested for four years, the company pays a bonus equal to 50 percent of the employee's own savings. An investment for ten years qualifies for a bonus of 200 percent. An alternative for the employee is a commitment to periodic savings that will accrue a 25 percent bonus at the end of the four-year period. The four-year period can be waived in certain specified circumstances, such as marriage, emigration, or house purchase. Under this plan, the employer secures exemption from the payment of tax and social security contributions on that part of the employee's earnings that go toward savings.

The second type of plan is profit-sharing savings, whereby the employer allocates a sum to the employee that is directly or indirectly related to profits. The annual allocation must not exceed f 750 ($366) per worker. The employee can use the money either to purchase shares or to secure interest in a savings account in a bank. Any such money is frozen for a period of seven years, subject to the usual exemptions for marriage, house purchase, and emigration.

Wage-savings plans are based on collective agreements and are compulsory for those employees covered by the agreements. For each individual, the employer can withhold a sum of up to a maximum of 2 percent of the earnings on which social security contributions are charged, which means currently up to f 1,065 per year ($520). The savings are used to buy shares in the company or are placed in a savings account. All such funds are administered by a fund controlled jointly by the unions and management that are ty to the collective agreement. The savings are frozen for a period of seven years, but dividends and interest can be paid to the employee immediately. Employees are exempt from tax and social security contributions on these savings, while employers are exempt from their social security contributions but have to pay tax at a flat 15 percent rate.

---

[11] "Savings and Profit-Sharing Schemes in the Netherlands," pp. 13-15.

One major wage-savings plan is that for the twenty thousand employees in the printing industry.[12] This was negotiated in July 1969. An amount equal to 1 percent of the individual's wage is placed each year in a fund, which is held on behalf of those individual employees. The fund's assets are frozen until the employee retires, although in certain circumstances, such as disablement, distribution can occur earlier. The unions see the plan, not as a supplementary pension, but as a method of asset formation for employees. The funds are controlled by a joint union-management board, which decides on investment policy. A similar arrangement applies to eight thousand workers in the canal-dredging industry.[13]

A survey conducted by the Central Bureau of Statistics in 1974 indicated the relative popularity of the different types of plans.[14] There were 2,429 bonus-savings plans, 1,255 wage-savings plans, and only 438 profit-sharing savings plans. A total of 884,000 employees were covered by savings plans, and this constituted 31.6 percent of employees in establishments with over ten employees, the sample to which the survey was restricted. In 1975, the average savings per employee was f 469 ($185; 1975); wage-savings plans provided the highest amount. Industries showed some differences and ranged from f 348 ($138; 1975) in building to f 579 ($229; 1975) in banking and insurance.

Vermogensaanwasdeling (VAD)

The Netherlands has also attracted attention in recent years because of the proposal for collective worker asset formation, the Vermogensaanwasdeling (VAD) plan.

Dutch unions have a long record of interest in this subject. In 1952, the Catholic union federation, NKV, put forward a policy favoring the transference of a portion of profits to employees by means of industrywide funds.[15] Initially, the Socialist union federation, NVV, was lukewarm to these proposals and claimed that they would have no significant impact on the distribution of wealth. In 1962, however, the two federations, together with the Protestant federation, CNV, started joint discussions on the issue and, in 1964,

---

[12] Derek Robinson, *Incomes Policy and Capital Sharing in Europe* (New York: Barnes and Noble, 1973), pp. 87–88.
[13] *Ibid.*, p. 84.
[14] "Ruim 4800 Bedrijven Hadden Eind '74 een Spaarregeling," *Onderneming* (Verbond van Nederlandse Ondernemingen), November 5, 1976.
[15] Solomon Barkin and Derek Robinson, *Workers' Negotiated Savings Plans for Capital Formation* (Paris: Organization for Economic Cooperation and Development, 1970), p. 25.

agreed on a common platform.[16] The employers responded by arguing that voluntary agreements were preferable to legislation.

The union proposals consisted of two separate models. The first was a proposal for a collective investment fund financed by a levy on the "excess profits" of firms. This idea is the direct antecedent of the VAD plan. The second involved a payment additional to normal wages to be made by the employer to a fund, which would then invest it on behalf of the employees. This differs from the first proposal mainly in its lack of direct relationship to profits.

In the period from 1964 to 1975, Dutch unions continued to pursue the matter and gradually concentrated attention on the excess-profits levy. In May 1975, the government took up the proposal and laid before Parliament a document on incomes policy, which included a provision for the excess-profits levy. In 1976, a draft law incorporating the VAD plan was approved by the government and sent to the Council of State to ascertain its views.

1975 Proposals

The 1975 document prescribed that 10 percent of a company's excess profits should be transferred to employees but did not clarify how such profits would be calculated.[17] The allocation of money was to be divided into two parts. The first would be invested for the employees of the firm concerned and would be held for a blocking period of some years. The other part would be placed in a national investment fund that would be used to improve such social benefits as pensions. The plan met with considerable employer hostility and was also not universally welcomed by the unions, especially those in nonprofit sectors.

1976 Proposals

By 1976, the proposals had been somewhat clarified.[18] First, the plan would apply only to companies that were liable to pay corporation tax and had pretax profits of at least f 250,000 ($94,554; 1976). Once companies fell within the ambit of the law, however, their total profits would be taken into account in making the required calculations. Other companies could be excluded from the plan by administrative order, a provision apparently designed

---

[16] Ibid., p. 26.
[17] "Incomes Policy in the Netherlands," *European Industrial Relations Review*, No. 18 (June 1975), pp. 8–10.
[18] Verbond van Nederlandse Ondernemingen, "Dutch Capital Gains Sharing Bill: Comment" (The Hague, 1976).

primarily to remove certain seghents of public enterprises liable for corporation tax. Multinational corporations would be assessed only on profits arising out of their Dutch operations.

The assessment would be based on profits minus various compensating allowances:
1. the amount of profit for which a deduction to prevent double taxation had been granted in the relevant financial year;
2. the amount of corporation tax levied during the financial year;
3. earnings deficits suffered during the preceding year or one of the three subsequent years; and
4. a return on the equity capital, provided that this was not a negative figure.

The calculation of this return on capital was fixed as equal to the average yield of a mix of certain state bonds plus a risk premium of 2 percent. The determination of this figure each year would be the responsibility of the Ministry of Social Affairs. Equity capital was defined as the sum of
1. year-end capital less items of taxable capital, which are disregarded when profits are calculated or which are used to obtain the profit for which a deduction to prevent double taxation can be granted;
2. the difference between the current value of the items constituting equity capital and the book value for tax purposes of such items; and
3. the nominal value of capital growth certificates issued.

The value of buildings, transport, and similar items would be determined by raising or lowering the historic costs of such assets by a percentage of such cost to be determined by the Ministry of Social Affairs and by deducting an amount for depreciation from the resulting figure.

The draft legislation was to be made retroactive to the 1975 financial year. It proposed that 10 percent of the "capital growth," as defined above, for that year should be transferred to a Capital Growth Sharing Fund. For 1976, the percentage was to rise to 12 percent; thereafter, it could increase to 18 percent by 1979. The Dutch employers' organization, VNO, estimated the 1975 yield from the plan at about f 1,300 million ($514 million; 1975).

Once the amount for each company had been calculated, it would be handed over to the fund in the form of shares in the company. If a company was unquoted, it was to issue "capital growth certificates" to the fund, and if the fund agreed, quoted companies could do likewise. These certificates could not be sold or transferred by the fund without the permission of the company.

After the company transferred the shares or certificates, they would be split into two parts. The first would be divided equally among all the employees of the particular firm, subject to a maximum individual holding equivalent to 2 percent of the salary taken into account for social security contributions. This is the same restriction that is applied to savings plans. The individual holding would be frozen in the fund for an unspecified period of time. This portion could constitute up to one-half of the total payments, provided that the total came to less than 5 percent of the company's wage bill, inclusive of social security contributions. Once this total exceeded 5 percent, only 20 percent of the additional payments could be used for the company's work force. This provision was designed to equalize holdings between employees of companies with different levels of profitability. This company holding would be eventually distributed to the workers in the form of certificates of participation in the central fund, which would be quoted on the stock exchange, and which the employees could therefore sell if they so wished after a period of time had elapsed. This blocking period was not quantified in the bill but was to be laid down later by administrative order.

The second part of the payment would be the direct property of the fund without any individual entitlement attached to it. The fund would administer the money as the collective capital of all Dutch workers, except civil servants and the self-employed. The fund would be given freedom to decide the use of the money, but it was generally expected that much of it would be applied for extra pension payments and for other disbursements, including higher sickness or unemployment pay.

The fund would be a legal entity with between five and fifteen members who would be appointed solely by employees' organizations for a period of office of four years. The major share of the seats would most likely be held by the FNV, the body created by the amalgamation of the NVV and NKV.

Reaction to the Proposals

The government's action generally received a warm welcome from the unions, but employer opposition was strong. The employers' organization, VNO, described the situation in the following terms: "The bill on capital growth sharing, which was submitted to the Second Chamber on June 22, is one of the worst conceivable contributions the government could have made towards realizing a socio-economic climate within which a policy covering a number of years can be fruitfully pursued."[19]

In particular, it criticized the bill for its failure to define the details of key sections, for its failure to specify how the fund's capital should be used, and for its retroactive application. In general, the bill was regarded as marking a decided increase in power over the economy for the Dutch trade union movement.

Modified VAD

The bill did not complete its legislative passage before the 1977 general election. Although the Labor party made gains in the election, it had to enter into a period of bargaining over the formation of a coalition with the Christian Democrats and the smaller Democrats '66. During the course of these negotiations, agreement was reached on modifications to the VAD proposals after the mediation of a Dutch academic, Willem Albeda.[20] Although Albeda is a Christian Democrat, he was known to be favorably inclined toward the principles of the VAD plan.

It was agreed that there should be a reduction in the size of companies to be covered by the plan to those with pretax profits of f 200,000 per year ($97,561). This brought more firms within the scope of the legislation. In addition, the contribution rate for companies was raised to 20 percent, with a 1 percent per year rise for a period of four years. Opponents of the plan did, however, win some concessions. The first year of application of the plan was to be 1977 rather than 1975. This was welcomed by companies, although to some degree, it merely reflected the delay in implementing the plan. Companies were to be allowed to set the individual VAD levy against corporation tax, and it was agreed that there would be a limitation on the size of the fund's shareholding in any individual company. It was also accepted that the balance between payments into the collective fund and the company funds should be equal. This represented a decrease in payments to the central fund, although the amount of the reduction depended on the level of profitability, which had been a factor in the previous formula.

The agreement was interpreted differently by various parties. The Labor party's concessions were not very great, and employers seemed disappointed by the failure of the Christian Democrats to lessen significantly the impact of the plan.

---

[19] *Ibid.*, p. 1.
[20] "New Proposal on VAD," *IDS International Report*, No. 54 (August 1977), p. 4.

1978 Proposals

Negotiations on the formation of the Labor party coalition collapsed, however, and a new center-right coalition was formed in December 1977. This did not signal the death of the VAD concept, a fact emphasized by the appointment of Albeda as minister of social affairs.

The government produced its own proposals in April 1978.[21] It separated the collective asset-formation aspects of VAD from the individual benefits. It lowered the threshold for inclusion in both parts of the plan to companies with profits of at least f 100,000 ($48,780) per year, a sharp fall from the f 250,000 ($121,951) proposed by the previous government. This profit level, however, was to be indexed to keep pace with inflation. It was estimated that about two thousand companies would come within the legislation's scope. The calculation of excess profit was similar to that in the earlier version of VAD, although the risk premium above the return on the portfolio of government bonds was raised from 2 to 3 percent. For 1977, this would have created a total return on equity figure of about 11 percent.

The levy was fixed at 12 percent of profits for the individual part of VAD. There were provisions whereby payments to written profit-sharing plans that had been established prior to April 1978 would be deductible from a company's VAD payments. The individual maximum entitlement was raised to 3 percent of the maximum wage over which social security contributions were payable, which was f 1,536 ($749) in 1977 and f 1,677 ($818) in 1978. Any amount that could not be distributed to employees in a particular year because of the individual maximum could be used over the following six years to make future payments if the level would not otherwise reach the 3 percent ceiling. Any balance remaining after the six-year period would accrue to the company.

A major change in the proposals came in the method of distributing the employee's entitlement. This was made more flexible, and the company could decide the method of distribution, although the works council could give advice on the issue. The distribution could be in the form of shares, cash, or VAD certificates (a kind of deferred debenture). The VAD certificates would be subordinated to all other creditors but preferred to shareholders. They would attract a fixed annual interest, based on the effective interest rate on long-term government bonds plus 1 percent. Thus, the rate for 1977

---

[21] The Netherlands, Ministry of Social Affairs, *Nieuw Wetsontwerp Vermogensaanwasdeling naar Tweede Kamer* (The Hague, 1978).

would have been about 9 percent. Individual entitlements would still be subject to a seven-year blocking period.

The plan was designed to take effect retroactively to January 1977. Additional tax benefits were introduced for companies; in particular, they were allowed to offset their VAD payments against corporation tax.

By October 1978, the government was able to announce its proposals for the collective side of the VAD plan.[22] This would involve another levy of 12 percent on excess profits, subject to a maximum of 3 percent of total taxable profits. The levy was to commence in April 1979 but would apply to profits made after the beginning of 1978. Profits were to be calculated in the same manner as under the individual VAD plan. The levy was also to be treated as a direct tax; thus, foreign companies operating in the Netherlands could claim a foreign tax credit for the payment. Initially, the government would make a one-time payment to the fund to provide its initial capital. The plan was designed to operate for an experimental three-year period.

The fund would be managed by a board of twenty members, twelve nominated by the unions and eight by the government. This board would be appointed for a four-year period and would have the power to decide how the fund should invest its assets. The fund would be used for two major purposes. First, it would finance early retirement plans agreed upon by companies and unions. Second, it could make payments to improve general pension arrangements. In this case, any pension institution seeking to improve benefits would receive a participation certificate in the fund, which could only be cashed after a blocking period.

VAD'S FUTURE AND IMPACT

The reaction to the new proposals was mixed. On the union side, the FNV sharply attacked the bills as an attempt to water down collective asset formation to mere individual profit sharing. It felt that the latter, if desired, could more effectively be introduced through regular collective bargaining.[23] It also criticized the tax concessions as pushing some of the VAD burden from companies

---

[22] Verbond van Nederlandse Ondernemingen, "The Dutch VAD Bills" (The Hague, 1978).

[23] "FNV Dissatisfied with Capital Gain Sharing," *FNV News*, No. 7 (May 1978), pp. 8-9.

and onto taxpayers as a whole. This critical view of the proposals was shared by the Labor party.[24]

This adverse reaction by the unions, however, did not mean that the proposals were entirely welcomed by the employers. The VNO's comment on the bill was appropriately entitled "dissatisfaction remains."[25] The VNO felt that the risk premium was still too low, it disliked the retroactive nature of the bill, and it felt that the proposals as a whole would still have a negative effect on investment and employment. The VNO was particularly critical of the collective part of the VAD plan. Its views received apparent corroboration from a study commissioned by the Dutch government in 1977. Conducted by McKinsey and Company, the study highlighted a number of the factors that discouraged foreign investment in the Netherlands.[26] Along with high wage costs and social security payments, VAD was cited as a significant disincentive to investment.

The political fate of VAD is still uncertain, and there have been further delays in the bill's passage through Parliament because members of the government coalition parties have pressed for amendments. The intention had been to pass the legislation by April 1979, an optimistic deadline. The government seems to have managed to produce a bill that, by satisfying nobody, stands some chance of not progressing into law. There is also some evidence that VAD is not electorally popular. A survey conducted by NIPO, an opinion research organization, showed a marked voter preference for individual company profit sharing over collective plans.[27] The Labor party and unions, however, may reluctantly accept the 1978 bill and hope that they can amend it in the future to increase the importance of the collective aspect. In any case, the plan still remains a comprehensive attempt to redistribute Dutch company profits, and its effect on the operation of the Dutch private sector will serve as an important test of the possible impact of collective investment proposals in other countries.

---

[24] "Dutch Profit-Sharing Changes Allow Companies Tax Relief," *Financial Times* (London), May 3, 1977, p. 2.
[25] Verbond van Nederlandse Ondernemingen, "Ontevredenheid Blijft," Press Release of April 27, 1978 (The Hague).
[26] "Foreign Companies Weigh Pros and Cons of Dutch Investment," *Business Europe*, December 15, 1978, pp. 396-97.
[27] F. A. Hoogendijk, "Werknemers Willen VAD Niet," *Elseviers*, April 29, 1978, pp. 95-97.

CHAPTER IX

United Kingdom

The United Kingdom is a predominantly industrial and commercial country and has the smallest agricultural sector in Western Europe. It has a smaller number of self-employed than any Western European country, except Sweden, a fact that reflects its small agrarian sector, although the latter is not a sufficient explanation for the phenomenon. In the period since 1945, the country has had a low rate of investment and savings and has experienced well-publicized economic difficulties, including a high rate of inflation in the period 1973-77. This inflation rate has been matched only by Ireland's, whose economy is closely interrelated with the United Kingdom, and by Italy's.

In per capita Gross Domestic Product (GDP), the United Kingdom has fallen behind its main European competitors, and among members of the European Community (EC), only Ireland and Italy are lower. The country has experienced persistent investment shortages, which have contributed to the picture of a low-wage and low-productivity economy. The United Kingdom's traditional export industries have been those that have declined throughout the Western world, such as shipbuilding. This has led to serious balance-of-payments difficulties and to a steady fall in the value of the pound against other Western European currencies since the 1960s. The discovery and exploitation of offshore oil reserves seems likely to offer an essentially temporary respite, during which period the United Kingdom's future situation will be determined by its ability to tackle its structural economic problems.

Industrial structure has been based on heavy industries, which have been declining throughout the Western world, a decline that in the United Kingdom has been exacerbated by outdated manufacturing methods, to which economic critics have drawn attention. In the 1970s, the rate of economic growth has been low, and levels of unemployment have been high.

Government expenditure is relatively high, as Table V-2 illustrates. Taxation is high and progressive, and there are wide welfare provisions. The public sector is a significant element in the

United Kingdom's economy. Between 1945 and 1951, a number of basic industries, such as coal, railways, and airlines, were brought under public ownership. Since the mid-1960s, a number of other industries have also been taken over, including steel, aerospace, shipbuilding, and British Leyland, the major vehicle manufacturer. Under both major political parties' rules, this process has gone forward primarily for the rescue of ailing industries. As a result, the public sector is less healthy economically than in many other European countries.

TRADE UNIONS AND POLITICS

British labor relations have received considerable attention. The country's strike record is in practice not as bad as often depicted, but the pattern of short, unpredictable strikes that are not officially called by the unions means that industrial action has a greater effect on production than a straight comparison of days lost would suggest. The labor force is over 50 percent organized, and union strength in this respect has increased significantly in the 1970s, particularly among white-collar employees. The political strength of the unions also springs from their close association with the Labour party, affiliation to which is mainly through trade unions. The central trade union federation, the Trades Union Congress (TUC), embraces virtually all organized employees and, unlike most of its counterparts in Europe, has no rival federation. In this respect, its position is closest to those of the Deutsche Gewerkschaftsbund (DGB) and the Landsorganisationen i Danmark, although there are fewer organized workers in the United Kingdom outside the TUC than there are in Germany outside the DGB.

The strike pattern arises partly because labor relations is characterized in certain industries by the power of shop stewards at plant level to call strikes. The unions often neither wish nor would be able to take disciplinary action against unofficial strike leaders. Only a small minority of British strikes are officially called by the unions, although this does not necessarily mean that the strikes are opposed by the official leadership. Decentralized collective bargaining has been identified by many economists as a contributory factor in British inflation since the 1960s. As a result, governments have sought periodically to apply pay policies designed to limit the size of wage settlements. Such policies were not highly successful before 1975, and indeed, the Conservative government was defeated in a general election in 1974, which was called after the National Union of Mineworkers (NUM) called a strike in defiance of government policy. Between 1975 and 1977, the Labour government and unions agreed on a policy of pay restraint that was effective in reducing the size of wage settlements and in contributing to the lowering of the rate of inflation.

Since the Second World War, the Labour party has enjoyed approximately the same amount of time in government as the Conservative party, although since 1964, the former has been in power for eleven out of fifteen years. For most of the postwar period, politics has been essentially based on a two-party system; the only confusion has arisen from the small centrist Liberal party. In the 1970s, the political situation has become more volatile, and instead of three political parties, there are now seven represented in Parliament. The most important factor has been the development of national consciousness among the minority nations of the United Kingdom. The Scottish Nationalist and the Welsh Nationalist (Plaid Cymru) parties have both secured seats in Parliament and have pressed for a greater decentralization of political power. The situation in Northern Ireland since 1968 has also altered the traditional political balance. The main Protestant party, the Ulster Unionists, has been traditionally allied with the Conservative party, but this link has been greatly weakened by the events of the 1970s. The Ulster party now acts as a separate force in Parliament and has often refused to support the Conservatives. The Catholic representatives from Northern Ireland are more divided, but the major party, the Social Democratic and Labour party, generally supports the Labour party.

No major political group has exhibited any close interest in profit sharing except the Liberal party, which was the major instigator of proposals passed by Parliament in 1978 to provide tax benefits to company plans. The Labour party briefly showed interest in collective fund proposals in 1973, but the interest has not been maintained. Increased interest in union representation on company boards and in union representation on pension funds could, however, lead to a revival of interest in profit sharing.

COMPANY PROFIT SHARING

In the United Kingdom, individual company profit-sharing plans are limited in number. Prior to 1977, the only companies with over 10,000 employees to have such plans were Imperial Chemical Industries (ICI), Boots Limited, Kodak, Tate and Lyle, Barclays Bank, the National Westminster Bank, and the Blue Circle Group. There are also a limited number of share-option or share-purchase plans, including ones for Brooke Bond Liebig and Allied Breweries.[1] In addition, during 1977, new profit-sharing plans were introduced by Marks and Spencer and the House of Fraser, and a new share-option plan was introduced by Rowntree Mackintosh. One of the most famous profit-sharing experiments, that at John Lewis Partnership, a retail firm, has been extensively researched.[2] In this company, all the equity capital is held in trust on behalf of the 23,500 employees, and after allowance for preference dividends and retained earnings, all profits are distributed to employees. In total, probably only a small percentage of the country's labor force is covered by any form of profit-sharing plan.

The plans differ somewhat in form. Brooke Bond, in the food sector, allows employees to purchase shares by installments taken out of salary. When the employee has paid for the number of shares that he has contracted to purchase, the company will give him additional shares equal to one-fifth of the shares purchased. The shares carry full dividends even before they are fully paid for, although no voting rights are given until the payments are completed.[3] Allied Breweries, a beer and spirits manufacturer with over thirty thousand United Kingdom employees, introduced a share plan in 1974. This gives an option to purchase shares at a discount, but it is only open to about twelve thousand of the company's labor force because it requires employees to be over age twenty-five and to have at least five years' service.[4]

Rowntree Mackintosh, the chocolate and food manufacturer, introduced a share-option plan in 1977 open to all employees with over five years' service. It provides that employees can exercise an option to use money saved over a five-year period to purchase shares at the price fixed at the beginning of the five-year period. Employees are given six months in which to decide whether to exercise the option. They have to purchase a minimum of fifty shares and must pay out at least £ 240 ($505).[5] At the current share price (April 1979), fifty shares would cost only £ 209 ($440), and so the minimum purchase would have to be fifty-eight shares. The

---

[1] D. Wallace Bell, *Financial Participation* (London: Industrial Participation Association, 1973), pp. 60-75.
[2] Allan Flanders, Ruth Pomeranz, and Joan Woodward, *Experiment in Industrial Democracy* (London: Faber, 1968).
[3] Bell, *Financial Participation*, pp. 42-43.
[4] Industrial Participation Association, *Examples of Profit Sharing, Added Value Bonus Schemes, and Employee Share Schemes in British Companies*, IPA Resource Paper (London, 1977), p. 3.
[5] Unless otherwise specified, the exchange rate used is $1=£ 0.475 as of April 10, 1979.

total shares available under the plan are limited to 7.5 percent of the issued ordinary shares.[6]

The Rowntree plan, like that of Allied Breweries, utilizes the government-run "Save As You Earn" (SAYE) plan, which allows employees to contract to save over a five-year period and to receive a tax-free bonus at the end of the period. In both companies, the employee takes out an SAYE contract, and if he decides not to purchase shares with his savings, he can withdraw his money in the normal manner provided by that plan. An SAYE contract requires a minimum payment of £ 1 ($2.10) per week and a maximum payment of £ 5 ($10.53) per week.[7]

Cash Distributions

Many of the straight profit-sharing plans distribute payments in cash. A recent study suggested that 71 percent of companies with profit-sharing plans operated on a cash-distribution basis.[8] Boots Limited, the retail and manufacturing drug company, introduced a plan in 1959 that is open to all employees with over twelve months' service, currently some forty-one thousand out of sixty thousand employees. Eight and one-half percent of United Kingdom pretax profits are distributed annually to staff, the allocation being based on salary and length of service.[9] At Kodak, which has operated profit-sharing plans since 1912, an annual cash distribution is made to the twelve thousand employees at a level decided by management. The payment is termed a "wage dividend" and is not usually directly related to profits and, in recent years, has usually been based on total earnings. This policy is directly related to Eastman Kodak's policy prior to 1960 in the United States (see chapter II). The Blue Circle Group, a cement manufacturer, distributes for its thirteen thousand employees an annual cash payment determined on a basis decided by the board. Tate and Lyle, the sugar company, also distributes cash payments based on profits for its twelve thousand employees.[10]

In 1974, two major banks introduced profit-sharing plans. At National Westminster Bank, provided pretax profits exceed £ 100

---

[6] Rowntree Mackintosh, *U.K. Employee Share Option Scheme* (York, England, 1977).

[7] *Ibid.*, pp. 12–14.

[8] Peter A. Reilly, *Employee Financial Participation* (London: British Institute of Management, 1978).

[9] Bell, *Financial Participation*, p. 64.

[10] D. Wallace Bell, director of Industrial Participation Association, interview in London, January 5, 1978.

million ($211 million), a bonus is paid equal to 3 percent of the first £ 100 million and 5 percent of the remainder. Some fifty thousand employees are eligible, and the payment, which is proportionate to salary, is made annually.[11] The 1978 payment was £ 25 ($53) per £ 500 ($1,053) unit of salary, which provided a payment of about £ 125 ($263) for the employee who earned average wages. The maximum cutoff point for which units could be credited, previously £ 6,000 per year ($12,632), was raised.[12]

Barclays Bank provides 4 percent of annual pretax profits and distributes this annually in cash or shares. Employees above a salary level of £ 3,500 per year ($7,368) are obliged to take their allocation in the form of shares, and this arrangement covers about half of the bank's employees. The remaining employees are given the choice of cash or shares. The payment is related to salary but cannot exceed 15 percent of annual salary.[13] The employee can sell his shares immediately, and evidence shows that about one-third do so. Payments were 4.5 percent of salary in 1974 and 2.9 percent in 1975.[14] In 1976, this rose to 4.1 percent, and in 1977, 5.7 percent.[15] To avoid dilution of existing shareholding, a maximum of 5 percent of the issued share capital is available to the profit-sharing plan. The company apparently believes that the effect of the plan, which is scheduled to be reviewed in 1983, has been positive. One manager was quoted as saying:

> I think people are already identifying more closely with the bank as a result of the profit sharing scheme. The staff are more interested in how much profit we make and they are keener to compare one year's results with those of the previous year.[16]

The plans at both banks were introduced after consultation with the National Union of Bank Employees (NUBE), which has taken a positive attitude toward such plans. This also helps account for the fact that two other major banks, Midland and Lloyds, recently followed the industry pattern and introduced profit-sharing plans. At Midland, 4 percent of pretax profits are available for distribution, with maximum payments limited to 15 percent of salary.[17]

---

[11] *Ibid.,* p. 70.
[12] "Profit-Sharing Payments Announced," *IDS Report,* No. 279 (April 1978), p. 28.
[13] Industrial Participation Association, *Examples of Profit Sharing,* p. 4.
[14] "Barclays Bank: A Share Deal for Employees," *Financial Times* (London), February 6, 1978, p. 5.
[15] "Profit-Sharing Payments Announced," p. 28.
[16] "Barclays Bank: A Share Deal for Employees," p. 5.
[17] "Profit-Sharing on the Way at Midland Bank," *IDS Report,* No. 276 (March 1978), p. 25.

This is strictly comparable to the Barclays Bank plan. At Lloyds, the distribution is made in the form of cash for those below a certain salary level or of shares for those above but is available only to employees with at least five years' service.[18]

The major retail company, Marks and Spencer, a recent convert to profit sharing, established a plan in 1977.[19] This provides that all profit in excess of £ 100,000 ($210,526) should be available for distribution each year in whatever manner and amount the board thinks fit. The plan is open to employees with over five years' service, which accounts for some seventeen thousand out of forty-two thousand employees. The distribution is made annually in the form of shares, and the allocation is proportionate to the employee's salary. Thus, each employee receives share certificates worth 4 percent of his gross earnings over the previous year less tax. In 1978, it was estimated that the average participating employee received shares valued at about £ 60 ($126). As soon as the shares are issued, the employee is free to sell them if he wishes. The distribution each year is at the discretion of the company's board.[20]

Another major retail firm, the House of Fraser, which has twenty-five thousand employees, followed the example of Marks and Spencer and introduced a plan in 1978. The plan aims to make available about 1.2 million shares per year for distribution to employees over a ten-year period. Shares worth up to £ 2,000 ($4,211) are distributed annually on a basis related to salary. Many employees, however, receive amounts which are much lower, under £ 100 ($211). The overall allocation is 4 percent of profits, and the plan is open to employees at least twenty-five years old and with one year's service or under age twenty-five with five years' service. A five-year blocking period is provided before an employee can receive his shares, which in the interim are held by a trust.[21] Employees leaving within less than three years of when the shares are allocated to them are not allowed to collect them.

Imperial Chemical Industries (ICI)

The largest company with a profit-sharing plan is the chemical company ICI, which is one of the largest United Kingdom cor-

---

[18] John Elliott, "Swelling Tide of Employee Share Schemes," *Financial Times* (London), February 19, 1979, p. 10.
[19] Industrial Participation Association, *Examples of Profit Sharing*, p. 18.
[20] Paul Taylor, "Marks and Spencer Profit-Sharing Scheme," *Financial Times* (London), May 4, 1978, p. 8.
[21] John Elliott, "Retailers Launch Profit Sharing," *Financial Times* (London), April 22, 1978, p. 3.

porations and one of the five largest chemical companies in the Western world. The company operated a share-purchase plan from 1927, but in 1946, it set up a committee to investigate ways of improving productivity, which recommended the establishment of a profit-sharing plan. The plan commenced in 1954 and was amended in 1958 because it had proved unable to accommodate adequately the effect of a stock split.[22]

The plan is established under a trust deed and is under the control of nine trustees, who include employee representatives nominated through the company's consultative system. The trustees are necessary under the provisions of section 54 of the 1948 Companies Act, which makes it illegal for a company to provide money for investment in its own shares, except in accordance with an arrangement for share purchase by trustees for the benefit of its own employees. All employees are eligible to join the plan, which is not, however, a part of the employee's contract of employment and over which the company maintains full control.

The plan originally provided for a total sum to be set aside for distribution equal to 22 percent of the total pretax amount paid by the company in dividends and interest on all forms of stock. The actual rate of bonus was then decided each year by the board, which took profits into account but also considered other factors. No bonus, however, was paid if the dividend rate was less than 5 percent. The bonus is divided in proportion to total salary, and tax is deducted by the company. The net amount per employee is then handed over by the company to the trustees, who purchase new company stock at market price for each worker. The shares were initially handed over to the employee when he had accumulated forty shares or after two years, whichever was the earlier. During the period when the stock was being held by the trustees for the individual, the dividends were also credited to his account. In 1962, the plan was modified to distribute shares to the employees in the year of issue.

The participation rate in the plan was high from its introduction. In 1954, 72.5 percent of employees were involved, rising to 78.6 percent in 1957. The average payment after tax was £ 25.20 in 1954 and £ 40.84 in 1957.[23] These sums constituted about two weeks' pay for most individuals. By 1975, participation had risen to over 80 percent, and average payments were £ 112 ($248; 1975), or about

---

[22] Imperial Chemical Industries, *The Profit-Sharing Scheme of Imperial Chemical Industries Limited*, 2d ed. (London, 1959), pp. 5-6.
[23] *Ibid.*, p. 20.

twice the average weekly United Kingdom male industrial wage.
The company has always made modest claims for its plan. It takes pains to stress that the plan is neither a cure for bad industrial relations nor a substitute for an effective wage structure. Such benefits as the plan may bring are seen to be more long term, such as underlining the common interest between shareholder and employee. To achieve this, ICI believes that the actual bonus paid has to be set at a significant monetary level.

The plan has received some criticism, and in September 1975, a "joint working party" drawn from both management and employees was set up to consider the operation of the plan and to recommend modifications. The initiative for the establishment of this working party lay in a request from the employees' side of ICI's consultative machinery.

The committee examined a number of areas of difficulty. One of these was the question of the employees' lack of understanding of the basis for determining the bonus level. The company had originally related payments solely to dividends because this relation seemed easier to explain than a relation to "profits," which might be susceptible to different definitions, as well as to short-term fluctuations. Over a period of time, however, it had modified this calculation to make the bonus less dependent on one indicator. As the working party pointed out, one of the main criticisms of the plan was that "the bonus rate is decided each year by the ICI Board on a basis which is not known by the vast majority of employees and is not demonstrably linked to business performance."[24]

The working party understood that the main criterion in recent years for determining the bonus was the ratio of trading profit before taxes to assets employed. The report placed overriding importance on the need to find a simple published formula, even if this then had to be changed from time to time. It recognized the need for a criterion that was not too heavily affected by inflation. The working party's suggestion was a formula of added value divided by employee costs. This ratio would then be converted into a bonus rate in a manner simple enough to allow employees to calculate their own entitlement. The initial proposal was that, if the ratio fell below 1.54, no bonus would be paid, but the bonus would then rise to a maximum of 15 percent at a ratio of 2.42 or above. The working party calculated that, if this formula had been applied over the previous ten years, the rate of bonus would have followed a

---

[24] Imperial Chemical Industries, "ICI Employees' Profit-Sharing Scheme," Report of the Joint Working Party (London, 1976), p. 4.

similar pattern to that which it did in practice, but at a level 19 percent higher on average.

The problems faced by all efforts to produce a simple standardized formula were quickly demonstrated when, after the report was presented in December 1976, the year's bonus was announced at a level 11 percent higher than the new formula would have yielded. The working party accordingly produced a supplementary report in April 1977 and revised its proposal so that no bonus would be paid below a ratio of 1.42, and the 15 percent maximum would be reached at 2.26.[25]

The working party also sought to tackle the general issue of the manner in which the individual could relate his own effort to the bonus plan. It felt that no plan was likely to have a direct effect on motivation but felt that the plan was valued by existing employees and was an important background factor in securing a more cooperative environment. It also felt a more extensive educational program might further aid employee identification. In addition, the working party investigated the possibility of calculating the bonus on a divisional or plant basis rather than on a whole company basis. Although this might have brought the plan closer to individuals, it was rejected because it would have led to differing payments and would have subverted the common interest of employees, especially where plant performance was affected markedly by factors other than employee effort. The working party did, however, recommend that the unit on which profitability should be based should no longer be only the ICI companies that participated in the profit-sharing plan but should be the ICI group as a whole. This recommendation seemed a rather reluctant one. The management representatives in particular seemed to have felt that a considerable amount of extra work would be required to prepare detailed figures based only on the participating profit-sharing companies, and in the past, although the company had based its calculations on this unit, it had not published figures. The working party felt, however, that such figures were needed if employees were to have faith in the plan. The main effect of the change was to include overseas ICI plants in the calculation.

The question of whether the issue of shares should be replaced by cash payments was also discussed. This matter arose because of the tendency of employees to sell their shares soon after receiving them. The figures showed that, by September 1971, when statistics

---

[25] Imperial Chemical Industries, "Employees' Profit-Sharing Scheme," Supplementary Report of the Working Party (London, 1977).

on the subject were discontinued, some 60 percent of the shares issued had been sold by recipients. When the plan was established, ICI had opposed cash payments because the worker might see the payment merely as an extension of ordinary wages to be quickly spent and thus would not feel any increased identification with the company. The working party reaffirmed this view and felt in addition that such a change would affect adversely the company's cash flow, because the money would no longer be invested in the company.

The working party also examined the issue of whether the bonus should continue to be linked to salary level. It felt that this was "one of the most difficult and controversial areas."[26] The decision was one against any change in the principle but in favor of a modification allowing all employees earning less than £ 3,000 per year ($6,316) to receive an entitlement as if they had earned that amount. The report also upheld the use of a probationary year of service with the company for membership eligibility but recommended that no such period should be applied to reengaged employees. Improved provisions for leavers were recommended, as was the election, rather than the nomination, of trustees.

The report as a whole gave cautious approval to the plan but suggested that it should be reviewed thoroughly every ten years, with the bonus formula reviewed every five. The report projected the costs of its proposed changes at about 19 percent, plus £ 500,000 ($1,052,632), above the level of the existing plan.

The attitude of the unions toward the plan has generally been neutral. When the plan was first introduced, the company was careful to discuss it informally with the unions in advance of its introduction. The unions were known to have "a somewhat reserved attitude"[27] toward profit sharing, but no direct opposition was encountered.

Most of the proposals contained in the report have now been implemented by ICI, and the 1978 bonus was calculated on the new basis. The effect of the government's profit-sharing proposals in 1978 may, however, require a further review of the plan.

SHARE-PURCHASE AND SHARE-OPTION PLANS

Share-option plans grew in the early 1960s after a legal judgment against the Inland Revenue prevented them from being taxed at

---

[26] Imperial Chemical Industries, "ICI Employees' Profit-Sharing Scheme," Report of the Joint Working Party, p. 15.
[27] Imperial Chemical Industries, *The Profit-Sharing Scheme of Imperial Chemical Industries Limited*, p. 16.

income tax rates. They were, however, almost solely limited to senior executives. The 1966 Finance Act tightened the regulations on these plans, and thereafter, their introduction slowed down. Under the 1973 Finance Act, however, share-purchase and -option plans have become more attractive, provided that they are open to all employees with five years' service or more. Maximum employee contribution levels of £ 20 per month ($42) are also stipulated, and the purchase of the shares at a discount is allowed. This tax change does seem to have encouraged some firms to look at share-purchase plans in a fresh light, although progress has been slow.[28]

A few companies have accordingly introduced share-purchase plans. BOC International, the air products company, has provided a plan that has been utilized by about 10 percent of the company's sixteen thousand United Kingdom employees; while in the electrical engineering field, BICC's plan has led sixty-five hundred employees out of thirty-four thousand to become shareholders.[29] Both plans take advantage of the tax benefits available under the SAYE plan. This requires the employee to save for a minimum of five years before he can activate his option to purchase company shares. The option allows purchase of the shares at the previously agreed price with the money accumulated by savings over the five-year period. Tax is, however, payable on the difference between the market price at time of receipt of the shares and the previous option price.

GOVERNMENT INITIATIVE

The prospect for significant tax changes to encourage profit-sharing plans was raised in 1978 by the political situation. The Liberal party, on whose parliamentary votes the Labour government depended, has long favored profit sharing. In 1977, it persuaded the government to set up an inquiry into the issue with the aim of producing a "Consultative Document."

The Consultative Document on profit sharing was issued at the beginning of February 1978.[30] It discussed the possible changes in the tax treatment of arrangements under which an employee may acquire shares in the company for which he works. It analytically separated profit-sharing plans from share-ownership plans that need not relate to profit levels. It recognized that any encouragement of wider share ownership would involve some distortion of the tax sys-

---

[28] Bell, *Financial Participation*, pp. 39–47.

[29] "Share Savings Plans in the U.K.," *European Industrial Relations Review*, No. 35 (November 1976), pp. 8–9.

[30] United Kingdom, Inland Revenue, *Profit Sharing: Tax Relief*, Consultative Document (London, 1978).

tem in favor of those employed in the corporate sector. It rejected, however, any tax relief for profit sharing unrelated to share ownership, for this would be equivalent to a payment of wages free of tax.

The current tax situation was described. Typically, under profit-sharing plans, any amount paid as a bonus is taxed as income. Where an employee or director purchases company shares on which restrictions are imposed (e.g., on voting rights, transferability), he is liable to income tax on the growth in value of those shares from the date of acquisition to the earliest of (1) the date he ceases to own the shares, (2) the date at which restrictions cease to apply, or (3) seven years after acquisition of the shares.

The growth in value of the shares is treated as income for the year in which the liability arises. If the shares were acquired at a discount, the latter is chargeable to income tax at the time the shares are acquired. The amount charged to income tax as growth in value is taken into account in computing the gain or loss for capital-gains tax purposes.

The document discussed three possible methods of providing tax relief for share acquisition. Method I was that a company could allocate a part of its profits as bonus, deduct tax, and use the net amount to purchase its shares, which would then be credited to its employees. The market value of these shares could be reduced by a discount of up to 37 percent. The employee would have to hold the shares for five years but would be free from income tax on their growth in value and on the discount. When the shares are sold, any capital-gains tax would be charged on the market value of the shares at the time of acquisition and not on the discounted price. In order for this plan to attract tax relief, it would have to meet certain criteria. First, it would have to be open to all employees with a specified length of service, and second, to prevent the advantages accruing mainly to the better-paid, there would have to be a limit on the value of shares that could be acquired by any one employee in a year.

Method II was the "share-incentive" plan. Under this, the employee could acquire shares on favorable terms provided that the plan set the same conditions as for the first method. The employee, however, would have to use money from his own resources, which, as the document discouragingly stated, "many employees may be unable to do."[31]

Method III was that the company would make an allocation each year out of its profits, which would be used to purchase shares at

---

[31] *Ibid.*, p. 5.

their full value. The shares, although theoretically applied to individuals, would in fact be held by a trust on their behalf. The employee could not sell his allocation for five years, except in specified circumstances such as redundancy or death. When sold, the proceeds would be divided into two parts for tax purposes. There would be a charge to income tax on the sale proceeds to the extent that they did not exceed the original acquisition cost. This income tax charge would be tapered on the basis of the length of time the shares had been held. For instance, if the shares were held between five and ten years, only 50 percent would be chargeable. Any excess of the proceeds over the acquisition cost would be charged to capital-gains tax. Dividends would be paid to the employee from the outset and would incur income tax in the normal way. Voting rights would also be exercisable by the employee from the beginning. The maximum shareholding under this method would be set higher than under method I so that the maximum amounts after tax would be comparable.

Various conditions would have to be met by any plan that received tax relief.

1. The shares would have to be in the company employing the participants, a company controlling that company, or a company that was a member of a consortium that owned the employing or controlling company and owned not less than 15 percent of the ordinary share capital of that company.
2. The shares would have to be quotable on the stock exchange or would have to be shares in a company that was independent. This excluded the use of shares of unquoted subsidiaries.
3. The shares would have to be in a class, the majority of which had not been acquired by directors or employees, unless in pursuance of an offer to the public.
4. The dividends would have to be the same as for other shares of the same class.
5. The plan would have to be open to all United Kingdom employees with at least five years' service, although there would be nothing to preclude less restrictive participation requirements.
6. The total value at the time of acquisition of all shares acquired by an individual in any year would be £ 415 ($874) under methods I and II and £ 500 ($1,053) under method III.
7. Under methods I and II, the minimum price at which shares could be acquired would be 63 percent of their market value.

In addition to the conditions imposed generally on plans, there were certain conditions that would be applied to participants. They would have to keep the shares for five years, except in the event of death or loss of employment from injury, disability, or redundancy. Under methods I or II, if the plan shares were in a "close company," participants could not have any material interest in that company during the five-year blocking period or at any time during which the shares are subject to restrictions and, under method III, could not have such interest until the shares had been sold. A close company is broadly defined as a company controlled by five or fewer persons.

Reaction to the Proposals

After the publication of the Consultative Document, there was a period of discussion before these proposals were finalized. There was little comment from union quarters, although the TUC general secretary contrasted unfavorably the lack of progress on proposals for union representation on company boards with the speed of production of the Consultative Document.[32] In general, although most unions had little enthusiasm for the proposals, they did not actively campaign against them. The third largest union, the General and Municipal Workers Union, usually regarded as politically moderate, did sharply attack the profit-sharing proposals as having no advantages for employees. Its view was that employees should be paid for their labor directly in wage benefits, and that the amounts involved were insignificant.[33]

Not only were the unions unenthusiastic about the proposals, but the employers seemed no more favorable. The largest employers' federation, the Confederation of British Industry (CBI), published its own views; it did not see profit sharing as a major method of increasing employee involvement in companies.[34] Profit sharing might make a useful contribution to employee participation programs, but the CBI did not view it as an alternative to other measures. Employers also feared that, in the long term, shareholders' rights might be jeopardized if employees seek to expand the level of their benefits under a profit-sharing plan.

A number of other managerial organizations criticized specific aspects of the government proposals. The British Institute of Management criticized the plan for forcing employees to hold shares

---

[32] John Elliott, "Budget Will Have Concessions on Employees' Share Stakes," *Financial Times* (London), February 3, 1978, p. 32.

[33] Pauline Clark, "Shun Profit-Sharing Schemes, Says GMWU," *Financial Times* (London), May 5, 1978, p. 8.

[34] Confederation of British Industry, *Financial Participation in Companies* (London, 1978).

over a long period. It believed that this would reduce the incentive effect of plans and reduce the identification that employees would feel with employers.[35]

Clear support for the proposals was therefore confined to the Liberal party, whose enthusiasm for method III was the vital factor in its incorporation in the 1978 Finance Act. The Labour party, while not enamored of the proposals, saw little reason to oppose them. The Conservative party, however, broadly in favor of wider share ownership, produced its own paper in 1977. In addition, one of its members of Parliament, Julian Ridsdale, introduced an unsuccessful bill into Parliament early in 1977 to provide tax benefits to plans.

Government Action

The 1978 Finance Act included provisions broadly on the basis of method III for tax relief for plans.[36] The government, therefore, firmly committed itself to the promotion of profit sharing, but only where it was accomplished through the medium of share ownership. Tax relief became available in April 1979.

Under the act, a company can make available to each employee an amount of up to £ 500 ($1,053) each year in shares. All employees with five years' service must be eligible, and the employee can request to receive his allocation in cash, which is taxable in the normal way. Shares must be held in trust for five years, except in such events as injury or death. If an employee leaves his job voluntarily, his shares continue to be held by the trust until the expiration of the five-year period. The tapered income tax provisions outlined in the Consultative Document were modified, both initially and again during the bill's passage through Parliament. In the final version, shares held between five and seven years are subject to tax on 50 percent of their value; between seven and ten years, 25 percent; and over ten years, no charge. The excess of sale receipts over acquisition costs is liable to capital-gains tax. The Inland Revenue is responsible for approving proposed plans.

The new provisions have created some problems for companies that already have profit-sharing plans. Lloyds modified its plan to give employees below a certain salary level a choice of shares or cash instead of having to take the latter.[37] Under the House of Fraser

---

[35] "To Heel, Brothers," *Economist*, May 13–19, 1978, p. 127.
[36] 1978 Finance Act (c. 42).
[37] Elliott, "Swelling Tide," p. 10.

plan, a highly paid individual could receive an allocation of £ 2,000 ($4,211) worth of shares, far in excess of the government's proposed upper level for tax relief of £ 500 ($1,053), and this required modification. ICI has had to amend its plan to qualify for tax relief under the act. The major difficulty was that, under the ICI plan, shares were immediately handed over to the employee, who was free to sell them at once. In the future, employees will be able to choose whether to continue to receive shares on this basis or to take up to £ 500 in shares under the new arrangement, which will mean that they have to hold them for five years. By dividing the plan into two parts, ICI has also ensured that higher-paid employees can receive more than the £ 500 limit of shares by taking shares under each part.[38]

COLLECTIVE PLANS

British unions have been slow to imitate European proposals for collective asset-formation plans. In 1973, the Labour party suggested a plan whereby companies would place 1 percent of their equity each year in a workers' fund in which all United Kingdom employees would be entitled to share. Such shares would not be available to be cashed for seven years. The plan was opposed by Labour's left wing, however, and no action was taken on it after Labour came to power in 1974.[39]

The TUC has shown some signs of interest in union control over investment. Its proposals, supported by the government, for 50 percent union representation on the boards of pension plans may be partially seen in this light. In the face of Liberal party hostility to this proposal, there is no immediate possibility of its implementation. The TUC's evidence to the Wilson Committee, which has been reviewing the functioning of British financial institutions, suggested greater union involvement in investment policy and some proposed means of achieving this. In general, other proposals of the Meidner or VAD type have had little impact in the United Kingdom.

CONCLUSION

Although the political situation has brought it to the fore, profit sharing still lacks a firm base of support. There has been some growth of plans in recent years, but mainly in the white-collar banking sector and in the retail industry, where unionization is weak.

---

[38] John Elliott, "ICI Adapts Profit Scheme to Gain Tax Relief," *Financial Times* (London), January 10, 1979, p. 7.
[39] "All Capitalists Now," *Economist*, June 16, 1973, p. 74.

Neither employers nor unions generally have shown much inclination to take any initiatives in this regard. The TUC may generate more interest in collective plans, although their fate elsewhere in Europe does not offer a promising model.

CHAPTER X

France

Although the French economy has not been immune to the economic difficulties of the 1970s, France is an atypical European country in many respects. As Table V-4 illustrates, France's agricultural sector is larger than those in other European countries, except those in Ireland and Italy, and French farmers have formed a powerful political lobby. In part because of its agrarian sector, France is less dependent on foreign trade than any other Western European country. Its trading links are also more diversified than those of many of its European Community (EC) partners. Less than one-half of its trade is with other EC countries, and it maintains close trading links with those underdeveloped countries that were formerly French colonies.

The country has been able to balance its agrarian sector with rapid development of industry. This has been aided by a generally good record in the fields of investment and savings. There are a number of large and successful French companies, such as Michelin and Peugeot. Increasing demand for labor in the 1960s led to considerable immigration of workers, but this has slowed since 1973. The labor force participation rate is comparable with those of France's main competitors.

As Table V-2 shows, the level of government consumption is low by European standards. Welfare provisions are less developed than in most of Europe, and personal taxation is considerably lower. The government has, however, become more directly involved in industry. Two major French companies, Renault, the vehicle manufacturer, and Elf Aquitaine, the oil company, are state-owned. The largest French company, the Compagnie Française des Pétroles (CFP), is 35 percent state-owned. In addition, the state has a high level of ownership in banking and financial institutions, including the Banque Nationale de Paris and Crédit Lyonnais.

Although per capita Gross Domestic Product lags behind the levels in some Western European countries, such as Germany, France is still firmly at the upper end of the spectrum, well ahead of the United Kingdom and Italy. The major problems faced by France over the last twenty years have largely arisen from political events, and the stability of the economy has been a factor in reducing the impact of political changes over recent years.

TRADE UNIONS AND POLITICS

France is unusual in its political and union structure as well. Unlike other major Western countries, except Italy, it has a powerful Communist party, which regularly secures about 20 percent of the vote in national elections, and its main union federation, the Confédération Générale du Travail (CGT), is Communist-led. Social democracy, which dominates the political left in most of Europe, has proven less substantial in France and Italy. One result in France has been twenty years of political dominance by parties of the center-right. The political power of unions has been accordingly reduced, a factor enhanced by the labor movement's own internal divisions. The CGT, which claims 2.4 million members, has been the most important group, but like the French Communist party, it has been less flexible in its relations with other groups on the left than has its Italian counterpart, the Confederazione Generale Italiana del Lavoro. This has reduced the number of occasions on which the union movement could present a united front on political or economic issues. The CGT's closest relations have been with the Confédération Française Démocratique du Travail (CFDT), which claims to have about 800,000 members. The two federations agreed on common programs of action in 1966, 1970, and 1974 and have cooperated on a number of issues.[1] The CGT has welcomed this approach. As its secretary-general, Georges Séguy, has written:

> La CFDT, au cours des dix dernières années, a suivi incontestablement un·chemin qui autorise à envisager avec optimisme le rapprochement de nos deux centrales. . . . En admettant que le pouvoir politique doit appartenir à la classe ouvrière en alliance avec les autres forces progressistes transformatrices de la société et que les moyens principaux de production et d'échange doivent être collectifs, la CFDT a levé un important obstacle sur la voie de nos convergences.[2]

The CFDT's move to the left, to which Séguy refers, has been very pronounced over recent years. Indeed, one of the major causes of the friction that does develop occasionally between the CGT and CFDT is the tendency of the former to believe that it is being out-

---

[1] Confédération Française Démocratique du Travail, *Textes de base* (Paris, 1975), pp. 123–34.
[2] Georges Séguy, *Lutter* (Paris: Editions Stock, 1975), p. 310.

maneuvered from a leftward direction by the latter. This may seem surprising at first glance when it is recalled that the CFDT traces its origins to the Catholic union federation, founded in 1919. This federation split in 1964, and the minority retained the original name, Confédération Française des Travailleurs Chrétiens (CFTC), but kept only about two hundred thousand of the members. The creation of the CFDT marked a conscious effort to secularize the federation, and in 1968, the federation adopted a more radical approach than the other union federations during the events of that year. The move to the left and towards *le socialisme autogestionnaire* ("socialism under workers' control") as an ultimate objective has continued since.[3]

Force Ouvrière (FO), which claims to have nine hundred thousand members, was formed in 1948 as a breakaway from the CGT by anti-Communist elements.[4] In many ways, the FO has adopted the least political and most industrial orientation of any of the French union federations and appears, as a result, to have made some gains in membership over recent years.[5] The FO has not been eager for cooperation with the CGT, which has led the latter to criticize its leadership. The CFDT has also criticized the FO position and stressed that there is a risk that it will become an increasingly right-wing body whose opposition to united trade union action objectively aids the employers.[6] The FO, on the other hand, is critical of the tendency of the CGT and CFDT to act for political reasons, not trade union ones.[7]

In addition to the four federations above, there is also the white-collar Confédération Générale des Cadres (CGC), whose influence is probably greater than its claimed 260,000 members would suggest.[8]

Membership figures for French unions are probably less reliable than for almost any other EC country, except Italy. All the figures quoted above are those claimed by the federations. For instance, the

---

[3] Edmond Maire and Jacques Julliard, *La CFDT d'Aujourd'Hui* (Paris: Editions du Seuil, 1975); Edmond Maire and Claude Perpignon, *Demain L'Autogestion* (Paris: Editions Seghers, 1976).

[4] Val R. Lorwin, *The French Labor Movement* (Cambridge, Mass.: Harvard University Press, 1956), pp. 119-30. Lorwin's book, although dated, is still the best account in English. In French, see Jean Daniel Reynaud, *Les Syndicats en France* (Paris: Editions du Seuil, 1975).

[5] Alain Bergounioux, *Force Ouvrière* (Paris: Editions du Seuil, 1975); André Bergeron, *La Confédération Force Ouvrière* (Paris: EPI, 1972).

[6] Maire and Julliard, *La CFDT d'Aujourd'Hui*, pp. 127-28.

[7] André Bergeron, *Lettre Ouverte à un Syndiqué* (Paris: Albin Michel, 1975), p. 157.

[8] Confédération Générale des Cadres, *Voici La Confédération Générale des Cadres* (Paris, 1973), p. 2.

CFDT claims to have the most accurate figures and believes that its real membership is just under one-half that of the CGT and over twice that of the FO.[9] It seems clear that many of those who consider themselves supporters of a particular union do not actually pay dues to it on a regular basis, which would be the standard by which membership would be judged in most countries. Even taking the claimed membership figures of the different federations, the French unions only organize about 23 percent of the working population, and the true figure is probably lower. Membership is not the sole criterion, of course, for the strength of an organization, but it has a substantial impact.

The relatively low membership figures were reflected in the unions' reaction to the wave of strikes and unrest in 1968. The unions lacked control over protesting workers and were themselves often the targets of attack for responding belatedly to the workers' demands. The unions' weakness is also illustrated by their tactics in negotiation and in strike situations. The national centers lack the funds and organization to maintain long strikes and so have resorted consistently to the use of short demonstration stoppages.

France is a country in which the language of class struggle is deeply embedded. In many respects, it is also one of the least egalitarian countries in Europe. The differentials in earnings between blue-collar workers and higher-paid managers and professionals are greater in France than in most other Western European countries.[10] Wealth ownership is concentrated, and many employees, for motives that are not overtly ideological, seem suspicious of such proposals as share ownership. This perhaps accounts for the slow growth of individual profit-sharing plans in France and for the Gaullist attempt to find some way of integrating employees into the capitalist system by introducing a compulsory profit-sharing plan.

PROFIT-SHARING LEGISLATION

France has a legislative framework for profit sharing that dates back to 1959. At that time, the government sought to promote voluntary agreements within companies to provide to employees payments based on profits, dividends, or a portion of the gain resulting from increased productivity. If the plan was based on either profits or dividends, an annual payment could be made either in cash or in shares. If the system was based on productivity im-

---

[9] Maire and Julliard, *La CFDT d'Aujourd'Hui*, pp. 19-20.
[10] Malcolm Sawyer, *Income Distribution in OECD Countries* (Paris: Organization for Economic Cooperation and Development, 1976), pp. 14-15.

provements, a cash payment would be made every three months. The benefits disbursed under this plan were taxable. Concern arose, however, that the voluntary system was not functioning effectively, and in 1965, the government announced that it would take a new initiative.

This led in 1967 to the passage of Ordonnance No. 67–693, which makes profit sharing compulsory for all companies with over one hundred employees and allows smaller organizations to sign voluntary agreements. The government's aim in providing the legislation is outlined in the preamble to the ordinance, in which the need to involve workers in the operation of companies is spelled out. The development of more harmonious industrial relations is also projected:

> L'intérêt des travailleurs suppose le maintien d'une économie prospère; l'intérêt de notre economie est lié à une large diffusion des fruits de l'expansion, l'intérêt de notre société, enfin, rend indispensable que patrons et salariés, qui concourent ensemble au développement des entreprises, partagent le prix de leurs efforts communs.[11]

The law was also intended to increase the level of investment in the economy and the level of personal savings. The latter aim was explicitly encouraged by the passage of a parallel ordinance designed to give tax benefits to savings plans, which could either be integrated with the profit-sharing system or kept separate from it.[12]

The law, and the subsequent decrees made under it, which were later embodied in the French Labor Code, provides that companies should set aside a certain portion of each year's profit for investment on the employees' behalf. The amount to be set aside is calculated by a formula that takes after-tax profit, subtracts an allowance for the company of a 5 percent return on capital, and then multiplies the remaining amount by a factor calculated by dividing the total salary bill by value-added. This is an attempt to take into account the relative capital/labor intensity of the business. The actual sum paid is one-half of the figure resulting from the above computation. It is specified in the legislation that any payment under this plan is quite distinct from regular pay. The formula provides a minimum payment, and unions can seek to negotiate more favorable arrangements. The CFTC, for instance, has suggested eliminating the final halving of the figure. In practice, it

---

[11] "Ordonnance No. 67–693 Du 17 Août 1967 Relative à la Participation des Salariés aux Fruits de l'Expansion des Entreprises," *Journal Officiel de la République Française*, August 18, 1967.
[12] "Ordonnance No. 67–694 Du 17 Août 1967 Relative aux Plans d'Epargne

is not clear that unions have been very successful in making major improvements.

Lengthy definitions of profit, capital, and value-added are set forth in the law. Profits are to be based only on a company's operations in France and in the four overseas departments: Guadeloupe, Martinique, Guyane, and Réunion. Foreign multinationals are only assessed for operations in this area. Applying the same principle, the definition of capital excludes capital invested in operations outside this defined area.

If both employees and management agree, it is possible to use a less complicated formula and to modify some aspects of the agreement if the resulting payment is at least as good as under the statutory formula. An agreement embodying a different arrangement from that specified in the legislation is termed an *accord dérogatoire*. Any simplified proposal has to be examined by the Centre d'Etude des Revenus et des Coûts (CERC) for its approval.[13] The CERC is a body established in 1966 to provide economic information and to undertake research. Although it is under the general direction of the Commissariat Général du Plan, it is best characterized as a semigovernmental body with some degree of independent status. When considering agreements, its composition is the president and council members of the CERC; plus five employee representatives, one from each union federation; five employers; and three independent experts.[14] Any formula approved by the CERC requires the ultimate sanction of the Ministry of Labor and the Ministry of Economics and Finance, but any formula rejected by the CERC cannot be approved. The CERC has also developed a role of interpretation of agreements on points where the original law requires clarification.

The sum placed aside as a result of these calculations is called the Réserve Spéciale de Participation (RSP). These funds may be used in a number of ways according to the agreement reached at plant level by the two sides.

This agreement, the *accord de participation*, is central to the whole process. In general, the agreement is made between management and the works councils *(comités d'entreprise)*. It was reported that, at the end of 1975, 83 percent of all agreements had been concluded in this manner. The remainder were concluded either

---

d'Entreprise et Modifiant La Loi No. 65-997 du 29 Novembre 1965," *Journal Officiel de la République Française*, August 18, 1967.

[13] For a description of the CERC's work, see "La Participation des Salariés aux Fruits de l'Expansion," *Documents du Centre d'Etude des Revenus et des Coûts*, No. 27 (1975); No. 31 (1976).

[14] "La Participation des Salariés aux Fruits de l'Expansion," No. 27, p. 4.

directly with the unions (13.4 percent of the cases) or with the works council and unions as joint signatories.[15] The agreement may be made either with union representatives external to the company or with internal representatives alone. The agreement specifies the formula for calculating the reserve, its allocation, and the method of investing the funds. Since 1973, the only exception is that, in companies with under fifty employees, the employer could on his own initiative propose the introduction of a plan, and this could be approved by two-thirds majority vote of the employees.[16]

Investment of the RSP

The RSP can be used in one (or more than one if feasible) of five specified ways.
1. The issue of the company's shares to employees. This can be either in the form of shares bought on the stock market or in the form of the issue of new stock if the existing shareholders agree.
2. The issue of company debentures with a fixed rate of interest.
3. The opening of a current account by the company detailing the employee's holding. This also has a fixed interest system and is basically a less formalized version of the debenture system.
4. The investment of the money in a mutual fund or SICAV *(Société d'investissement à capital variable)*.
5. The investment of the money in a *fonds commun de placement* (FCP), which is a type of mutual fund, set up specifically for the workers in the company concerned. In practice, this requires that the company should have sufficient employees to support its own fund, and this usually means at least five hundred. The FCP must be managed by an external *société de gestion*, often a bank.

The advantage of an FCP over an SICAV is that it offers a larger degree of control over investment to the employees of the company. Even when an external managing body is chosen, an internal *conseil de surveillance* must monitor its activity.[17] This body consists of employee representatives, but if they agree, it can also include employer representatives.

---

[15] France, Ministry of Labor, "La Participation: Situation des Accords au 31 Décembre 1975," *Travail Informations*, No. 34 (December 13–19, 1976).
[16] "La Participation des Salariés aux Fruits de l'Expansion," No. 27, p. 19.
[17] "Décret No. 67-1112 du 19 Décembre 1967 Fixant les Conditions d'Application de l'Ordonnance No. 67-693 du 17 Août 1967 Relative à la Participation des Salariés aux Fruits de l'Expansion des Entreprises," *Journal Officiel de la République Française*, December 21, 1967, and January 28, 1968, Article 11.

Employee Accounts

The actual amount attributed to the employee is calculated in proportion to his annual salary up to a maximum cutoff point, which is fixed at a level of four times the pay on which social security payments are calculated.[18] The maximum cutoff point is therefore currently at a level of Fr 192,000 ($44,037) per year.[19] There is also a parallel provision for a maximum annual allocation to the individual employee, which is one-half of the social security maximum pay, or Fr 24,000 ($5,505) per year currently.

The parties are allowed to modify the formula that relates the allocation to salary, but only within certain limits. The CERC has ruled that egalitarian efforts to attribute the same amount to all employees, regardless of salary level, are not admissible.[20] Formulas relating allocation solely to length of service have also been rejected by the CERC, partly because they were held to be likely to inhibit the mobility of labor.[21] A premium related to length of service is permitted, but the CERC will judge its size based on the situation of the particular employer. As a general principle, however, the CERC has decided that at least 50 percent of the payment must be directly related to salary level. The ceiling of four times social security earnings can be somewhat reduced but never increased. The CERC again examines the particular situation and so, in some cases, allows a reduction to a ceiling of twice the level and, in others, allows a floor to be put in to raise the allocation of the lower-paid. If there are a large number of workers paid at or near the legal minimum wage, which is one-half of the social security level, then a formula may even be allowed that sets the ceiling equal to the social security level. To qualify for entry into the plan, the employee has to have a minimum of three months' service with the company.

Irrespective of the particular method of using the money, the capital accumulated in the employee's name must not be touched for five years, except in the specified circumstances of layoff, retirement, death, disablement, or marriage. The interest can, however, be paid to the employee, and he must receive a statement detailing his holding each year.

In order to provide a stimulus to comply with the law, there is a provision that, if there is no agreement within one year of the company's coming within the legislative framework, the Ministry of

---

[18] *Ibid.*, Article 6.
[19] Unless otherwise specified, the exchange rate used is $1 = Fr 4.36 as of April 10, 1979.
[20] "La Participation des Salariés aux Fruits de l'Expansion," No. 31, pp. 64–65.
[21] *Ibid.*, pp. 65–66.

Labor will compel the undertaking to transfer the relevant money to current accounts in the employees' names. Such accounts are, however, blocked for eight years and earn only 5 percent interest.[22] The employer's tax exemption for the sums paid is also halved. Up to December 1975, 196 such orders had been issued by the ministry under the authority that it had been given by Article L 442-12 of the Labor Code.[23] The ministry claims that most of these cases do not arise from a breakdown of negotiations but occur in situations in which there is neither a works council nor recognized unions.

Tax Incentives

Tax incentives are a major part of the plan. The employee pays neither income tax nor social security contributions on his allocation. The employer receives exemptions from profits and income tax for his payments into the RSP. In addition, the employer can set up a reserve for investment equal to the employees' share of the profits. If this is used within one year to finance the acquisition of assets, it is also tax-deductible.[24]

Management of the Fund

Within the enterprise, the plan is usually managed by a *commission de participation*, which comprises both employee and employer representatives. The creation of this committee and the nature of its membership are not obligatory, and if it does not exist, the works council will assume its functions. In general, both parties are represented on the body. There is legal provision, however, that the number of employer representatives cannot exceed one-half of the committee. The size of membership is not fixed but seems to vary between three and thirteen.[25] If there is also a *conseil de surveillance* for an FCP or a savings plan, then its members are appointed by the *commission de participation*.

If disputes arise out of the profit-sharing arrangements, these are

---

[22] "Ordonnance No. 67-693," Article 11; "Décret No. 68-104 du 31 Janvier 1968 Fixant le Taux de l'Intérêt Alloué aux Comptes Courants Mentionnés à l'Article 11 de l'Ordonnance No. 67-693 du 17 Août 1967 Relative à la Participation des Salariés aux Fruits de l'Expansion des Entreprises et de l'Intérêt Prévu à l'Article 29 du Décret No. 67-1112 du 19 Décembre 1967 Fixant les Conditions d'Application de Cette Ordonnance," *Journal Officiel de la République Française*, February 2, 1968.

[23] "Ordonnance No. 67-693," Articles 7 and 8.

[24] France, Ministry of Labor, "La Participation: Situation des Accords au 31 Décembre 1975."

[25] Confédération Française des Travailleurs Chrétiens, *La Conclusion des Accords de Participation* (Paris, 1972), p. 73.

first dealt with by the commission. When it meets for this purpose, it must have an equal number of employee and employer representatives. If it fails to agree on the necessary course of action, there is provision for the dispute to be referred to outside arbitration. If there is no *commission de participation*, disputes are referred to a *commission de conciliation*, which consists of two employee representatives, appointed by the works council, and two employer appointees.

Where a *commission de participation* has been established, it has to meet at least twice a year to monitor the agreement. This task involves informing the employees about the calculation of payments and being consulted about the report that the employer has to make to employees each year about the plan's operation. The report has to cover the basis of calculation for the amount of the RSP and information on the management and use of the funds in the reserve.[26]

The law also allowed for a transition period lasting until the beginning of 1970, during which any existing profit-sharing plan could remain in separate existence provided that it yielded benefits at least as good as those under the statutory plan, and provided that it was the result of an agreement between the employer and his workers. Plans set up under the 1959 legislation could also be brought into the new framework in a similar fashion.

EFFECT OF THE LEGISLATION

The 1959 voluntary plan has had little impact. By 1977, only 234 voluntary agreements had been signed, and these covered only 125,000 employees. The largest company to have implemented such a plan is probably Ferodo, the manufacturer of motor and aircraft components, which established its plan in 1960 but later integrated it into the 1967 framework.[27]

The impact of the 1967 law can be measured in various ways. The coverage of the plan is quite extensive. By December 1975, a government survey showed that there were 9,581 agreements, covering 10,769 undertakings, which employed 4.73 million workers, or approximately 22.5 percent of the country's labor force.[28] The survey

---

[26] "France: An A to Z of Employee Shareholding and Profit Sharing," *European Industrial Relations Review*, No. 53 (May 1978), p. 8.
[27] "Décret No. 67-1112," Article 25.
[28] For these figures and the subsequent statistical data, see France, Ministry of Labor, "La Participation: Situation des Accords au 31 Décembre 1975"; and France, Ministry of Labor, "La Participation: Résultats Financiers de la Participation en 1973 et Répartition de la Réserve Spéciale de Participation," *Travail Informations*, No. 35 (December 20-26, 1976).

showed that 19.6 percent of these agreements had been concluded in firms of under one hundred employees. The number of agreements in these small companies has increased steadily since the inception of the plan; in March 1972, only 13.6 percent of the total were found in such undertakings. The total number of agreements has also grown steadily and, in 1972, stood at 5,526 agreements. The rate of increase has, however, apparently slowed down and, in 1975, was 3.1 percent for both the number of agreements and the number of undertakings covered.

The limited percentage of the labor force covered is a natural consequence of the provisions of the legislation. First, the law applies primarily to the private sector, and second, it is mandatory only for firms with over one hundred employees. In the private sector in France, it is estimated that there are only 12,000 undertakings with over one hundred employees out of a total of 1.8 million private firms. In any case, a firm has to make a minimum 5 percent return, and a number of otherwise eligible companies have not come within the scope of the legislation because they have failed to make this return.

In practice, 79 percent of the companies with agreements are *sociétés anonymes* ("limited companies"). Agreements in firms with over 500 employees constitute 16.9 percent of the total but cover 3.13 million workers, or 66 percent of the total covered by profit-sharing plans. Therefore, when measured against its potential coverage, the law's actual coverage has been fairly extensive.

Public Sector Coverage

A later decree brought a number of specified public sector organizations within the ambit of the law.[29] The criteria for inclusion are that the organization should be separated from the direct governmental machinery, should be industrial or commercial in character, and should be relatively free to set its own prices so that its profitability reflects its real economic performance. The companies brought within the plan include a number of banks and financial institutions, such as the Banque Nationale de Paris and Crédit Lyonnais, as well as industrial or transport undertakings, such as Air France and Renault.

---

[29] "Décret No. 69-255 Du 21 Mars 1969 Fixant les Conditions d'Application aux Entreprises Publiques et Sociétés Nationales de l'Ordonnance No. 67-693 du 17 Août 1967 Relative à la Participation des Salariés aux Fruits de l'Expansion des Entreprises," *Journal Officiel de la République Française,* March 23, 1969, and May 11, 1969.

Investment Choice

In the choice of investment method, the preference of employees seems fairly clear. The number of agreements based on share acquisition has been very small. In December 1975, only 1.3 percent of all agreements utilized this method. The options that provide a fixed rate of interest have proved far more popular and account for 50.9 percent of the agreements; the SICAV and FCP options account for another 47.9 percent. Even the politically moderate CGC has advised its members that these latter mutual fund options offer the safest investment method.[30] The CFDT and FO have also advised their members to utilize the mutual fund options. The CGC, along with the other unions, has criticized the fixed interest options as providing the employer with cheap financing.[31] The CGT, in complete contrast, has been unwilling to be seen to support the capitalist system in any way and so has recommended the fixed interest options to its members; this policy accounts for these options' widespread use.[32]

The amount of money involved has been relatively small. The average allocation available for withdrawal in 1974, the first year a worker could take out part of his capital (i.e., the 1969 allocation), was only Fr 353 ($73; 1974). The actual total individual allocation by 1973 had reached Fr 699 on average ($157; 1973). At that time, the total amount of all RSPs was Fr 2,176 million ($489 million; 1974), an increase of nearly 60 percent over the 1970 figure of Fr 1,373 million ($248 million; 1970). Naturally, the individual allocation had grown less rapidly (by 40 percent) as the number of employees involved increased. In 1974, some 72 percent of employees cashed in their holdings, a somewhat higher rate of withdrawal than had been expected.

The complex method of calculating the RSP seems to have created certain difficulties. The 1976 government survey showed that, of the first 9,385 agreements, 3,372 (36 percent) had been monitored by the CERC because the calculation differed from the standard formula laid down in the ordinance.

---

[30] Jean-Paul Trarieux, "Les Contrats de Participation aux Fruits de l'Expansion Doivent Etre Negociés Avant le 31 Décembre," *Le Creuset* (Confédération Générale des Cadres), No. 555 (September 20, 1969), p. 4.
[31] Jean-Paul Trarieux, "Le Point de Vue de la CGC," *Le Creuset* (Confédération Générale des Cadres), No. 531 (August 24, 1968), pp. 4-5.
[32] Derek Robinson, *Incomes Policy and Capital Sharing in Europe* (New York: Barnes and Noble, 1973), p. 93.

Overall Impact

The consensus seems to be that the legislation has not had the impact that was hoped for in 1967. The main employers' federation, the Confédération Nationale du Patronat Français, has consistently supported the legislation, but there has been less enthusiasm on the union side. The Communist CGT has opposed the plan on the grounds that it merely makes more money available to employers to invest, which would otherwise be secured by employees in direct wage benefits, at the same time that it gives employers tax concessions on their contributions. The only union federation clearly in favor of the plan is the small CFTC, the rump of the Christian federation.[33] With around two hundred thousand adherents, compared to about four million in the three main federations, the CFTC's support has not had a major impact. This can also be illustrated by the lack of effect of its preference for share-acquisition plans; it feels that the plans lead to greater employee involvement in companies. The CFTC has consistently claimed that unions have not taken the initiative in reaching agreements and have shown little interest in them.[34] Other union federations' attitudes appear to support this conclusion. It is, for instance, significant that in a two-hundred-page handbook for its active members dealing with conditions of work, social security, wage issues, and other subjects, the CFDT does not bother to mention profit sharing at all.[35]

In the various industrial sectors, the legislation has had a differential effect caused by differences in their profitability and capital intensiveness. Thus, by 1973, the total RSP per worker was highest in the chemical industry (Fr 1,170: $263; 1973) and electrical construction (Fr 1,030: $231; 1973), while it was much lower in such industries as domestic service (Fr 229: $51; 1973), catering (Fr 236: $53; 1973), the non-food retail sector (Fr 330: $74; 1973), and clothing (Fr 389: $87; 1973).[36]

SAVINGS PLANS

A law passed in 1965 had aided savings plans *(les plans d'épargne)* for employees by providing tax benefits, although only if there was a ten-year blocking period. The 1967 law provides that savings

---

[33] Confédération Française des Travailleurs Chrétiens, *Les Accords de Participation des Travailleurs aux Fruits de l'Expansion des Entreprises* (Paris, 1968).

[34] Confédération Française des Travailleurs Chrétiens, *La Conclusion des Accords de Participation* (Paris, 1972), p. 4.

[35] France, Ministry of Labor, "La Participation: Résultats Financiers."

[36] Confédération Francaise Démocratique du Travail, *Guide Pratique 1977* (Paris, 1976).

plans can be set up either within the framework of the profit-sharing agreement or outside of it.[37] Thus, if a company has under one hundred employees or does not make the necessary level of profits, it can still establish a savings plan. If the savings plan operates within a company with a profit-sharing agreement, the plan can still adopt different methods of investment for the RSP and allow individuals to choose their preferred investment method rather than have them submit to a collective decision.

Payments into the savings plan can come wholly from the employer, wholly from the employee, or jointly. Savings plans, unlike the profit-sharing system, can be established unilaterally by the employer, although agreements are also allowed, and in any case, an individual is free not to participate. The savings plan can be set up as part of the *accord de participation*. The plan must invest in a similar range of options to that for the profit-sharing plan and must have a similar five-year blocking period, except in the specified circumstances of layoff, retirement, death, disablement, or marriage.

A savings plan is subject to organizational controls similar to those for the FCP. A *conseil de surveillance* must be appointed, and a managing body must be created, either internally or externally.[38]

PROPOSALS FOR CHANGE

The major "Sudreau Report" on company reform and labor relations praised the manner in which the law had encouraged employees to take a wider interest in the operation of their companies.[39] The report did not recommend any major alterations in the means of calculating payments or in the tax benefits given to the plan. It did, however, suggest that an optional additional RSP could be negotiated at company level. This could be based on a range of criteria, similar to the 1959 legislation, and there would not need to be a ceiling on the amount distributed to the individual employees. The report recommended that employees have the option of obtaining immediate payment of amounts acquired under the compulsory participation plan, although they would lose the tax benefits if they chose to take the payments at once.[40]

The report also drew attention to the insignificant degree to which

---

[37] "Ordonnance No. 67-694."
[38] *Ibid.*, Article 5.
[39] "The Reform of the Enterprise in France: Report of the Research Committee on Company Reform," Official English Translation of the "Sudreau Report" (Philadelphia: Industrial Research Unit, The Wharton School, University of Pennsylvania, 1975), p. 140.
[40] *Ibid.*, pp. 144-45.

the plan had encouraged employees to become shareholders of their companies. The report suggested measures to make this option more attractive and to make it available in unquoted companies by the issue of "shares" with a nominal value. The report also recommended that the legal provisions should be gradually extended to all companies, not just those with over one hundred employees.

One result of the compulsory plan has been to discourage attempts to create voluntary profit-sharing arrangements outside the scope of the legislation. This factor seems to have influenced another recent government report, which argued the case for assistance to encourage employee shareholding. The government set up a group in October 1977, chaired by Paul Delouvrier, chairman of Electricité de France.[41] The report of this committee was made public early in 1978. It stressed the failure of voluntary share-ownership plans, such as that introduced in 1973, to encourage stock-purchase plans, which had been applied in only fifteen companies. The report's proposals generally followed the line of the Sudreau report. There is little evidence that these proposals have significantly advanced efforts to overcome union hostility to share-ownership plans.

The government has shown signs of wishing to encourage wider share ownership. The 1970 "stock-option" law has been used only in about forty companies and is usually limited to senior executives.[42] The 1973 law has also often been limited to higher-paid employees. In June 1978, the French president, Valéry Giscard d'Estaing, declared his support for further measures, including a one-time free distribution of shares for 1979.[43]

In October 1978, the government announced the introduction of legislation on share distribution. This would require that all companies quoted on the stock exchange, and which had declared dividends in two of the previous three years, should issue shares to their employees in 1980. Companies that subsequently met these criteria between 1980 and 1984 would also have to make a share distribution. The distribution was expected to involve 850 companies, employing 2.25 million workers, and the average share payment was anticipated to be Fr 1,380 ($317).[44] The value of shares to be issued would be limited to a maximum of 3 percent of a

---

[41] "New Proposals on Employee Shareholding and Participation," *European Industrial Relations Review*, No. 51 (March 1978), pp. 15–16.
[42] "France: An A to Z of Employee Shareholding," p. 9.
[43] "La Réunion de Presse du Président de la République," *Le Monde*, Sélection Hebdomadaire, June 15–21, 1978, p. 4.
[44] "French Shares for Workers Plan," *Financial Times* (London), November 1, 1978, p. 1.

company's capital. The shares would be blocked for between three and five years, and there would be a ceiling of Fr 5,000 ($1,147) on the value of shares allocated to any individual. An individual employee would be eligible to receive shares if he had at least two years' service with the company. The company could allocate shares in relation to status and seniority, but no worker could receive more than three times the lowest individual allocation of shares. A key feature of the plan was that the government would provide companies with a credit equal to the market value of the shares issued. This credit would be repayable over a ten-year period.

The reaction of the unions was predictably cool. The CGT attacked the proposal as a "gadget" that would cost employers nothing.[45] The more moderate FO also attacked the plan.[46] The plan still has to pass into law, but its initial reception does not suggest that it will have any noticeable effect on French industrial relations.

CONCLUSION

In France, the attempt to impose a system of profit sharing by law has produced mixed results. France remains the only European country that has sought to implement a comprehensive system of individual profit sharing.

As chapter XI indicates, some European countries have not shown great interest in profit sharing, but despite this, the European Community (EC) has begun to develop its own policy on the subject. It is evident that, in the process of policy formulation, the EC will assess carefully France's experience with its legislation, for it stands as the major model in Europe of legislated personal asset formation.

---

[45] "Participation: Un Nouveau Gadget," *La Vie Ouvrière* (Confédération Générale du Travail), November 6-12, 1978, p. 22.
[46] "French Government Plans for Employees' Shares," *International Trade Union News* (International Confederation of Free Trade Unions), November 15, 1978, p. 21.

CHAPTER XI

The European Community and Other European Countries

There are a number of European countries in which profit sharing has had only a limited impact. The reasons for this situation vary considerably. Ireland has the largest agrarian sector in Europe and the smallest percentage of employees in manufacturing. Its unions are highly organized and have a reputation for militancy. Their policies are similar to those of British unions, a number of whom have members in Ireland. As such, they have not been enthusiastic toward profit sharing. In Italy, the unions and employers have not shown much interest in profit sharing, and unlike the Gaullists in France, the Italian political parties have not been anxious to fill this vacuum. In Switzerland, not a member of the European Community and ever the odd man out in Europe, profit sharing has only made limited progress. Luxembourg has an economy whose total employment is only fifteen hundred thousand, and whose main industry, steel, is not a noted profit sharer in any country.[1] Belgium shares some of the same social attitudes as France but is, on the face of it, the most surprising omission from the list of countries with active profit-sharing arrangements.

It is not possible, therefore, to isolate any simple factors that lead countries to show little interest in profit sharing. Other than the United Kingdom, Belgium has, in contrast to Ireland and Italy, the smallest agricultural sector in Western Europe. The size of the public sector in these countries is generally smaller than the European average, a fact that might on its face seem to offer more scope for private sector profit sharing. Investment and savings ratios span both the high and low end of the European spectrum, and although all the countries except Switzerland have a high level of union organization, so have countries with collective proposals

---

[1] Although Luxembourg is a member of the European Community, it is omitted from consideration here because there is no evidence of a significant number of profit-sharing plans at company level or of collective investment proposals by the unions in Luxembourg.

such as Sweden and Denmark. Ireland and Italy are the two poorest countries in the European Community (EC), while Switzerland is one of the two richest countries in Europe. The reasons for the lack of interest in profit sharing shown by these countries must be sought by examining the special circumstances of each.

SWITZERLAND

Switzerland has neither extensive individual company profit-sharing plans nor significant proposals for collective investment funds.

Nestlé, the largest of the Swiss multinationals, does have a plan that provides a bonus to all headquarters staff with at least three years' service, which is equal to 8 percent of the dividend paid to stockholders. This is paid in cash to those who earn less than SF 500 ($289) per week.[2] For those who earn more, part is given in the form of bonds that represent one-tenth of a share and can be converted into actual shares when ten-tenths have been accumulated. The Swiss operating companies of Nestlé operate a slightly different system, related directly to profit and not to dividends. Each general manager can choose his own plan, but usually, the bonus paid is only equivalent to about two weeks' salary.

Ciba-Geigy, the chemical multinational, which is the second largest Swiss company after Nestlé, also has a stock-ownership plan. After four years' service, an employee can purchase one share of the company at a cost of SF 200 ($116), and thereafter, he can purchase an additional share at the same price every two years. These shares are currently worth about SF 712 ($412). The employee can sell every third share he receives, but he has to keep all the remaining shares until he retires or leaves the company. Voting rights on the stock are given during this period when his holding is blocked.

The largest retail food chain in the country, the Federation of Migros Cooperatives, which has thirty-five thousand employees in nearly 450 stores, has also experimented with profit sharing through the payment of an annual stock bonus. Employees become eligible for payments only after three years of service, although at that point, benefits are made retroactive to the commencement of service. An employee's entitlement can be cashed only at the termination of employment. The plan, which was introduced in 1971, was mainly designed to reduce the high rates of labor turnover that the company had been experiencing. The plan does not, however, seem

---

[2] Unless otherwise specified, the exchange rate used is $1 = SF 1.73 as of April 10, 1979.

to have had any great success in attaining this objective.[3]

One of the most interesting Swiss plans is that practiced by Hoffmann-La Roche, the fifth largest Swiss company.[4] The plan is profit-related in that the amount available for distribution to an employee each year is equal to the dividends paid on one company share. The company, however, has an unusual structure of ownership and so has avoided making employees into shareholders directly. The company's capital consists of 16,000 paid-up shares and 54,400 "bonus certificates" *(Genusscheinen)*, including 6,400 issued in 1971.[5] The company's original capital was set at SF 8 million in 1920. This was fully repaid between 1928 and 1943 and then replaced by two issues of share certificates; since then, the company's capital structure has remained unchanged. The company has, therefore, relied heavily on self-financing.

Thus in 1971, when the company decided to introduce a profit-sharing plan, it did so by setting up a separate Profit Sharing Foundation, which was financed initially by a direct grant from the company of SF 22 million ($15.35 million; 1971). Retired employees of the company received immediately a one-time cash payment of SF 250 ($61; 1971) per year of service at a total cost of SF 5 million ($1.22 million; 1971). The current employees receive SF 400 ($97; 1971) per year of service, but this money is invested and only paid out at retirement. One of the aims of the plan was said to be the provision of additional retirement income, and so this plan constitutes an unusual European example of this goal. The employee's account is increased each year by the annual company contribution based on the dividend and by the interest accruing to his invested account. The company has estimated that, if dividend growth and interest both equaled 5 percent per year, an employee with twenty years' service would retire with SF 26,000 ($6,318; 1971), and with forty years' service, SF 137,000 ($33,293; 1971).[6]

There are stringent conditions, however, to discourage employees from leaving the company. Any employee who leaves with under ten years' service, except in the cases of retirement or death, would receive nothing. Employees who leave with over ten years' service are entitled only to one-third of their holdings, and even this depends on the agreement of the foundation's council to this payment's being made.

---

[3] "Swiss Workers Don't Want Shares," *Financial Times* (London), November 7, 1975, p. 8.
[4] "Vermögensbildung durch Gewinnbeteiligung," *National-Zeitung Basel*, May 27, 1971, p. 21.
[5] *Jane's Major Companies of Europe* (New York: Franklin Watts Inc., 1975), p. C254.
[6] "Vermögensbildung durch Gewinnbeteiligung," p. 21.

The foundation is legally distinct from the company. It is governed by a council of nine members, five of whom are indirectly elected by the participating employees. Votes are proportional to the size of the employee's holding in the fund. The other four council members are appointed by the company. Changes in the plan, however, require a two-thirds majority vote of the council. The council is responsible for investing the funds and for administering the plan.

BELGIUM

Belgium does not have many company profit-sharing plans, nor does it have any active campaign for collective investment plans.

Petrofina, the Belgian petroleum multinational, is a rare example of a company that does have a plan. It was instituted in 1967 and primarily provides for a distribution of shares to employees on the occasion of a stock increase or capital expansion. Thus in 1976, one hundred thousand shares were made available to staff at a discounted price, and this offer was oversubscribed two and one-half times. There is also a more regular plan, which provides that any employee with two years' service in the company can receive a certain percentage of his pay in the form of shares. Whatever amount the employee decides to take, the company will provide an equal amount free of charge. There is a maximum limitation on the amount of pay that can be taken in this form, which rises from 1 percent with two years' service to 6 percent for those with twenty or more years of service. The shares are blocked for a period of five years, and the two sets of shares (the employee's and the employer's matching amount) are kept in separate accounts. At the end of five years, the employee can sell his shares, but if he does so, he loses the employer's contribution of shares.

The unions have not favored this plan, but some 80 percent of eligible staff have taken advantage of it. The idea for the plan was imported from the United States, where Petrofina, like many American oil companies, has a similar plan for its United States employees. Management retains total control over the plan, which is in no sense collectively bargained.[7]

ITALY

In Italy, there seems to be no widespread use of individual company profit-sharing plans, which are opposed by much of the trade union movement.

---

[7] Company official, interview in Brussels, May 16, 1977.

There was some interest among unions in various plans in the 1950s and 1960s. The Catholic union federation, Confederazione Italiana Sindacati Lavoratori (CISL), put forward a plan that aimed to set aside part of pay increases to be paid in savings certificates if the workers so wished. The plan would, therefore, have been voluntary as far as the worker was concerned, but the employer would pay the money into a fund controlled by the participating unions. The CISL envisioned such plans' being arrived at by means of collective bargaining and suggested that they would aid economic growth by providing an additional source of funds for investment.[8]

The reaction of the other union federations was not very favorable. The Communist Confederazione Generale Italiana del Lavoro opposed the plan totally, while the Socialist Unione Italiana del Lavoro claimed that it was not opposed in principle, but that it thought the plan framed by the CISL would reduce unions' wage-bargaining power.

In any case, proposals of this kind confronted the legal obstacle that mutual funds were illegal. In October 1963, therefore, the CISL proposed a bill to set up a special investment fund to act as the depository of workers' savings. The fund would have had a majority of trade union representatives on its managing body. The bill continued to be moved around the legislature for some time, but it was not finally passed. Since that time, there appear to have been few further developments of interest in this subject, and by 1969, the investment-wage proposal was no longer even included in the CISL program.[9]

IRELAND

There is no widespread use of profit sharing at company level or any union proposals for collective investment funds in Ireland. There are a few plans, most notably for the Guinness brewing company, Irish Distillers, Harp Lager, and the Bank of Ireland.[10] The largest plan is that for the Guinness Group, which covers about twenty-eight hundred employees. This plan, which dates back to 1964, distributes part of the profit annually to participating em-

---

[8] Solomon Barkin and Derek Robinson, *Workers' Negotiated Savings Plans for Capital Formation* (Paris: Organization for Economic Cooperation and Development, 1970), pp. 22-25.

[9] Derek Robinson, *Incomes Policy and Capital Sharing in Europe* (New York: Barnes and Noble, 1973), p. 89.

[10] "Ireland Profit Sharing: The Company Approach," *European Industrial Relations Review*, No. 50 (February 1978), pp. 15-16.

ployees. The part for distribution is calculated by first subtracting 30 percent from total profits for reinvestment and then subtracting 5 percent from the remaining figure, which represents interest on capital employed. Of the remaining profit, 12.5 percent is distributed to employees, a sum totaling £ 1.68 million ($3.02 million; 1976) in 1976-77. Individual allocation is related to salary.

EUROPEAN COMMUNITY

With the exception of Sweden and Switzerland, and of course the United States, all of the countries studied here are members of the EC. The EC has been playing an increasingly interventionist role in the economic and social affairs of its members. There has been some speculation that the EC will take a major initiative in the area of worker asset formation. The European Commission has been working on a draft directive on the subject, and there are signs that the work may be nearing completion, although any initial proposal is likely to be followed by prolonged debate.

It seems possible that, faced with the variety of existing practices in member states, the commission may, without favoring any particular system, confine itself to specifying that countries should adopt some form of asset formation. There are different policy lines that would spring from following, for example, either the French or German models. Although it is not easy to establish the likely nature of any proposal, some guidance can be derived from the commission's working paper on the subject, which was presented to the tripartite conference in Luxembourg in June 1976.[11]

The working paper cited the major objectives for any policy on personal asset ownership as
1. a fairer and less uneven distribution of wealth,
2. the provision for individuals of "some degree of financial independence and greater security in the face of life's many risks and burdens,"[12]
3. the encouragement of home ownership by more families,
4. a higher overall level of savings to finance investment,
5. the achievement of fuller participation by households in total savings,
6. more extensive use of medium- and long-term investments by personal savers, and
7. the encouragement of price and general economic stability.

---

[11] Commission of the European Communities, *Policy on Personal Asset Ownership* (Brussels, 1976).
[12] *Ibid.*, p. 6.

The paper discussed the policies pursued by a number of European countries and carefully avoided statements favoring any particular system. It did, however, produce some basic principles that it felt any policy should follow.
1. Savings should be blocked for some period of time;
2. Government encouragement to asset formation via capital premiums was considered preferable to tax exemptions, which were felt to benefit relatively high-income groups the most;
3. In view of the policy's social objectives, there should be a ceiling either on savers' income or on the amount of savings receiving favorable treatment; and
4. Any policy should be interlinked with general policies on wages and inflation.

The report also examined the issue of the more traditional forms of profit sharing and share ownership and mentioned the latter without committing itself either for or against it. The report merely mentioned union opposition to it on double-risk grounds and looked more favorably at proposals to distribute to employees a certain percentage of a firm's profits. If the EC's policy were to be based on a single company system, it should not discriminate between different categories of workers. The collective fund concept was also mentioned as a possible option, but with no commitment in its favor and no definite proposal on its management structure.

It has been reported that the European Trade Union Confederation has taken a skeptical attitude toward the EC initiative, while the European Employers Federation has given the plans a cautious welcome.[13] The attitude of the latter, however, should be seen in the light of the federation's opposition to any legal imposition of profit sharing. Thus, there does not seem to be strong support for an EC initiative, although the enactment of asset-formation legislation in the Netherlands and in other countries could perhaps stimulate EC interest in sponsoring a program.

---

[13] "Wealth to the Workers," *Economist*, October 16, 1976, p. 71.

CHAPTER XII

Conclusion

Profit-sharing, stock-ownership, and asset-formation plans are thus found in a variety of different environments and serve a range of purposes. In the United States, asset-formation (savings) plans are mainly an addition to the fringe benefit package. In Europe, they are sometimes a means by which governments seek to influence the savings patterns of employees. In neither context are they a source of major controversy in their own right. Judgments on the degree to which they meet their different aims are not easy to make. As an aid to saving, they are clearly a positive factor, albeit, in view of the amounts of money involved, a relatively marginal one. The impact of any single fringe benefit, separated from the total compensation policy of a company, is almost impossible to determine. The force of example and the relatively low cost to companies seem to have helped the spread of savings and thrift plans in the United States.

Profit-sharing and stock-ownership plans go beyond a mere fringe benefit. They constitute an ideological policy based on underlying assumptions and values about the operation of a economic system. Two fundamental aspects of the capitalist economic system are the generation of profits and the use of shareholder funding. Company plans are not only based on the desirability of these aspects but also on the desirability of imbuing the employees with the values that underpin the economic system. The success varies among countries. It seems clear that plans have been most successful in the United States and Germany and least successful in a number of countries where the capitalist system has been considerably modified and where employers no longer appear to feel confident in actively proclaiming the values of that system.

Profit sharing further seeks to stress the common interest of employees and employers in the successful operation of their businesses. It is apparent that few would deny that there are some common interests between the two groups. The problem is that profit sharing sometimes appears to seek to deny that there are also antagonistic interests. This criticism cannot validly be leveled at the more sophisticated supporters of profit sharing, such as the Profit Sharing Research Foundation. Moreover, many companies that have achieved commercial success have been able to make their profit-sharing plans sufficiently attractive to appear to be a clear aid to employee performance.

In many respects, the major benefit to employers from profit sharing lies in its perceived impact on employee attitudes. It is often believed that, under an arrangement that transfers to them a portion of profits, employees will feel that they are being more fairly treated, and that they are more fully participating in their company. The gains that companies expect to secure from profit sharing, such as higher productivity and better labor relations, are dependent on the plans' modifying employee attitudes. This makes the attainment of the employers' objective heavily dependent on convincing employees of the value of profit sharing and on making them aware of the relation of their own work effort to the company's results.

Doubts over the impact of profit-sharing plans on individual employees have caused some companies to abandon plans. General Electric operated profit-sharing plans between 1915 and 1932 and again from 1934 to 1967. The attitude of General Electric management was summed up in the following way:

> Our experience with profit sharing plans in General Electric demonstrated that many an individual employee seemed to realize that his performance on the job had little or no effect on what he got from the general profit sharing plan. He apparently felt that fellow workers who were slack on their jobs seemed to enjoy about the same profits from a general profit sharing plan as workers who were efficient. Thus the plan tended to kill rather than create individual incentive.[1]

IBM's attitude toward profit sharing seems similarly based on the view that such plans do little to motivate individual employees. IBM believes firmly that, beyond minimum compensation, employees should be paid according to their performance as individuals. IBM, therefore, avoids any means of payment based on an automatic formula that would fail to differentiate between employees. It seems possible to argue that smaller companies might experience more positive results from profit sharing. The doubts of companies such as IBM lie in the practical aspects of profit sharing's performance rather than in any objection to its ideological base.

This indeed is a typical situation in the United States, where company profit sharing is a thriving reality; it not only is widely

---

[1] General Electric, *Super News*, Vol. IV, No. 26 (October 3, 1961), p. 1.

Conclusion

accepted but has had a significant financial impact on employees. In Europe, except for Germany, profit sharing has not gained the same level of acceptance, nor has it involved as large a sum of money as in the United States. In the United States, the range of pretax profits that are shared falls usually in the range of 10 to 24 percent.[2] In Europe, this level is rarely attained.

The United States is a profoundly individualistic country. Its history and its pattern of immigration have reinforced this. Indeed, it is interesting to speculate on the social and political attitudes of Europeans who chose to come to America. It might seem possible to argue that those who came were more individualistic and more personally ambitious than those who stayed behind. Whether this has been a factor or not, Europe has developed a much more collectivist outlook. This outlook has been reinforced by the much stronger class consciousness of Europeans. Class, too, is often seen as an inherent social fact, which is unchanged by economic status; Americans, however, see class more typically in terms of income alone. The strength of class boundaries in Europe, particularly between the elite and other groups in different countries, is much greater than in the United States and can less readily be overcome by economic success.

Many American companies covered by our inquiry have been confronted with the decision of whether to extend profit sharing to their overseas subsidiaries. The reaction has been mixed. Some companies, such as Sears Roebuck, consider profit sharing such a basic element of their philosophy that they would not contemplate being without profit-sharing plans abroad. Other companies either have decided that it would not be appropriate to export profit sharing or have encountered difficulties when they attempted to do so.

One major problem in Europe has been the failure of some countries to provide sufficient tax advantages to make profit-sharing plans attractive to companies and their employees. It has been fundamental to the growth of profit sharing in the United States that such plans attract taxation benefits. This has not always occurred in Europe. In countries where there is a legislative framework for profit sharing, such as France, it may prove difficult to operate a plan that has a different form from that envisioned by the legislation, and such a policy may not accord with the company's aims. There can also be problems where foreign subsidiaries are small or

---

[2] Profit Sharing Council of America, *Guide to Modern Profit Sharing* (Chicago, 1973), pp. 52-53.

cannot fairly be considered as separate profit centers. In this case, to base the calculations for profit sharing on the subsidiary alone may pose problems, and if the base is small, slight fluctuations may have a disproportionate effect on the amount of profit available to be shared.

There is a range of problems associated with the wide role of trade unions in many European countries. There is a tendency for profit-sharing companies that are nonunion in the United States to find that profit sharing in a unionized environment overseas raises different issues. In many cases, companies may not wish to bargain over profit sharing but may find that it is not easy to resist efforts by unions to secure a say in this area. In many countries, there are legislative rules on the content of collective bargaining that may make it difficult for a company to maintain unilateral control over its plan.

Profit sharing on an individual company basis involves the possibility of differential rewards for employees of companies whose profitability varies. This is, of course, inherent in the concept of profit sharing. Yet, this possibility flies in the face of the egalitarian views on income distribution held by trade unions, and indeed by others, in many European countries. In Sweden, rejection of company profit sharing in favor of a collective approach is explicitly based on this attitude. In this regard, it is interesting to relate attitudes toward profit sharing to the structure of income distribution in society. A recent study by Sawyer shows that, among members of the Organization for Economic Cooperation and Development, Sweden is the country with the most even spread of income.[3] Its closest rivals among the countries we have examined are the United Kingdom and Belgium. All three countries are distinguished by a relative lack of interest in profit sharing. The most uneven distribution of income occurs in France and the United States, and the latter is one of the few countries to have witnessed no major trend toward equalization over recent years.[4] The role of both countries in relation to profit sharing has been more favorable than in the first group of countries.

One problem for companies may be the very fact that profit sharing focuses attention on profits. In the United States, this focus is the very intention of profit sharing. In Europe, however, many unions are explicitly opposed to the capitalist profit motive, and other unions may implicitly consider that profits are in some sense

---

[3] Malcolm Sawyer, *Income Distribution in OECD Countries* (Paris: Organization for Economic Cooperation and Development, 1976).
[4] *Ibid.*, pp. 26–29.

not legitimate. High profits may therefore be, not a goal to be attained, but a target to be attacked.

There can be other difficulties. The use of profit sharing may draw added attention to the accounting policies of multinational companies. It was recently reported, for instance, that Chase Manhattan Bank was facing criticism from its French employees that they were not receiving as much as they should from the profit-sharing plan because Chase was transferring funds from France to the United States to reduce its tax liability.[5]

In order to have profit sharing, one needs profits. This statement might seem trite, but in Europe, many employees work in the public sector, where there are no profits to share, and their views can have a strong influence over general trade union policy. Even within the private sector, companies with low profits are unlikely to prove successful profit sharers. In the United States as well, adverse experience with one company in the field of profit sharing may affect attitudes in another company. Thus, one company found that only two of the unionized plants that it purchased rejected its profit-sharing plan. Both of these plants were organized by unions that drew their unfavorable view from their experiences with profit sharing at other companies. Adverse experience with a profit-sharing plan can occasionally lead to direct industrial conflict. For example, difficulties with the Kellogg's profit-sharing plan led to a strike at the company's cereal plant in Battle Creek, Michigan, in October 1978.[6]

In the United States, some unions have not been keen to become embroiled in management decision making. In some cases, such unions have considered profit sharing as posing an insoluble dilemma. This attitude was most effectively summarized by Marvin Miller, former assistant to the president of the United Steelworkers of America, in 1964:

> It seems to me that a union which accepts a profit sharing plan gets itself into this position: either it must demand a voice in areas where it has never demanded a voice before and where in general it does not want a voice: or it must be willing to have its return for its employees under that plan regulated unilaterally by company decisions.... the Steelworkers Union is not interested in doing either.[7]

---

[5] "An Overseas Tax Ploy Irks Chase Employees," *Business Week*, October 2, 1978, p. 95.

[6] "Kellogg Co. Estimates Unauthorized Strike Cut Plant Output 90%," *Wall Street Journal*, October 18, 1978, p. 5.

[7] Statement of Marvin Miller, then assistant to the president of the United Steelworkers of America, before the National Industrial Conference Board meeting of January 16, 1964.

Despite this attitude, there is a risk for employers that a collectively bargained profit-sharing plan might lead to the union's demanding more influence over the decisions that affect profits. When the United Automobile Workers put forward profit-sharing proposals to the auto companies in 1958, the business community was suspicious of the union's motives, which they saw as involving an attempt to secure indirectly a role in managerial decisions.[8] It may not be necessary to go as far as this in order to believe that, when profit sharing becomes a subject for collective bargaining, this may lead to an increased union interest in business decisions. The whole purpose of collective bargaining is to limit managerial freedom of action, and in the field of profit sharing, this could have far-reaching ramifications.

Although profit sharing can develop in the direction of greater union and employee influence over managerial policy, this is not an inherent part of its impact. It is often claimed that profit sharing increases employee involvement and democracy at the workplace. Any definition of democracy, however, must include the concept of having a voice in the determination of important decisions. On this basis, a unilateral company profit-sharing plan adds nothing to industrial democracy.

Indeed in Europe, one of the spurs to collective investment funds lies in the belief that they are a democratizing force in industry, which individual plans are not. In many cases, whether one believes this depends on whether one thinks that unions are genuine representative organizations, the extension of whose influence also involves the extension of employee influence. In Europe, industrial democracy has often come to be equated with an increased role for unions, and the proposals for collective investment funds flow from this.

There has been considerable debate on the impact of profit sharing. It is difficult to isolate the variables and impossible to quantify the issue. On a macroeconomic level, it would seem that, as long as it is on a deferred basis, profit sharing has a beneficial, but marginal, effect on the rate of savings in the economy. Stock-ownership plans also have the effect of spreading direct involvement in investment at company level but are also marginal in their impact.

Collective funds would certainly represent an important accretion of power to trade unions, but how far-reaching their economic effects would be is less clear. Unions are generally cautious investors

---

[8] U.S. Chamber of Commerce, Economic Research Department, *Reuther's Profit-Sharing Demand* (Washington, D.C., 1958).

Conclusion

of their own assets.⁹ If this attitude extends to collective funds, unions might merely end up investing in a manner similar to other institutional investors, such as pension funds and insurance companies. The innate conservatism of these bodies may have been a restraint on economic growth, and collective funds might suffer from the same problem, although the beneficial effects of any application of additional investment funds might outweigh this.

In any case, the criticism of such funds is not generally made on this basis. It is the aspect of economic power that is central. It has been rare for unions to use their influence over pension funds and other resources to effect changes, but instances have been increasing. In the United States, the campaign by the Amalgamated Clothing and Textile Workers Union to organize the J. P. Stevens Company led to union threats to withdraw its funds from Manufacturers Hanover Trust Company.¹⁰ In Europe, union-influenced pension funds in countries such as Sweden and Germany have considerable economic power. Apart from specific cases, such as J. P. Stevens, it is not always clear what unions could do with their investments that would significantly undermine the economic system or increase union power. The avoidance of particular types of investments—for example, in companies with interests in South Africa—is often cited as a potential example of union pressure. Yet, much of the activity on this front has come from non-trade union groups, even though the issue is one that unites unions of many different persuasions. The use of economic power to encourage union recognition may be a potential factor in the United States, but in Europe, where unionization is much heavier, it seems unlikely to be a major facet of the policies of collective funds.

The possibility has been raised that collective funds will be tempted to place investments in accordance with social, rather than economic, criteria, a criticism leveled by employers in countries such as Denmark. The funds would, however, probably face the same pressures as pension funds to avoid bad investment risks, although the possibility of "social" investments seems real. Once again, the attitude toward such investments depends partly on one's political values. That a part of an investment portfolio should be set aside for social purposes is a policy demand increasingly being made on other investment institutions. There is clearly a limit

---

⁹ Geoff Latta, "Trade Union Finance," *British Journal of Industrial Relations,* Vol. X, No. 3 (November 1972); Leo Troy, "American Unions and their Wealth," *Industrial Relations,* Vol. 14, No. 2 (May 1975).

¹⁰ "Today Manny Hanny, Tomorrow the World?" *Forbes,* March 20, 1978, pp. 37-39.

to the degree to which this can be followed without significantly lowering investment return.

Whether the funds will lead to a major shift of economic power is not clear. In many cases, institutions already own large parts of companies, and there has been some growing criticism of this situation, which is advanced further in Europe than in the United States.[11] The intervention of pension funds in matters such as takeovers and mergers has begun to curtail managerial freedom of action. On one level, collective funds would provide an additional element of strength to unions in these situations. At another level, however, the steady growth of collective fund holdings, envisioned in countries such as Sweden and Germany, would transfer economic control of private companies to a mixture of institutions, where union influence either could be strong, as in pension funds, or could be dominant, as in collective funds. In this context, the political battle over investment funds is a battle over the ultimate nature of the economic system. In Europe, that system has profoundly changed, although the effects of this change have not always been totally realized. The concepts of individual entrepreneurship and private individual shareholding are increasingly under attack.

The Marxist analysis of capitalism has always proposed the view that the system would be destroyed as a result of its own internal contradictions. It would be ironic if this destruction took the form of institutional control of companies through a lack of discrimination in the raising of capital. This growth of "collective control" might have a number of results, but much would depend on whether the collective funds sought to apply their power as shareholders to the running of companies. The decline of shareholders' control over companies has been widely seen as a major trend of the twentieth century and has led to the development of concepts such as the "managerial revolution." The growth of institutional shareholding could reverse this trend and impose considerable limitations on managerial freedom of action. It is not yet clear that institutional investors either recognize their power or wish to exercise it, but the potential very obviously exists. What that potential is for, is less clear. As the *Economist* of London commented about British pension funds, "Their potential power has more in common with the corporate than with the socialist state."[12] This may also be the result with collective funds. Power is likely to accrue to investment managers and advisers, and it is not certain that lay trade unionists will

---

[11] "A Private Corporate State," *Economist*, November 4-10, 1978, pp. 11-15.
[12] *Ibid.*, p. 11.

Conclusion

be able to control this process. The issue of accountability of fund managers may arise in a sharp form as their power increases. In theory, however, collective funds represent a great addition to union power.

An actual appraisal of the collective fund concept in practice cannot, of course, be made until such plans have operated for some period of time. The VAD plan is therefore likely to be the focus of much attention.

The verdict on individual profit sharing draws on a wider range of experience, but this does not increase its decisiveness. The subject has been studied most frequently by those with an interest in finding for or against profit sharing, and verdicts have often been made in black and white terms. The truth seems somewhere between the two extremes. In some situations, profit sharing has met the objectives that companies set out to achieve. In other situations, it has been less successful. Its success is integrally related to the economic and social structures of particular countries, and this creates its diversity.

Although it is possible that phenomena may exist that no longer serve any perceived needs, the widespread use of profit sharing in the United States suggests that it does meet the aims of companies and serves as a valued fringe benefit to employees. Any judgment on profit sharing in Europe must take into account the significant degree of political opposition to individual profit-sharing plans. Employees are, of course, unlikely to refuse a payment that they see as additional to normal remuneration; however, acceptance of the payment does not necessarily imply support for the policy underlying it. Many European workers have shown a marked reluctance in their personal investment decisions to assume the risks inherent in share ownership. This risk is basically a function of profits, and in Europe, employees seem to see in profits little relevance to themselves. In the United States, much closer interest has been evinced. The increasing divergence between economic and social conditions of the United States and Europe has had a profound impact on profit sharing. It requires from companies that seek to implement such plans in Europe a degree of caution greater than that required in implementing plans in the United States.

Appendix

A number of countries outside of Western Europe and North America have had considerable experience with profit sharing. This experience is briefly summarized here.

VENEZUELA

The information in this section is based on a study by Cecilia M. Valente, *The Political, Economic, and Labor Climate in Venezuela.*[1] In Venezuela, legislative provision for profit sharing was first enacted in 1936 and is now regulated by the 1975 Ley del Trabajo. The law provides for annual bonus payments, which are referred to as *utilidades.* Each enterprise has to distribute 10 percent of net profits to workers each year, and the payment must constitute at least fifteen days' pay but should not exceed two months' pay. If a company takes a loss in a particular year, it may still be ordered by the federal executive to make a payment to its employees.

The calculation of net profits in principle allows certain deductions for general business expenses and interest. Some expenses are not always allowable as deductions, including contingency expenses and provision for income taxes and legal reserves.

The payment is allocated to each employee in relation to his salary level. The law decrees that 75 percent of the payment is made directly to the employee, while the remaining 25 percent is deposited in a bank account in the employee's name. This latter part of the profit-sharing payment can only be withdrawn after five years or when the amount in the account reaches B 2,000 ($466).[2] Certain exceptions are allowed in the event of permanent disability or house purchase.

Some collective agreements also make provision for profit-sharing payments, which as a result can exceed the maximum level laid down by the legislation. In 1977, for example, an agreement between the metalworkers' federation (FETRAMETAL) and the Mack Truck Company established annual payments of sixty-five days' wages per worker. Insofar as such payments are provided on a guaranteed basis, the plans clearly can no longer be regarded as genuine profit-sharing plans. A Ministry of Labor study in Venezuela concluded that, in practice, "worker-distributed profits are directly related to actual net income only in the case of a small proportion of firms."[3]

---

[1] Cecilia M. Valente, *The Political, Economic, and Labor Climate in Venezuela,* Latin American Studies, No. 4d (Philadelphia: Industrial Research Unit, The Wharton School, University of Pennsylvania, 1979).

[2] The exchange rate used is $1 = B 4.29 as of April 10, 1979.

[3] Valente, *The Political, Economic, and Labor Climate in Venezuela,* p. 138.

An analysis of profit-sharing payments by sector in 1976 showed that the average payment per employee ranged from B 481 ($112) in personal services to B 5,995 ($1,400) in the petroleum industry. Slightly over two-thirds of industries fell in the range of B 1,000 ($233) to B 3,000 ($699).

MEXICO

The information in this section is drawn from *The Political, Economic, and Labor Climate in Mexico*, by James L. Schlagheck.[4] Since 1963, companies in Mexico have been obliged by law to distribute a portion of their annual profits to their employees. The amount of the collective share is set by the tripartite National Committee on Profit Sharing. In 1977, this amount was set at 8 percent of taxable corporate income. Profits are defined in a broad manner with limited exclusions only for pension fund earnings, dividends, and certain gains from the exchange or sale of corporate securities. A company cannot offset a "loss" year against a "profit" year.

The allocation to each employee is divided into two parts; 50 percent is distributed to employees on the basis of the number of days worked each year, and 50 percent, on the basis of salary level. Boards composed of management and labor representatives in equal numbers determine the specific share of each employee. Any dispute at this board level can be referred to the area labor inspector. The payment is made in lump-sum form, with no attempt to block a portion of it for any period of time.

PERU

The information in this section is drawn from *The Political, Economic, and Labor Climate in Peru*, by Nancy R. Johnson.[5] In 1970, the General Law of Industries introduced a system of profit sharing and a number of other measures. The law covered all employees with at least three months' service who worked at least four hours a day. Companies were compelled to distribute 15 percent of their pretax income to employees collectively in the form of shares in the enterprise and an additional 10 percent of pretax income in the form of cash. It was intended that total employee share

---

[4] James L. Schlagheck, *The Political, Economic, and Labor Climate in Mexico*, Latin American Studies, No. 4b (Philadelphia: Industrial Research Unit, The Wharton School, University of Pennsylvania, 1977).

[5] Nancy R. Johnson, *The Political, Economic, and Labor Climate in Peru*, Latin American Studies, No. 4c (Philadelphia: Industrial Research Unit, The Wharton School, University of Pennsylvania, 1978).

ownership should build up to a level of 50 percent of total company equity. The law was part of a general attempt to introduce a large measure of employee control over the management of companies.

This radical system was modified in February 1977, primarily to reduce the potential for employee shareholders to secure ownership of a company. The 15 percent distribution was no longer to be in the form of regular voting shares in the company. The distribution was split into two parts, 13.5 percent of income going in the form of nonvoting shares and 1.5 percent in cash. Moreover, the share allocation was to be made on an individual basis instead of a collective basis. Workers could sell their shares after six years. In addition, the maximum share of a company's equity permitted to employees was decreased from 50 percent to 33.3 percent.

In 1979, the law was again weakened, by Decree Law 22229. One-half of the 13.5 percent of income allocated to shares must in the future be paid in company shares, and the other half can be allocated to a range of investment options from which the individual worker can select. Workers can also sell shares freely without any blocking period.

CHILE

Industrial and commercial companies must set aside 10 percent of their net taxable profits for distribution to blue-collar workers.[6] The profit to be distributed is that amount which exceeds 10 percent of net worth. This profit share *(participación en las utilidades)* cannot exceed 6 percent of an individual worker's annual wages. The payment can only be made to employees who are members of a legally recognized trade union. One-half of this payment is distributed to the union to finance a range of welfare provisions. The other half is distributed to union members who have worked at least 70 percent of the working days in the year.

These provisions do not apply to corporations *(sociedades anónimas)*, which must set aside 6 percent of their capital in the form of shares, which are paid over to the union.

There is also a system known as the *gratificación annual*. In essence, this is a bonus of 20 percent of net taxable profits, as defined above. The bonus for each employee is limited to 25 percent of the annual salary and also may not exceed 4.75 times the minimum wage. In the provinces of Tarapacá, Antofagasta, and Magallanes, this limit is 25 percent higher.

[6] Organization of American States, *A Statement of the Laws of Chile in Matters Affecting Business* (Washington, D.C., 1977), pp. 148–49.

An employer can avoid the obligation to relate payments to profits by agreeing to pay a bonus to employees equal to 25 percent of salaries.

JAPAN

The information in this section is based on "Industrial Relations in Japan: A Summary Analysis," by Herbert R. Northrup.[7] Profit-sharing plans are not, in a formal sense, common in Japan, although it is normal for companies to provide large semiannual cash bonuses to employees, and these are based largely on profits.

Employee stock-ownership plans are far more common, and 61.6 percent of all companies and 81.1 percent of companies listed on the stock exchange with over five thousand employees have such plans. Most companies that have such plans encourage employees to form a stockholders' society, which in a unionized firm is usually done by agreement with the union. The company often provides financial assistance to the stockholders' association in the form of payment of administrative expenses and broker's fees.

Employees who wish to purchase stock can allocate a certain amount of their income for this purpose, and some companies will supplement the employee contribution. For instance, Nissan Motor Company and Sharp Electronics both provide shares worth 5 percent of the value of shares purchased by the employee. Matsushita Electrical contributes 20 percent of the cost of all stock allocated to employees.

Many large companies in Japan also provide assistance to employee savings. The companies act as banks for employee savings but pay a rate of interest above that which would be offered by commercial banks. The plans are heavily concentrated in large companies. In 1976, a Ministry of Labor survey showed that less than 2 percent of all companies had such plans, but these companies employed 6.5 million workers, or around 16 percent of employees covered by the survey. There is some evidence of a decline in interest in such plans. Sharp, for instance, is one company that discontinued its plan by agreement with the union soon after it established its stock-ownership plan.

---

[7] Herbert R. Northrup, "Industrial Relations in Japan: A Summary Analysis," Paper prepared for the Japan Society (Philadelphia: Industrial Research Unit, The Wharton School, University of Pennsylvania, 1978.)

Index

AB Sveriges Investeringsbank, 93
Accelerated Capital Formation Bill. See entry under United States
Accord de participation, 149, 157
Accord dérogatoire, 149
Adam, Hermann, 80n
Adler, M. J., 48n
AEG-Telefunken, 82
AFL-CIO, 58
Air France, 154
Aktiengesellschaften, 76
Aktiengesetz, 81
Akzo, 113, 115
Albeda, Willem, 122-23
Alfa Romeo, 66
Allied Breweries, 129, 130
Amalgamated Clothing and Textile Workers' Union, 22, 173
AMC. See American Motors Corporation
Amdur, James A., 31n, 32n
American Brands, 6
American Federation of Labor, 15, 24. See also AFL-CIO
American Free Enterprise System, 4
American Motors Corporation, 25-26
Amsted Industries, 55
Antofagasta, 182
Arbeitsgemeinschaft zur Förderung der Partnerschaft in der Wirtschaft, 84
A/S Atlas, 94
Asset-formation plans, 1-2, 7-8. See also Collective asset formation; Employee savings plans; European Community, asset-formation plans; France, employee savings plans; Germany, asset-formation plans; Netherlands, employee savings plans
  aim, 8
  definition, 7
  ideological basis, 1-2
Association for the Promotion of Profit Sharing. See entry under United States

Backaus, Karl, 82
Bank America, 23
Bank of Ireland, 164
Bankers Trust Company, 29, 38n, 62n
  and studies on employee savings plans, 36-44

Banque Nationale de Paris, 144, 154
Barclays Bank, 128, 131, 132
Barkin, Solomon, 84n, 85n, 86n, 118n, 164n
BASF AG, 74, 82
Bayer AG, 74, 82
Joh. Friedrich Behrens, 82
Belgium, 160
  Christian and Socialist union federations, 65
  income distribution, 170
  profit-sharing plans, 163
  Protestant union federations, 65
Bell, D. Wallace, 129n, 130n, 137n
Bell and Howell, 22
Bennett, Keith W., 56n
Bergeron, André, 146n
Bergounioux, Alain, 146n
Betriebsräte,
  defined, 75
BICC, 137
Binns, W. Gordon, Jr., 51n
Bloom, Gordon F., 3
Blue Circle Group, 128, 130
BOC International, 137
Boots Limited, 128, 130
British Institute of Management, 140
British Leyland, 66
Brooke Bond Liebig, 129
"Brother-sister" corporations, 53
Brotherhood of Railway Clerks, 59
Brower, F. Beatrice, 17n
Bundestag, 89
Burck, Charles G., 55n, 58n, 62n
Bureau of Labor Statistics. See entry under United States
Burlington Industries, 18
Burritt, Arthur W., 15n, 16n
Burrows, A. C., 4n
Bushman, Ronald M., 49n, 57n, 61n

Capital gains, 46. See also Employee savings plans, tax considerations; Employee stock-ownership plans, tax considerations; Profit-sharing plans, tax considerations
Capital-sharing plans. See Profit-sharing plans
Carlsson, Torsten, 101n
Carter Hawley Hale Stores, 22, 23
CBI. See Confederation of British Industry

183

CDU. *See* Germany, Christian Democrats
Centre d'Etude des Revenus et des Coûts, 149, 151, 155
Centrist parties, 7
CERC. *See* Centre d'Etude des Revenus et des Coûts
CFDT. *See* Confédération Française Démocratique du Travail
CFP. *See* Compagnie Française des Pétroles
CFTC. *See* Confédération Française des Travailleurs Chrétiens
CGC. *See* Confédération Générale des Cadres
CGIL. *See* Confederazione Generale Italiana del Lavoro
CGT. *See* Confédération Générale du Travail
Chase Manhattan Bank, 21, 23, 171
Chile,
profit-sharing plans, 181–82
Christelijk Nationaal Vakverbond, 65, 114–15, 118
Christian Democrat party. *See* entry under Germany; Italy; Netherlands
Ciba-Geigy, 161
CISL. *See* Confederazione Italiana Sindacati Lavoratori
Clark, Pauline, 140n
Class vesting, 41–42. *See also* United States, Employee Retirement Income Security Act
CNV. *See* Christelijk Nationaal Vakverbond
Codetermination, 70, 75, 96
Collective asset formation, 8–9, 172–74. *See also* entry under Denmark; European Community; Germany; Sweden; United Kingdom; Vermogensaanwasdeling plan
Colletti, Jerome A., 24n
Comités d'entreprise, 149
Commissariat Général du Plan, 149
Commission de conciliation, 153
Commission de participation, 152–53
Communism,
and profit sharing, 4
Communist party. *See* entry under France; Italy
Compagnie Française de Pétroles, 68, 144
Companies Act of 1948. *See* entry under United Kingdom
Confederation of British Industry, 140
Confédération Française Démocratique du Travail, 145–47, 155, 156

Confédération Française des Travailleurs Chrétiens, 146, 148, 152n, 156
Confédération Générale des Cadres, 146, 155
Confédération Générale du Travail, 3, 65, 145, 155, 156, 159
Confédération Nationale du Patronat Français, 156
Confederazione Générale Italiana del Lavoro, 3, 65, 145, 164
Confederazione Italiana Sindacati Lavoratori, 65, 164
Conference Board. *See* entry under United States
Congress of Industrial Organizations, 25. *See also* AFL-CIO
Congress of Trade Unions. *See* entry under Ireland
ConRail. *See* Consolidated Rail Corporation
Conseil de surveillance, 150, 152, 157
Conservative party. *See* entry under United Kingdom
Consolidated Rail Corporation, 50
Construction Workers' Union, 85
Constructive receipt, 34
Consultative Document. *See* entry under United Kingdom
Conte, Michael, 61n
Cooper, Walter J., 17n, 18n
Crédit Lyonnais, 144, 154
CSU. *See* Germany, Christian Social Union
Cullingford, E.C.M., 75n, 85n
Curran, Joseph, 59
Czarnecki, Edgar R., 5n, 26n

DA. *See* Dansk Arbejdsgiverforening
Dáil Éireann, 66
Daimler-Benz AG, 74, 82
Danish Bank Rate, 94
Danish Companies Act, 97
Danish Parliament. *See* Denmark, Folketing
Danish Union of Engineering Workers, 95, 96
Dansk Arbejdsgiverforening, 95, 99n, 100n
Dart Industries, 19
Delouvrier, Paul, 158
Denmark, 9
central fund, 97–99
collective asset formation, 95–101
economic characteristics, 91–94
"Employees' Investment and Dividend Fund," 96

Index

Folketing, 96, 98, 100
Gross Domestic Product, 91
industrial characteristics, 91-94
investment trends, 93-94
"Joint Ownership (Employees) Bill," 96-101
labor force, 91
"Labour Market Supplementary Pension Scheme," 96
level of government consumption, 68
Liberal party, 92, 101
Ministry of Labor, 96n
profit-sharing plans, 94-95
and social criteria for investment of collective funds, 173
Social Democrats, 92, 96, 101
Socialist People's party, 100
and state ownership of companies, 94
taxation, 92
unions, 65, 92. See also Landsorganisationen i Danmark
welfare, 92
Dennis, C.L., 59
Depression, 16
Deutsche Angestellten-Gewerkschaft, 75
Deutsche Beamtenbund, 75
Deutsche Gewerkschaftsbund, 75, 88, 127
DGB. See Deutsche Gewerkschaftsbund
"DM 312" Act. See Germany, First Asset Formation Act
DSM NV, 68, 113

Eastman Kodak, 5, 15, 22, 23, 130
  Savings and Investment Plan, 11, 14
  Wage Dividend Plan, 11
EC. See European Community
Electricité de France, 158
Elf Aquitaine, 68, 144
Elliott, John, 132n, 140n, 141n, 142n
Emmet, Boris, 5n, 15n
Employee Retirement Income Security Act. See entry under United States
Employee savings plans, 28-45. See also asset-formation plans
  benefits of plans, 44-45
  contribution investment, 40
  cost to employer, 31, 39
  employee contributions, 38
  employee eligibility, 36-37
  employer contributions, 38-39
  lump-sum distribution, 34-35
  number in U.S., 29-31
  as money-purchase pension plans, 31
  and profit-sharing plans, 29, 31, 32
  and separation from service, 34-35
  and stock-bonus plans, 31
  and stock-ownership plans, 28-29
  tax considerations, 34-35, 36
  vesting provisions, 41-42
"Employees' Investment and Dividend Fund." See entry under Denmark
Employee stock-ownership plans, 1, 6-7, 46-62, 71, 167, 175. See also Employee savings plans; France, share ownership; Germany, share ownership; Japan, employee stock-ownership plans; United Kingdom, share ownership
  for acquisitions, 55
  advantages, 54-56, 60-62
  aim, 7
  and capital-intensive companies, 61-62
  and closely held companies, 57
  and collective bargaining, 59-60
  and company's fiduciary duty, 57
  and corporate financing, 47, 50, 51, 62
  definition, 6
  development of, 48-54
  disadvantages, 56-58, 60-62
  and double risk to employees, 7, 56
  effect on employees, 15-16, 54
  and employee savings plans, 28-29
  ideological basis, 6-7, 167
  for improving cash flow, 54
  and Internal Revenue Code qualifications, 49
  and labor-intensive companies, 61-62
  and leverage, 47, 56
  number in U.S., 48-49
  proposed U.S. legislative changes, 59-60
  and publicly owned companies, 57
  for refinancing debts, 54
  for spinning off subsidiaries, 55
  tax considerations, 49, 51-57
  tax-exempt trust, 47
  for transfer of stock ownership, 55-56
  and union attitudes, 58-59
  and unionization, 58-59
  U.S. legislative definition, 49-54
  vesting provisions, 52, 56, 60
Employee stock-ownership trusts, 47, 50, 51, 52, 54, 55, 56, 60
  credit relation to ESOPs, 51
  limits on debt, 50
Employer securities, 50, 52
  and special tax treatment, 35-36
Engen, Gunnar, 18n, 23n
Enka Glanzstoff, 115

ERISA. See United States, Employee Retirement Income Security Act
ESOPs. See Employee stock-ownership plans
ESOTs. See Employee stock-ownership trusts
Estel, NV, 113
E-Systems, 59, 62
Europe, 3, 6, 7, 8
 collectivist outlook, 169
 and implementation of profit-sharing plans, 169-70
 levels of government consumption, 66-67
 and profit sharing, 63-73, 167-75
 size and character of unions, 63-66
 structure of labor force, 69-70
European Commission. See entry under European Community
European Community, 68, 73, 91, 144, 159, 160-61, 165-66
 asset-formation plans, 165-66
 collective asset formation, 166
 European Commission, 165
European Metalworkers' Federation, 73
European Trade Union Confederation, 73, 166
Exxon, 29
 Thrift Plan, 32-33, 45

Fälldin, Thorbjörn, 107
Fannin, Paul, 59
FCP. See Fonds commun de placement
FDP. See Germany, Free Democrats
Federal Social Security Court. See entry under Germany
Federatie Nederlandse Vakbeweging, 65, 114, 121, 124
Federation of Migros Cooperatives, 161-62
Ferodo, 153
FETRAMETAL, 179
Finance Act of 1966. See entry under United Kingdom
Finance Act of 1973. See entry under United Kingdom
Finance Act of 1978. See entry under United Kingdom
Finance Court. See entry under Germany
Firestone, 116
First Asset Formation Act. See entry under Germany
Flanders, Allan, 129n
FNV. See Federatie Nederlandse Vakbeweging
FO. See Force Ouvrière

Fonds commun de placement, 150, 155, 157
Force Ouvrière, 146-47, 155, 159
Forsebäck, Lennart, 103n
Fortune, 54
Fox, Harland, 29n, 46n
France, 144-59, 160, 169
 Catholic union federation, 146
 Communist party, 65. 145
 economic characteristics, 144
 employee savings plans, 156-57
 Gross Domestic Product, 144
 and income distribution, 170
 industrial characteristics, 144
 Labor Code, 148, 152
 level of government consumption, 144
 Ministry of Economics and Finance, 149
 Ministry of Labor, 149, 150n, 152, 153n, 156n
 profit-sharing legislation, 147-56
 profit-sharing plans, 151-52, 155
 and share ownership, 71
 and state ownership of companies, 66, 68, 144
 trade unions and politics, 145-47
 union federations, 3
 union membership, 63, 146-47
Francis, Bion H., 31n
Free Democrats. See entry under Germany
French Labor Code. See France, Labor Code
Frenzel, Bill, 59

Galbraith, Evan G., 81n
Gallatin, Albert, 14
Gamble-Skogmo, 62
Gaullists, 147, 160
General and Municipal Workers Union. See entry under United Kingdom
General Electric, 25, 168
 Savings and Stock Bonus Plan, 28
General Law of Industries. See entry under Peru
General Motors, 25
 Savings-Stock Purchase Program, 28
Genusscheinen, 162
Germany, 3, 7, 74-90, 144, 167, 169
 asset-formation plans, 84-87
 Christian Democrats, 74, 84, 89
 Christian Social Union, 74, 89
 collective asset formation, 87-89, 173
 economic characteristics, 74
 Federal Social Security Court, 89
 Finance Court, 89
 First Asset Formation Act, 84-85

Index

Free Democrats, 7, 74–75, 86–87, 89
House Savings Law of 1952, 84
industrial characteristics, 74
National Bank Rate, 81
profit-sharing plans, 75–84
Savings Premium Law of 1959, 84
Second Capital Formation Act, 85–86
share ownership, 71–72, 80–81
Social Democrats, 86–89
and state ownership of companies, 74
Third Capital Formation Act, 86–87
unions, 65, 75
Gewerkschaft Öffentliche Dienste, Transport und Verkehr, 88
Gilman, Nicholas Paine, 14
Giscard d'Estaing, Valéry, 158
Gleitzke, Bruno, 84
Gompers, Samuel, 15, 24
Gränges, 105
Gratificación annual, 181
Green, William, 24
Gross Domestic Product, compared among countries, 66–68
Grünbaum, Henry, 95
Guadeloupe, 149
Guinness Group, 164
Guski, Hans-Günter, 76, 84n, 87, 88
Guyane, 149

Hannover, 87
Harp Lager, 164
Hartman, Bart P., 56n
Hearst, Peter, 55n, 61n
Helburn, I. B., 25n
Hesse, 87
Hetter, Patricia, 48n
Hettlage KGaA, 80
Hewitt Associates, 49n, 53–54, 62n
Hoechst AG, 74, 82
Hoesch Werke AG, 113
Hoffmann-LaRoche, 162–63
Hoogendijk, F. A., 125n
Hoogovens BV, 113
House of Fraser, 129, 132, 141–42
House Savings Law of 1952. *See* entry under Germany
Hyatt, James C., 49n, 54n

IBM, 46, 168
ICI. *See* Imperial Chemical Industries
IG Metall. *See* Industriegewerkschaft Metall
Imperial Chemical Industries, 128, 132–36, 142
Industrial democracy, 105
definition, 70
Industrial Participation Association. *See* entry under United Kingdom

Industriegewerkschaft Metall, 75, 77, 86–88
Industrirådet, 95n, 99n
Internal Revenue Code, 17, 31–36, 46, 49, 50, 52. *See also* Internal Revenue Service
Internal Revenue Service, 17, 18, 20–21, 32–33, 38, 43, 46, 57, 58. *See also* Internal Revenue Code
commissioner, 12n, 13n, 20n, 54n
International Labour Organisation, 91n
International Union of Electrical, Radio and Machine Workers, 25
Investment plans. *See* Employee savings plans
IRC. *See* Internal Revenue Code
Ireland, 160, 161
Congress of Trade Unions, 66
income distribution, 68
Labour party, 66
profit-sharing plans, 164–65
union federations, 65–66
union membership, 63
IRI, 68
Irish Distillers, 164
IRS. *See* Internal Revenue Service
Italy, 145, 146, 160, 161
Christian Democrat party, 65
Communist party, 65
income distribution, 68
profit-sharing plans, 163–64
Republican party, 65
Social Democrat party, 65
and state ownership of companies, 68
union federations, 3, 65, 145, 164
union membership, 63

Japan,
employee stock-ownership plans, 182
profit-sharing plans, 182
Javits-Humphrey Employee Stock Ownership Bill, 59
Jefferson, Thomas, 14
Jehring, J. J., 15n
Jewel, 23
Johnson, Nancy R., 180n
S. C. Johnson and Son, 4
Johnston, T. L., 101
"Joint Ownership (Employees) Bill." *See* entry under Denmark
Julliard, Jacques, 146n, 147n

Kampmann, Viggo, 95
Kapitalaufstockungsgesetz of 1959, 76, 81
Kellogg Company, 21, 171
Kelso, Louis O., 48, 59
economic views, 48, 60–61

Kelso, Bangert and Company, 58
Kelso plan, 48
KLM, 113, 116
Knowlton, P. A., 4
Küba Kühlerfabrik, 82
"Labour Market Supplementary Pension Scheme." *See* entry under Denmark
Labour party. *See* entry under Ireland; Netherlands; United Kingdom
Landsorganisationen i Danmark, 95, 96, 98, 99, 100, 101, 127
Landsorganisationen i Sverige, 65, 102, 107, 108-10, 111
wage solidarity policy, 103-4, 105. *See also* Meidner plan
Latta, Geoff, 173n
Laxton, David, 56n
Leber, Georg, 85
Lew, Michael, 57n
Lewis, John L., 25
John Lewis Partnership, 129
Ley del Trabajo of 1975, 179
Liberal party. *See* entry under Denmark; United Kingdom
Lief, Alfred, 15n
Lloyds, 131, 132, 141
LO. *See* Landsorganisationen i Danmark; Landsorganisationen i Sverige
Long, Russell, 48
Lorwin, Val R., 146n
Lower Saxony, 74, 87
Luxembourg, 160, 165
union federations, 65

McGill, Dan M., 31n
McKinsey and Company, 125
Mack Truck Company, 179
McMahon, P. C., 71n
Madison, James, 14
Magallanes, 182
Maire, Edmond, 146n, 147n
Managerial revolution, 174
Mannesman AG, 83
Manufacturers Hanover Trust, 23, 173
Marks and Spencer, 129, 132
Marriott Corporation, 19
Martinique, 149
Matsushita Electrical, 182
Mehr Commission, 107
Meidner, Rudolf, 102-11 passim
Meidner plan, 104-5, 106-7, 108, 109, 110-11, 142
Membership vesting, 42. *See also* United States, Employee Retirement Income Security Act

Metzger, Bert L., 2n, 11, 19n, 21n, 22n, 23, 24n, 54n
Mexico,
National Committee on Profit Sharing, 180
profit-sharing plans, 180
Meyer, Mitchell, 29n, 46n
Michelin, 144
Midkiff, Robert D., 19n
Midland, 131-32
Miller, Marvin, 171
Mitbestimmung, defined, 75
Money-purchase pension plans, 49, 50, 52
Monroe, Paul, 14n
Motorola, 22
Mueller, Rudolph, 81n
Mulach Steel Corporation, 56, 59

National Bank Rate. *See* entry under Germany
National Civic Federation. *See* entry under United States
National Committee on Profit Sharing. *See* entry under Mexico
National Labor Relations (Taft-Hartley) Act. *See* entry under United States
National Maritime Union, 59
National Pensions Insurance Fund. *See* entry under Sweden
National Union of Bank Employees, 131
National Union of Mineworkers, 127
National Westminster Bank, 128, 130
NATO, 91
NCW. *See* Nederlands Christelijk Werkgeversverbond
Nederlands Christelijk Werkgeversverbond, 116
Nederlands Katholiek Vakverbond, 114, 118
Nederlands Verbond van Vakverenigingen, 114-15, 118
Nestlé, 161
Netherlands, 7, 8, 10, 112-25
Catholic People's party, 115
Catholic and Socialist federations, 65, 114, 118
Central Bureau of Statistics, 118
and centralized wage agreements, 113-14
Christian Democrats, 115, 122
collective asset formation. *See* Vermogensaanwasdeling plan
Council of State, 119
economic characteristics, 112
employee savings plans, 117-24

Index

industrial characteristics, 112
Labor party, 115, 122-23
Ministry of Social Affairs, 120, 123
and overseas investment, 113
Parliament, 119
profit-sharing plans, 115-17
Second Chamber, 114-15
and state ownership of companies, 68, 113
union membership, 113-14
New York Stock Exchange, 46
Nilsson, Gunnar, 110
NIPO, 125
Nissan Motor Company, 182
NKV. *See* Nederlands Katholiek Vakverbond
Norgren, Christian, 93n
Norgren, Marie, 93n
Northern Ireland, 128
Northrup, Herbert R., 4, 182n
NUBE. *See* National Union of Bank Employees
NUM. *See* National Union of Mineworkers
NVV. *See* Nederlands Verbond van Vakverenigingen

OCE-Van der Grinten NV, 116
Olsson, Curt G., 101n
Ordonnance No. 67-693, 148
Organization of American States, 181n
Organization for Economic Cooperation and Development, 92n, 93, 112, 170

Pan Am, 58
Parliament. *See* Netherlands; Sweden; United Kingdom
Participación en las utilidades, 181
Peninsula Newspapers, 60
Penn Central, 58
J. C. Penney, 23
Peru,
  Decree Law 22229, 181
  General Law of Industries, 180-81
  profit-sharing plans, 180-81
Petrofina, 163
Peugeot, 144
Philips, 113, 115
Photo-Porst AG, 81, 82
Plaid Cymru. *See* Welsh Nationalist party
Plans d'épargne, 156
Pomeranz, Ruth, 129n
Porst, Hannsheinz, 81
Procter, Colonel William Cooper, 14
Procter & Gamble, 5, 14

Profit sharing,
  attitudes of unions, 24-26, 171-72
  and common interests of employees and employers, 3-4
  definition, 2
  effect on employee attitudes, 5, 15, 27, 168
  ideological opposition in Europe, 68
  ideological support, 2, 3-5, 167. *See also* profit-sharing plans, ideological basis
Profit-sharing companies,
  nature, 23-24
  nonunion status, 5
Profit Sharing Council of America, 11, 20n, 169n
  Planning and Research Committee, 11
  survey of profit-sharing plans, 20-21
Profit-sharing plans, 1-6, 11-27, 52, 167-72, 175. *See also* entry under Belgium; Chile; Denmark; France; Germany; Ireland; Italy; Japan; Mexico; Netherlands; Peru; Sweden; Switzerland; United Kingdom; Venezuela
  administration, 22-23
  deferred plans, 11
  differential rewards for employees, 170
  effect of decline in market values, 18
  employee contributions, 21
  focus on profits, 170-71
  ideological basis, 11, 14-16, 167
  immediate cash plans, 11
  investment policies, 21-22
  legal difficulties, 19
  major difficulties, 171-72
  and power of institutional investors, 174-75
  religious origins, 14
  and retirement income, 20
  tax considerations, 17-18
Profit Sharing Research Foundation, 11, 168
  comparison of profit-sharing and pension plans, 18-19
  study of chain department store industry, 24
PSCA. *See* Profit Sharing Council of America
PSRF. *See* Profit Sharing Research Foundation
Public utilities,
  and employee savings plans, 31

Raad van Overleg Middelbaar en Hoger Personeel, 114

Raspe and Paschen, 82
Regional Rail Reorganization Act. *See* entry under United States
Reilly, Peter A., 130n
Renault, 66, 144, 154
Réserve Spéciale de Participation, 149, 150, 152, 155, 157
Retirement income, 3, 17-18
Reum, Sherry Milliken, 55n
Reum, W. Robert, 55n
Réunion, 149
Reuther, Walter, 59
Revenue Act of 1978. *See* entry under United States
Reynaud, Jean Daniel, 146n
R. J. Reynolds, 19
Rhineland-Palatinate, 87
Ridsdale, Julian, 141
Robinson, Derek, 84n, 85n, 86n, 96n, 118n, 155n, 164n
Roscow, James P., 18n
Rosenthal AG, 80
Rowntree Mackintosh, 129-30
Royal Porcelain Manufacturing, 95
RSP. *See Réserve Spéciale de Participation*
Ryan, John J., 55n

Saarbergwerke AG, 74
SAF. *See* Svenska Arbetsgivareföreningen
Safeway Stores, 22, 23
Salzgitter AG, 74
Samuels, J. M., 71n
Samuelson, Paul A., 48, 60, 61n
San Francisco, 48
SAP. *See* Sweden, Social Democrats
Sapiro, Alan E., 58
"Save As You Earn" plan, 72, 130, 137
Savings plans. *See* Employee savings plans
Savings Premium Law of 1959. *See* entry under Germany
Sawyer, Malcolm, 147n, 170
SAYE. *See* "Save As You Earn" plan
Schiller, Bernt, 98n, 100n
Schlagheck, James L., 180n
Schneider, Hans J., 76
Schotta, Charles, Jr., 23n, 26
Scottish Nationalist party, 128
Sears Roebuck, 3, 5, 15, 18, 19, 20, 23, 169
SEB. *See* Skandinaviska Enskilda Banken
Second Capital Formation Act. *See* entry under Germany
"Second-tier" subsidiaries, 53

Séguy, Georges, 145
Share-ownership plan. *See* Employee stock-ownership plan
Sharp Electronics, 182
Shell, 29, 113
SICAV. *See Société d'investissement à capital variable*
Siemens AG, 74, 82
Signode, 20
Skandinaviska Enskilda Banken, 101-2, 105
Snyder, Linda, 62n
Social Democrat party. *See* entry under Denmark; Germany; Italy; Sweden; United Kingdom
Socialdemokratiska Arbeterpartiet. *See* Sweden, Social Democrats
Socialisme autogestionnaire, 146
Socialist People's party. *See* entry under Denmark
Sociedades anónimas, 181
Société de gestion, 150
Société d'investissement à capital variable, 150, 155
Sociétés anonymes, 154
South Africa, 173
South Bend Lathe, 55, 59
SPD. *See* Germany, Social Democrats
Standard Oil Indiana, 31
Standard Oil of California, 20, 22
Standard Oil of Ohio, 29
Statsföretag AB, 68, 92
J. P. Stevens, 173
Stewart, Bryce M., 17n, 18n
Stock-bonus plans, 46, 47, 50, 52. *See also* Employee stock-ownership plans
Stock-option plans, 46. *See also* Employee stock-ownership plans
Stock-purchase plans, 46, 58. *See also* Employee stock-ownership plans
Sudreau Report, 157-58
Sullivan, Donald E., 57n, 60
Svenska Arbetsgivareföreningen, 101, 104n, 105-7
Svenska Handelsbanken, 102
Sveriges Industriförbund, 105
Sweden, 8
 capital-formation levy, 110
 Center party, 107, 108, 110
 collective asset formation, 102-11, 173
 economic characteristics, 91-94
 Gross Domestic Product, 91
 Gross National Product, 92
 income distribution, 170
 industrial characteristics, 91-94

Index

investment trends, 93–94
labor force, 91
level of government consumption, 68
National Pensions Insurance Fund, 93
Parliament, 109
profit-sharing plans, 101–2
Social Democrats, 92, 93, 107, 108n, 111
and state ownership of companies, 68, 92–93
taxation, 92
union federations, 65, 92
welfare, 92
Swedish Union of Bank Employees, 102
Switzerland, 160
  level of government consumption, 68
  profit-sharing plans, 161–63

Taft-Hartley Act. *See* United States, National Labor Relations (Taft-Hartley) Act
Tannenbaum, Arnold S., 61n
Tappan Company, 19
Tarapacá, 182
Tate and Lyle, 128, 130
Tax Reduction Act of 1975. *See* entry under United States
Tax Reform Act of 1976. *See* entry under United States
Taylor, Paul, 132n
TCO. *See* Tjänstemännens Centralorganisation
Teague, Burton W., 55n, 58n
Texas Instruments, 5
Third Capital Formation Act. *See* entry under Germany
Thomas, Dana L., 48n, 55n, 56n
Thrift plans. *See* Employee savings plans
Thyssen AG, 74, 82
Tjänstemännens Centralorganisation, 111
Towers, Perrin, Forster and Crosby, 60
Trade Act of 1974. *See* entry under United States
Trades Union Congress. *See* entry under United Kingdom
Trade Union Bank, 87
Trade Union Institute of Economic Science, 84
TRAESOPs. *See* United States, Tax Reduction Act ESOPs
Trarieux, Jean-Paul, 155n
Triad Financial Reports, 60
TUC. *See* United Kingdom, Trades Union Congress

UAW. *See* United Automobile Workers

Ullsten, Ola, 111
Ulster Unionists, 128
Unilever, 113, 115
Unione Italiana del Lavoro, 65, 164
United Automobile Workers, 25, 26, 59, 172
United Kingdom, 7, 126–43, 145, 160
  Central Statistical Office, 72
  collective asset formation, 142
  Companies Act of 1948, 133
  Conservative party, 127–28
  Consultative Document, 137–41
  Department of Trade, 70n
  economic characteristics, 126–27
  Finance Act of 1966, 137
  Finance Act of 1973, 137
  Finance Act of 1978, 141–42
  Gross Domestic Product, 126
  General and Municipal Workers Union, 140
  government encouragement of profit sharing, 137–42
  income distribution, 68, 170
  industrial characteristics, 126–27
  Industrial Participation Association, 129n, 132n
  inflation, 126, 127
  Inland Revenue, 136, 137n, 141
  labor force, 91
  Labour party, 8, 128, 141, 142
  Liberal party, 7, 8, 128, 137, 141, 142
  Parliament, 128, 141
  politics, 127–28
  profit-sharing plans, 128–36
  share ownership, 71–72, 136–37
  Social Democratic and Labour party, 128
  and state ownership of companies, 66, 126–27
  Stock Exchange, 72
  strike pattern, 127
  Trades Union Congress, 127, 140, 142, 143
  unions, 65, 127–28
  Wider Share Ownership Council, 7
  Wilson Committee, 142
United Mine Workers, 25
United States, 3, 5, 7, 8, 11–62, 167, 173
  Accelerated Capital Formation Bill, 59
  Association for the Promotion of Profit Sharing, 14
  Bureau of Labor Statistics, 15
  Conference Board, 29
  Congress, 48, 66
  Department of Commerce, 51, 55

Economic Development Administration, 55
Employee Retirement Income Security Act, 11, 19, 29, 37, 41-42, 47, 50-51, 53, 57, 58, 60
employee savings plans. *See* main entry
employee stock-ownership plans. *See* main entry
income distribution, 170
individualistic outlook, 169
Joint Economic Committee, 46n, 48n, 50n, 56n, 59n, 60n
labor force, 69
level of government consumption, 66-67
National Civic Federation, 15, 24n
National Labor Relations (Taft-Hartley) Act, 60, 66
profit-sharing plans. *See* main entry
Regional Rail Reorganization Act, 50, 51
Revenue Act of 1978, 49, 54
Senate Subcommittee of the Committee on Finance. *See* United States, Vandenberg-Herring Subcommittee
Tax Reduction Act ESOPs, 52-54, 62
Tax Reduction Act of 1975, 51-52, 53-54, 62
Tax Reform Act of 1976, 52-54
Trade Act of 1974, 51
Treasury, 46
unions, 66
Vandenberg-Herring Subcommittee, 16, 24, 25n
U.S. Chamber of Commerce, 29, 31n, 172n

United Steelworkers of America, 171
Utilidades, 179

VAD. *See* Vermogensaanwasdeling plan
Valente, Cecilia M., 179
Vandenberg-Herring Subcommittee. *See* entry under United States
Veba AG, 74, 82
Venezuela,
profit-sharing plans, 179-80
Verbond van Nederlandse Ondernemingen, 116, 120-21, 124n, 125
Vermogensaanwasdeling plan, 10, 118-24, 142, 175
VNO. *See* Verbond van Nederlandse Ondernemingen
Volkswagen, 66, 74, 82

Waldenström, Erland, 105-7
Waldenström report, 105-7, 110-11
Walvoord, William, 56n
Wassner, Neil A., 58n, 61n
Welsh Nationalist party, 128
Westinghouse, 25
Wider Share Ownership Council. *See* entry under United Kingdom
Wilson Committee. *See* entry under United Kingdom
Windmuller, John P., 114n
Winn-Dixie Stores, 5, 21, 23
World War I, 15
World War II, 3, 17, 128
Württembergische Bank, 82

Xerox Corporation, 6, 18, 21, 22

Zenith Radio, 6, 18

Racial Policies of American Industry Series

1. *The Negro in the Automobile Industry,*
   by Herbert R. Northrup.   1968
2. *The Negro in the Aerospace Industry,*
   by Herbert R. Northrup.   1968
3. *The Negro in the Steel Industry,* by Richard L. Rowan.   1968
4. *The Negro in the Hotel Industry,* by Edward C. Koziara
   and Karen S. Koziara.   1968
5. *The Negro in the Petroleum Industry,* by Carl B. King
   and Howard W. Risher, Jr.   1969
6. *The Negro in the Rubber Tire Industry,* by Herbert R.
   Northrup and Alan B. Batchelder.   1969
7. *The Negro in the Chemical Industry,*
   by William Howard Quay, Jr.   1969
8. *The Negro in the Paper Industry,* by Herbert R. Northrup.   1969
9. *The Negro in the Banking Industry,*
   by Armand J. Thieblot, Jr.   1970
10. *The Negro in the Public Utility Industries,*
    by Bernard E. Anderson.   1970
11. *The Negro in the Insurance Industry,* by Linda P. Fletcher.   1970
12. *The Negro in the Meat Industry,* by Walter A. Fogel.   1970
13. *The Negro in the Tobacco Industry,*
    by Herbert R. Northrup.   1970
14. *The Negro in the Bituminous Coal Mining Industry,*
    by Darold T. Barnum.   1970
15. *The Negro in the Trucking Industry,* by Richard D. Leone.   1970
16. *The Negro in the Railroad Industry,*
    by Howard W. Risher, Jr.   1971
17. *The Negro in the Shipbuilding Industry,* by Lester Rubin.   1970
18. *The Negro in the Urban Transit Industry,*
    by Philip W. Jeffress.   1970
19. *The Negro in the Lumber Industry,* by John C. Howard.   1970
20. *The Negro in the Textile Industry,* by Richard L. Rowan.   1970
21. *The Negro in the Drug Manufacturing Industry,*
    by F. Marion Fletcher.   1970
22. *The Negro in the Department Store Industry,*
    by Charles R. Perry.   1971
23. *The Negro in the Air Transport Industry,*
    by Herbert R. Northrup et al.   1971
24. *The Negro in the Drugstore Industry,* by F. Marion Fletcher.   1971
25. *The Negro in the Supermarket Industry,*
    by Gordon F. Bloom and F. Marion Fletcher.   1972
26. *The Negro in the Farm Equipment and Construction
    Machinery Industry,* by Robert Ozanne.   1972
27. *The Negro in the Electrical Manufacturing Industry,*
    by Theodore V. Purcell and Daniel P. Mulvey.   1971
28. *The Negro in the Furniture Industry,* by William E. Fulmer.   1973
29. *The Negro in the Longshore Industry,* by Lester Rubin
    and William S. Swift.   1974
30. *The Negro in the Offshore Maritime Industry,*
    by William S. Swift.   1974
31. *The Negro in the Apparel Industry,* by Elaine Gale Wrong.   1974

Order from: Kraus Reprint Co., Route 100, Millwood, New York 10546

STUDIES OF NEGRO EMPLOYMENT

Vol. I. *Negro Employment in Basic Industry: A Study of Racial Policies in Six Industries (Automobile, Aerospace, Steel, Rubber Tires, Petroleum, and Chemicals)*, by Herbert R. Northrup, Richard L. Rowan, et al. 1970. *

Vol. II. *Negro Employment in Finance: A Study of Racial Policies in Banking and Insurance*, by Armand J. Thieblot, Jr., and Linda Pickthorne Fletcher. 1970. *

Vol. III. *Negro Employment in Public Utilities: A Study of Racial Policies in the Electric Power, Gas, and Telephone Industries*, by Bernard E. Anderson. 1970. *

Vol. IV. *Negro Employment in Southern Industry: A Study of Racial Policies in the Paper, Lumber, Tobacco, Coal Mining, and Textile Industries*, by Herbert R. Northrup, Richard L. Rowan, et al. 1971. $13.50

Vol. V. *Negro Employment in Land and Air Transport: A Study of Racial Policies in the Railroad, Airline, Trucking, and Urban Transit Industries*, by Herbert R. Northrup, Howard W. Risher, Jr., Richard D. Leone, and Philip W. Jeffress. 1971. $13.50

Vol. VI. *Negro Employment in Retail Trade: A Study of Racial Policies in the Department Store, Drugstore, and Supermarket Industries*, by Gordon F. Bloom, F. Marion Fletcher, and Charles R. Perry. 1972. *

Vol. VII. *Negro Employment in the Maritime Industries: A Study of Racial Policies in the Shipbuilding, Longshore, and Offshore Maritime Industries*, by Lester Rubin, William S. Swift, and Herbert R. Northrup. 1974. *

Vol. VIII. *Black and Other Minority Participation in the All-Volunteer Navy and Marine Corps*, by Herbert R. Northrup, Steven M. DiAntonio, John A. Brinker, and Dale F. Daniel. 1979. $18.50

SPECIAL REPRINT EDITION

Productivity Accounting, by Hiram S. Davis. A 1978 reprint edition of an outstanding, prescient analysis of the problem of defining and measuring productivity. Reprinted with the cooperation of the American Productivity Center, Inc. Foreword by Professor John W. Kendrick, foremost authority today on productivity analysis. 1955, 1978. $15.00

Order from the Industrial Research Unit
The Wharton School, University of Pennsylvania
Philadelphia, Pennsylvania 19104

*Order these books from University Microfilms, Inc., Attn: Books Editorial Department, 300 North Zeeb Road, Ann Arbor, Michigan 48106.

LIBRARY OF DAVIDSON COLLEGE